# About the Authors

**Jonathan V. Wright, M.D.**, is the author of *Natural Hormone Replacement for Women Over 45* and several other best-selling health books (over 600,000 copies sold). He is medical director of the Tahoma Clinic in Kent, Washington, and has treated over 2,000 patients with natural hormone replacement since 1982. Dr. Wright has also been a monthly medical columnist in *Prevention* (1976-1986) and *Let's Live* (1986-1996) magazines. Dr. Wright graduated from Harvard University and got his medical training at University of Michigan Medical School.

**Lane Lenard, Ph.D.**, has been a medical/science writer and editor for more than 22 years. During that time, he has been Articles Editor of *Science Digest Magazine*, Managing Editor of *Sexual Medicine Today*, and editor of several newsletters devoted to nutritional supplements and other health-related topics. He has also worked on countless educational and promotional projects for pharmaceutical industry clients. Prior to becoming a writer, he earned a doctorate in psychopharmacology and worked for several years as a researcher in drug development for a major pharmaceutical company.

**SMART** PUBLICATIONS™
PO Box 4667
Petaluma, CA 94955

fax: 707 763 3944
www.smart-publications.com

# Acknowledgements

**Lane Lenard, Ph.D.**
*for his scholarship and exceptional ability to critically evaluate
hundreds of research papers, extracting their basic meaning*

**John Morgenthaler**
*who encouraged and made possible the production of this book*

**Jennifer Morganti, N.D.**
*scholar, physician, and gifted organizer*

**Holly Hamm**
*ever-helpful co-ordinator and detail person*

**Lara Pizzorno**
*for fixing all our spelling, grammar, and punctuation*

*and especially to*
## Holly
(my wife)
*for her patience, support, and love*

*— Jonathan V. Wright, M.D.
Tahoma Clinic, Kent, Washington, 1998*

## ——— and to ———

**Jonathan Wright, M.D.**
*for your informed common sense views of science and medicine,
without which this book would never have happened*

**Phyllis** and **Katy**
*for your patience, understanding, encouragement, and advice during the preparation of this book and for your love always*

*— Lane Lenard, PhD
Shrewsbury, New Jersey, 1998*

# Maximize Your
# Vitality & Potency

## For Men Over 40

Jonathan V. Wright, M.D.
Lane Lenard, Ph.D.

**SMART** PUBLICATIONS™
PO Box 4667
Petaluma, CA 94955

fax: 707 763 3944
www.smart-publications.com

# Maximize Your Vitality & Potency
## For Men Over 40

by Jonathan V. Wright, M.D. and Lane Lenard, Ph.D.

Published by:
Smart Publications™
PO Box 4667
Petaluma, CA  94955

fax: 707 763 3944
www.smart-publications.com

Library of Congress Catalog Card Number: 98-86841
First Printing 1999
Printed in the United States of America
First Edition

ISBN: 0-9627418-1-7    $14.95  Softcover

## Warning - Disclaimer

# Table of Contents

# Preface

*Now I'd been on [testosterone pills] a year, faithfully; and it seemed as if there was a bit of an up in my spirits, a bit more optimism, maybe, and yet, and yet wasn't it all what the pessimistic doctors call suggestion?*

*I mulled back over my notes and had to admit that in the deepest biological sense, testosterone had authentic power. It could make hens crow and act like roosters; it could transform feeble and fuzzy-witted eunichoid humans into alert and hard-working males; it could put a healthy tan on human skin that was wrinkled and old and gray and pasty; it could make certain dwarfish boys grow into nearly normal young men; it could actually spark the human body's building of indispensable proteins; it could swell and harden feeble and flabby muscles in eunichoid men as well as in guinea-pigs; it could put sap of life into certain aging men.*

— Paul De Kruif
*The Male Hormone*, 1945

It's no longer a secret that an adult man's testosterone levels decline with age. Each man follows his own individual pattern. Some decline rapidly, some more slowly. Some start out at a relatively high "peak," others at a relatively low "peak." Sooner or later, though, the result is the same for all.

Eventually, nearly every man reaches a point where his testosterone no longer drives his sex life as well as he might like, and (just as importantly, but less well-known) no longer supports a wide variety of non-sexually related organs and tissues in an optimal way.

The relationship between gradually declining testosterone and a fading sex life is well-understood by every man (and every woman, too!), even if he or she doesn't have a degree in medicine. What's not generally appreciated by most men, and is just beginning to be appreciated by many practicing physicians, is that declining testosterone also shares a large part of the responsibility for a variety of other symptoms and diseases long thought to be part of "normal aging." These include heart disease, prostate disease (benign or cancerous), muscle and bone weakness, depression, high cholesterol, abdominal weight gain, and loss of mental acuity.

For years, the media have promoted "hormone replacement" for women, repeatedly reminding us that it will prevent a substantial portion of such serious age-related conditions as heart disease and osteoporosis. We're also starting to read and hear that "hormone replacement" may preserve women's mental functioning, too, not only stabilizing emotions and "nerves" during menopause, but also preventing a significant amount of senility and Alzheimer's disease at older ages. It's simply common sense — increasingly confirmed by volumes of scientific research — that if declining female sex hormones (estrogens and progesterone) contribute to these symptoms and diseases in women, declining male sex hormones, especially testosterone, might do the same in men.

Although the conventional medical wisdom hasn't quite come around to that point of view, more and more evidence suggests that, like hormone replacement in women, replacing men's testosterone as it declines can protect men from a variety of age-related conditions, including:

- Preventing the decline in sexual interest and ability or reinvigorating sexuality even if it has already begun to diminish.

- Preventing atherosclerosis, angina, heart attacks, strokes, and high blood pressure.

- Normalizing cholesterol and blood sugar.

- Keeping prostate glands healthy.

- Preventing the "low-grade" depression and "sour disposition" so common in men as they become grandfathers.

It is becoming clearer and clearer that the risks of these and many other "normal" symptoms of aging can be significantly lessened by appropriate replacement of testosterone, as well as by a variety of other natural means. There is no question that natural testosterone replacement is central to the treatment of all facets of "male menopause." For this reason, most of this book concerns the clinical uses of testosterone. But please don't forget that, for the best results, reversing or staving off the ravages of aging must involve a multifaceted strategy that includes an excellent diet, vitamin and mineral supplements, appropriate herbs, regular exercise, limited alcohol intake, complete elimination of tobacco and other drugs, stress reduction, and any other measures that promote "general good health."

# Natural Testosterone vs. Viagra® and Proscar®

| | Natural Testosterone | Viagra® | Proscar® |
|---|---|---|---|
| Enhanced erectile ability | yes | yes | no |
| Enhanced libido | yes | no | no |
| Prostate protection | yes | no | maybe |
| Cardiovascular protection | yes | no | no |
| Lower cholesterol | yes | no | no |
| Energy and vitality | yes | no | no |
| Feeling of well-being | yes | no | no |
| Reduced body fat | yes | no | no |
| Stronger bones/muscles | yes | no | no |
| Depression relief | maybe | no | no |
| Cognitive improvements | maybe | no | no |
| Unwanted side effects | no | yes | yes |
| Reduced libido | no | no | yes |
| Reduced erectile ability | no | no | yes |
| **Score** | 9/11 (-0/3) | 1/11 (-1/3) | -3/11 (-3/3) |

*Scorecard for natural testosterone compared to Viagra® and Proscar®. Natural testosterone has far more advantages and none of the disadvantages of the others.*

# Chapter 1
# The Day Impotence Became Hip

---

*"At my age, I want two girls at once; if I fall asleep, they have each other to talk to."*

*— Rodney Dangerfield*

Attitudes about the existence of and treatments for the age-related decline in male sexuality have been slowly changing for some time, but the FDA's approval of Pfizer Labs' new drug *Viagra*® (known generically as sildenafil citrate) on March 28, 1998 must stand out as a major milestone. We say this, not because FDA approval is all that monumental or because Viagra® is such a breakthrough drug. As we will show in the pages that follow, Viagra® may have its place, but it leaves much to be desired, and there are numerous natural alternatives that may be just as good and far safer. March 28, 1998 marked a turning point because that was the day that impotence, for ages the darkest and most shameful of the secrets held by the male sex, suddenly became "hip."

With the introduction of Viagra®, after years or even decades of pent up sexual frustration and disappointment, millions of men burst forth literally overnight from the closet of impotence. This phenomenon was not lost on the folks at Pfizer. Knowing a little something about the law of supply and demand, they have heavily advertised their new drug while pricing Viagra® pills at $10 a "pop."

Although Viagra® is officially marketed only at middle-aged men with erectile dysfunction, there is widespread recognition that its appeal transcends the ages of man (not to mention the ages of woman). Just days after Viagra's approval, *The New York Times* ran a major article on page 1 of its Business Section entitled "New Means To Make Men Feel Younger." The article predicted that Viagra® "...will not only aid impotent men but will also be used recreationally by baby boomers longing to recapture their youth. What 48-year-old man, after all, would not want to feel like a virile 18-year-old again?" wrote the *Times* reporter.[1]

In addition to its easily obtainable (apparently) prosexual benefits for many men, a large part of Viagra's success is probably due to the fact that it represents a *medical* solution to a problem that most men — not to mention their physicians and sexual partners — had always feared was, in essence, *psychological*. Before Viagra®, if a man couldn't "get it up" and "keep it up," it often meant he was lacking in some important, almost spiritual, way. It was his *fault*. And to admit this weakness would weaken him further still.

Viagra's message was that impotence was not a personal failure so much as a physiological problem, not much different from high blood pressure or heartburn. With most of the shame stripped away, men once too embarrassed to admit sexual inadequacy even to themselves, have shown that they are not only willing, but eager, to pay $10 for an erection.

Physicians, who also know a good thing when they see it, haven't been able to write Viagra® prescriptions fast enough. Thanks in part to Viagra®, Pfizer is enjoying unprecedented profits. In anticipation of Viagra's approval, Pfizer's stock price soared almost 30%. After approval, it rose even higher. And thanks largely to Viagra®, urologists, once a shadowy specialty, best known as the dreaded gloved finger responsible for ... *shudder* ... the digital prostate exam, not to mention prostate surgery and treatment of kid-

# A Viagra® Success Story

## *From the Internet...*

**I used Viagra** for the first time last night, and the results were everything you could hope for. I'm 43, an insulin-dependent diabetic for many years. I'm impotent. Have tried vacuum therapy, Prostaglandin E-1 and later switched to Caverject [an injectable (into the penis) drug that immediately produces an artificially hard, long-lasting, erection]. I take testosterone shots because my testicles crapped out years ago. Luckily, I'm married to a wonderful, beautiful, and very understanding wife. I took 50 mg. And unlike Caverject shots, where in 10 to 20 minutes you get a very rigid erection, this is more natural. As I became aroused from my loving wife, I achieved a very nice erection that felt natural. Not rock hard like you get from Caverject. After orgasm, my erection went down like a normal erection would. My wife made the statement that she felt like she was screwed by a man. Not by superman with a rock hard dick. It felt better to her. I haven't felt like this for years. Pfizer has a hit!

ney stones, have suddenly become a "glamour" specialty, the purveyors of easy, discrete, painless sexual satisfaction in a pill.

In a curious sort of way, the arrival of Viagra® has dragged impotence up from the depths of male shame and thrust it under the harsh floodlights of media exposure as a kind of anti-status symbol, even lending it an aura of geriatric hipness. In the midst of a tawdry sex scandal in which President Clinton was apparently demonstrating his still youthful sexual agility at every available opportunity, his recent electoral opponent, septuagenarian Bob Dole, proudly

proclaimed – on national television – that he, too, was a Viagra®
success story.

This may be a little hard to fathom, but it seems that in the
post-Viagra world we now inhabit, it has somehow become
"macho" to rise up out of impotence and *demand* (see box) that
your doctor prescribe — and your insurance company pony up for
— as many as 15 to 30 Viagra® pills a month. (Many insurance
companies limit reimbursement to about six pills a month, and others refuse to cover the drug at all, in effect, placing a *de facto* financial value on the role of sex in health and quality of life. Such is life
in the age of managed care.)

Beyond its sociological implications, though, Viagra® is the
perfect example of how the pharmaceutical industry approaches
many diseases and disorders – as an opportunity to reap enormous
profits from a patentable (and therefore, by definition, alien-to-the-
human-body) drug to influence the problem, without doing anything to correct the underlying cause of the disease. (No disease is
*ever* caused by the lack of a patentable drug.)

Age-associated impotence is really just one symptom of a
much larger *syndrome*,* known commonly as "male menopause."
As we will discuss later on, male menopause in many ways closely resembles the more familiar "female menopause." The box on
page 24 shows that the menopausal symptoms men and women
experience are more similar than they are different. It is highly likely that, just as virtually all women's menopausal symptoms grow
out of an age-related decline in the "female hormones," the **estrogens** and **progesterone**, men's menopausal symptoms (although
they "come on" much more slowly and variably) are related to a
comparable decline in the "male hormone," **testosterone.**

---

* A syndrome is medicalese for a collection of symptoms that tend to occur
together. It is common for all these symptoms to have a common root. For
example, the common cold, a syndrome characterized by such symptoms as
runny nose, sneezing, achiness, sore throat, and sometimes fever, is caused by a
single viral infection.

## "I Want My Viagra, and I Want It Now"

### *From the Internet...*

**What boggles my mind** is how any self-respecting uro could possibly not be up to speed by now on Viagra. I went to see my primary doctor today, and she refused to prescribe it for the same reason. Her eyes lit up when I mentioned it; said she had seen tremendous amount of interest and had a lot of requests for it. My unasked question was, "So why the f... haven't you educated yourself about it yet???" Of course, I'm too respectful to actually ask the question. I made an appointment with my uro yesterday, and the soonest I can see him is the 27th. I swear, if he uses the same excuse (which is entirely possible, judging by experience), I will refuse to pay for the visit. It took 3 visits and $400 before I had a prescription for Caverject in hand. This was long after I had been medically diagnosed with ED [erectile disorder]. I was his first Caverject subject, and he didn't know a thing about it when I first consulted him about it. I have no problem with his conservatism but no understanding at all of his ignorance. There's just no excuse.

For all its apparent value, though, Viagra® treats only one symptom of the whole-body decline in functioning that has been increasingly recognized as "male menopause." In fact, Viagra® treats only one symptom of age-related sexual dysfunction! Viagra® may give a man back his erections, but it won't increase his sexual desire. If there's no flame burning already, Viagra® isn't likely to spark one.

If a man has other symptoms of male menopause, such as depression, insomnia, progressively wasting muscles and bones, rising blood cholesterol levels, and an expanding waistline, Viagra®

won't do him any good either. If his prostate is growing larger, or if his heart and blood vessels are beginning to show signs of athero-sclerotic disease, Viagra® won't help a bit. In fact, depending on what other drugs he may be taking to treat these other manifesta-tions of the male menopause syndrome, he may not even be able to take Viagra®.

Fear not, though. If Viagra® relieves only one of the many symptoms of male menopause, the drug companies have ware-houses full of drugs for the other symptoms, too, from antidepres-sants, to antihypertensives, to anticholesterol agents, to weight-loss drugs, to sleeping pills, to prostate-shrinking drugs. Each is designed to treat one individual symptom – in isolation from the others – but none is designed to treat the underlying cause or caus-es of male menopause.

Of course, taking multiple powerful drugs is almost always problematic. Most of these powerful drugs can have disturbing, even dangerous, unwanted effects all by themselves. (Remember, by law, patentable drugs must be alien, and therefore intrinsically dangerous, to the human body…otherwise they can't be patented!) Put two or more of them together, and new avenues of trouble fre-quently open up. Take finasteride, which is marketed both as **Proscar**® (for treating benign prostate enlargement) and, at a lower dose, as **Propecia**® (for treating male pattern baldness). Finasteride may slow benign prostate growth, and it may even grow a little hair in some men, but it also causes several adverse effects, including *reduced libido* and *erectile difficulties* in a significant number of men. In other words, if you didn't need Viagra® before taking Proscar®/Propecia®, you may well need it afterwards.

Taking Viagra® along with certain heart medications (e.g., nitroglycerin and other nitrates) can cause a dangerous drop in blood pressure that has already killed several people. No one real-ly knows what happens (especially over months and years) when men take Viagra® and Proscar®/Propecia® together.

## Viagra® and Male Menopause

For all its faults (which we will enumerate later), Viagra® has focused a new light on impotence, directly, and on other aspects of male menopause, indirectly. It has allowed men to see their inability to achieve and maintain a satisfactory erection as due, not to some "failure" on their part, but to a disruption in their physiology, a dysfunction that can often be easily fixed by taking a pill. Viagra® is doing for impotence exactly what the wildly successful drug, Prozac® did for depression, shining a bright light on it and giving it a new acceptance, if not respectability. Suddenly, thanks to Viagra®, physicians have a new condition to treat – officially called *erectile disorder*, or in polite company, *ED* – for which, coincidently, they also have a new "cure."

One important benefit of this new post-Viagra attitude toward male sexuality has been a foot in the door for the idea that impotence and other aspects of male menopause may be due in large part to an age-related decline in the "male hormone," testosterone. Although this idea has been around in one form or other for thousands of years, until *very* recently, the existence of a hormonally driven male menopause analogous to that experienced by women was widely denied by the forces that rule mainstream medicine. Officially in this country,* it still does not exist, although incontrovertible scientific evidence to the contrary has finally begun a slow shift in attitude. The idea that replacing testosterone could help restore sexual function has generally been dismissed as "unproven" at best and "dangerous" at worst.

The unprecedented success of Viagra® may be the spark that ignites the transformation. One thing is certain. Pharmaceutical companies all over the world will be soon, if they are not already, spending billions researching the various aspects of male menopause and developing new drugs designed to meet the sexual

---

* No drugs are FDA-"approved" for treating male menopause, per se, although hundreds of drugs are approved for treating the various ailments associated with male menopause.

and other needs of aging men. As the *Times* reported, "The market for satisfying male ailments like impotence is largely untapped. Even though an estimated 30 million men suffer at one time or another from some degree of male erectile dysfunction, only 2.76 million visited doctors last year with the complaint...Of that number, 628,000 were new patients."[1] If you add in the other aspects of male menopause, almost every man becomes a potential candidate for treatment.

While we applaud the fact that Viagra® has helped propel us to the brink of an unprecedented explosion in knowledge and awareness in this area, the fact that much of this research will be aimed at developing the next generation of Viagras and Proscars is a little discouraging. It is apparent that conventional medicine is attempting to do for male menopause what it has already done for female menopause — turn it into a *disease* that can be *treated* only with expensive patented drugs. According to William Regelson, M.D., professor of medicine at Virginia Commonwealth University, and best-selling author of *The Superhormone Promise* and *The Melatonin Miracle*, research on treatments for menopausal men today is about where such research on female hormone replacement was about 15 years ago.[2] If men are going to be traveling the same path that women have already followed, we may be in for a bumpy ride.

## Better Safer, More Natural Ways

In this book, we suggest better, safer, more *natural* ways to restore sexual function without expensive or dangerous drugs by correcting the *underlying causes* of male menopause. We place the emphasis on *natural* for a reason. As we demonstrate repeatedly in the pages that follow:

- Scientific research, clinical experience, and ordinary common sense, confirm that sexual dysfunction as well as virtually all the other symptoms of male menopause can be traced, at least in part, to an age-related decline in testosterone.

"Irving, remember when we used to chase after young 'chicks' like that?"

"Oh, sure, I remember doing it....I just can't remember *why!*"

- Replacing testosterone with natural testosterone (not some other preparation masquerading as "testosterone"), as well as replacing other natural hormones when needed, and adding various nutritional, herbal, and botanical products, can be at least as effective, is almost always safer, and invariably costs less than conventional pharmaceutical solutions.

## Man's Worst Kept Secret...Finally Exposed!

For many men, the most disturbing sign of aging is the slow decline in sexual desire and ability. Rarely do we recognize it as a sign of male menopause, however. Instead we consider it to be just another "normal" milepost on the road from cradle to grave ...like muscles that slowly lose their strength and resilience and refuse to forgive overwork as they once did, ...like bones that become increasingly brittle and prone to fracture, ...like blood pressure and cholesterol levels that rise along with the risk of heart disease, and stroke, ...like the prostate gland, which seems to cause problems — ranging from discomfort to death — for nearly every man, should he live long enough. And then there are the more subtle changes of aging, like depression, and the loss of energy and vitality and mental acuity.

Scientific evidence strongly suggests that if a middle-aged or older man is losing interest in sex and/or is having difficulties performing sexually, his problems probably go a lot deeper than mere "sexual dysfunction." In fact, it's a safe bet that such a man is likely also to be experiencing one or more of the physical and mental changes now known to be directly related to a decline in testosterone.

We shrug these changes off. We deny them. We minimize them. We ignore them. We stuff them into the farthest recesses of our consciousness. Worst of all, though, we *accept* them.

Not only are *we* reluctant to talk about these problems, so are our doctors. Historically, medical science has largely ignored them, at least as manifestations of male menopause. If the roaring flames of energy, enterprise, and enthusiasm have dimmed to a faintly glowing ember; if sexual passion seems like a distant memory; if getting and maintaining an erection, once one of life's great pleasures, now feels like just another household chore; if muscles are growing weaker and bones thinner, conventional medical wisdom has offered little real help and even less consolation: *"Well, you're getting older, aren't you? What do you expect? Anyhow, what's all this got to do with testosterone?"*

The changes associated with male menopause are complex phenomena with a wide variety of possible causes. These can range from subtle hormonal imbalances, to atherosclerotic plaque clogging the arteries that serve the heart, brain, and penis, to an emotional "mid-life crisis," to the unholy trinity of American masculinity: worry, stress, and depression.

Whatever their causes though, their effects can be devastating, both physically and psychologically. For many men, they undermine the very foundation of what it means to be a man: strength ...energy ...vitality ...physical health ...mental acuity ...ambition, ...drive ...determination ...sexuality. These are all powerful talismans to give up and still think oneself a "man."

And to make matters worse, these losses tend to feed on one another, accelerating the decline. Chronic stress and worry can sap a man's strength as much as physical illness or painful joints and muscles, paving the way for depression and even impotence, all of which are almost certain to squelch any remaining sparks of sexual desire. And though it is common for men to deny these changes and keep them to themselves, they inevitably reverberate in their relationship with their spouse, piling on still more tension, stress, and loneliness that can just hasten the skid into illness and eventually death.

## The "Male Menopause" Syndrome

Although most men would prefer to think that menopause was something that only happened to their wives, scientific evidence says otherwise. We have chosen to use the term "male menopause" in this book, even though we recognize it as a bit of an oxymoron. The word "menopause" refers to the end of *menstruation*, a uniquely female condition. To avoid this confusion, some authors have chosen to use the name "andropause," "viropause," or even, redundantly, "male andropause." Thus, they make the obvious analogy to the female condition but add a distinctly male element. These approaches are perfectly valid and acceptable, and as far as we are concerned, all these names refer to the same syndrome. Nevertheless, we have decided to use the term "male menopause" in this book for three primary reasons:

First, most men have at least a vague idea what menopause means for the female sex. What men may not realize is that their experience, while different from women's in some ways, is also very similar in many other ways. We think the term "male

# Menopausal Symptoms and Associated Conditions in Men and Women

## Women

- Irregular menstruation
- Hot flashes
- Reduced libido
- Vaginal thinning/ dryness
- Painful intercourse
- Disturbed sleep
- Depression
- Fatigue
- Irritability
- Heart disease & atherosclerosis
- Osteoporosis
- Breast cancer
- Endometrial (uterine) cancer
- Thinning skin
- Slow wound healing
- Poor concentration/ memory lapses
- Reduced estrogen & progesterone

## Men

- Reduced libido
- Erectile dysfunction
- Ejaculatory problems
- Disturbed sleep
- Depression
- Heart disease & atherosclerosis
- Osteoporosis
- Prostate enlargement/ cancer
- Muscle weakness
- Fatigue
- Irritability
- Thinning skin
- Slow wound healing
- Poor concentration/ memory lapses
- Reduced testosterone

menopause" helps to focus more on the similarities than on the differences. (See box)

Second, using the word "menopause" helps emphasize the *hormonal* basis of the changes that men undergo, which all too often goes overlooked. In women, of course, menopause is the most obvious manifestation of the end of the ebb and flow of the "female hormones," the estrogens and progesterone, that began in adolescence and has driven the monthly menstrual cycle ever since. In men, the gradual decline in "male hormones" (or *androgens*), particularly *testosterone*, that begins in a man's late 40s or 50s, is now coming to be seen as the prime mover for nearly all the symptoms of male menopause.

Third, some words, although originally gender-specific, eventually come to transcend gender. One common example is "nurse." There is nothing more oxymoronic than "male nurse," yet every hospital has them. We believe menopause now falls into the same category.

As shown in the "Menopausal Symptoms and Associated Conditions" box, the hormonal fluctuations during the female menopause cause a variety of symptoms, such as hot flashes, sleeplessness, emotional swings, urinary incontinence, and thinning of the vaginal tissue that can cause pain during sexual intercourse. After menopause, women experience sharp increases in their risk of heart attack, stroke, osteoporosis, breast cancer, and memory loss.

Men also go through an age-related process of hormonal change that can profoundly affect their health and happiness. Unlike women, though, men who pass this way encounter no clear landmarks comparable to the cessation of menstruation, only a slow, almost imperceptible decline in various bodily functions. Like women, though, men often suffer subtle physical, mental, and emotional symptoms, including insomnia and depression, as well as a decline in sexuality and mental acuity. And also like women, menopausal men face a rapidly growing risk of serious "age-related" diseases, including heart attack, stroke, and even osteoporosis. Although breast cancer is very rare in men, prostate cancer is extremely common, and benign prostate enlargement is almost universal.

In women, the key hormones involved are the "female hormones," *estrogens* and *progesterone*. In men, of course, it is the "male hormone," *testosterone*.

The hormonal nature of "female menopause" has been recognized in medical circles for decades. Virtually all the symptoms and associated risks of menopause in women are now known to be directly or indirectly related to a decline in the *estrogens* and *progesterone*, which occurs as the ovaries shut down production between the ages of 45 and 55 years. Awareness of the mechanisms involved has made it possible to develop various medical, herbal, and nutritional measures to counteract this hormonal loss, thus helping to minimize the discomforts and risks associated with menopause.*

Where conventional medicine has been more than willing to embrace the fact that women go through important hormonal changes that can profoundly affect their mood, health, sexuality, and quality of life, it has historically been extremely reluctant to admit that the same might also be true of men. (Is there something "macho" about believing we have lots of testosterone flowing through our blood vessels?)

Although attitudes are changing, the existence of a male menopause is still far from established fact among many conventional physicians, who, as we mentioned earlier, usually prefer to attribute men's sexual dysfunction and other menopausal complaints to factors like stress, worry, depression, and that old standby, "normal" aging. They also prefer to view (and treat) prostate enlargement, benign and otherwise, as well as cardiovascular disease and osteoporosis as independent "age-related" diseases that have little or nothing to do with male menopause.

In fact, though, scientific evidence has been accumulating for more than half a century that males aged 40 and over do undergo a hormonal transformation analogous to that experienced by females. Where female menopause results from a relatively abrupt decline in the estrogens and progesterone, the symptoms of male menopause are caused by a more gradual fall off in testosterone.

---

* Please see *Natural Hormone Replacement for Women Over 45*, by Jonathan V. Wright, M.D., and John Morgenthaler. Petaluma, CA: Smart Publications.

# The Trouble With Female "Hormone" Replacement

**In women,** the standard pharmaceutical approach to menopause has long been "hormone replacement therapy" (HRT). HRT "replaces" the natural estrogens and progesterone the body has been making since puberty with a patented combination of horse estrogens (e.g., Premarin®) and a synthetic progesterone-like drug (e.g., Provera®).

By mimicking the effects of the missing hormones, these foreign (to the human body) agents are often able to relieve many menopausal symptoms. But, at what cost? As described in the book, *Natural Hormone Replacement for Women Over 45*[3], because these drugs and hormones are foreign to the human physiology, they do an incomplete job at best, and at worst, they may cause serious, even deadly, unwanted effects.

Consider, for example, that Premarin® relieves many common menopausal symptoms (i.e., hot flashes, vaginal thinning), protects against heart disease, and slows the progression of osteoporosis. At the same time, though, it promotes the growth of uterine and breast cancers. It also causes a wide variety of unpleasant effects, many of which may be countered by taking still other drugs, each of which comes with its own baggage.

Even more exciting is the fact that there is a growing arsenal of *natural* hormones, herbal remedies, and nutritional supplements that men can safely use to help restore sexuality while alleviating many of the discomforts and minimizing many of the dangers of this transformation.

## Trapped in the Pharmaceutical Model

Conventional medicine has finally begun to address these problems and hesitantly to accept the possibility that men really do experience a form of hormonally driven menopause. In addition to Viagra®, some physicians are even beginning to prescribe the new natural testosterone patch (as well as natural testosterone creams, gels, and sublingual tablets) for men with sexual dysfunction. That's the good news.

For the most part, though, conventional medicine remains firmly trapped in the pharmaceutical model of medical treatment when it comes to the male menopause syndrome, preferring to treat the various symptoms as unrelated diseases. Briefly, that model works like this: Identify a troublesome symptom; isolate it; understand its biochemical mechanisms; and then develop a chemical that specifically targets those mechanisms; patent the chemical; market it (and never mention that the symptom did not occur because of a deficiency of the patentable chemical). The results of this extremely successful – but seriously flawed – strategy fill pharmacy shelves and medicine cabinets the world over.

As more and more physicians come to recognize that many symptoms presently attributed to aging (and other causes) are actually due to "male menopause," perhaps the use of these patentable drugs will decline. Informed patients will very likely encourage physicians to move in this direction.

## Male Hormone Replacement

One of the brightest lights in the treatment of male menopause today is the use of *testosterone replacement therapy*. Having apparently learned something from its unhappy experience with women (see box), the pharmaceutical industry – and with it, conventional medical practice in this country – has begun to adopt *natural* testosterone as its standard. (In our opinion, it's malpractice not to do the same for women.)

Although *male hormone replacement* (*MHR*) has a long way to go before it becomes as commonplace as HRT, it is gratifying that the testosterone being used in all new products appearing on the market, from testosterone creams and gels to patented high-tech patches is, in fact, *natural* (identical-to-human) testosterone.

The various chemical analogues of testosterone are finally on their way out. Known as *testosterone esters* (e.g., testosterone enanthate, testosterone propionate, and testosterone cypionate) and *oral anabolic steroid drugs* (e.g., methyltestosterone), they have served as the only "legitimate" source of exogenous "testosterone" for treating menopausal men with sexual and other problems for the last 50 to 60 years. These synthetic "hormones" are actually man-made drugs based on the molecular structure of natural testosterone but modified slightly to make them more active or longer-lasting than natural testosterone and, of course, patentable. Like Premarin® and Provera® in women, these drugs produce a grossly unnatural hormonal environment in men's bodies that is associated with wild mood swings along with other serious and even deadly unwanted effects.

## Male Menopause, the Natural Way

There is no more important message in this book than this one:

*For restoring sexuality and the diverse  aspects of men's health known to deteriorate with age, natural testosterone, (and other natural androgens), as well as specific vitamins, amino acids, and herbal and botanical products are demonstrably more effective and safer in the human body than any synthetic "hormones" and pharmaceutical drugs. Used at physiologic doses (doses that produce levels in our bodies within the range naturally present) and on a schedule that closely follows nature's own timing, these natural products have been shown in study after scientific study to:*

- Enhance sex drive (libido)
- Restore the ability to achieve and sustain erections
- Protect against heart disease and stroke

- Reduce the risk of prostate disease (benign or cancerous)
- Increase energy
- Build stronger bones and muscles
- Relieve depression
- Lower cholesterol while raising HDL ("good") cholesterol
- Reduce weight
- Prevent age-related losses in mental acuity

In the remainder of this book, we will review much of this scientific research. We will also suggest which natural products would be most appropriate for which aspects of male menopause and how to use them to reap the greatest benefits with the least risk. Finally, we will explain how to obtain these products, including how to find a knowledgeable physician to prescribe them for you and guide you in their use.

## References

1.  Morrow D. New means to make men feel younger. *The New York Times*. March 31, 1998:B1-B2.
2.  Regelson W, Colman C. *The Superhormone Promise*. New York: Simon & Schuster; 1996.

# Chapter 2
# The Male Hormone

*"For it is the semen, when possessed of vitality, which makes us to be men, hot, well-braced in limbs, well-voiced, spirited, strong to think and act. For when the semen is not possessed of its vitality, persons become shriveled, have a sharp tone of voice, lose their hair and their beard and become effeminate, as the characteristics of eunuchs prove."*

*— Aretaeus of Cappadocia, 150 AD*

Testosterone is synonymous with masculinity. Of the hormones known as **androgens**, which are considered to be "male" hormones, testosterone is the Big Cheese, the Boss of Bosses, the Alpha Male, the Big Kahuna, Numero Uno.

People who wouldn't know the endocrine system from the New York City subway system will tell you with absolute certainty that testosterone is the stuff that makes a man a man. It is the *male* hormone, the chemical that makes men so different, not only from women, but also from little boys. And as we shall soon see, it is the gradual decline in testosterone that may be partly responsible for turning strong, vital, healthy, alert, vigorous, sexually active young men into frail, chronically ill, mentally dull, old codgers who haven't had an erection in decades and couldn't care less if they did.

We may take the existence of testosterone for granted today, but once it was a great mystery, the key to eternal youth, the Holy Grail of medical science, the path to the Nobel Prize. The hormone we now call testosterone was first identified and isolated only about 70 years ago. Until then, while it was clear that something important resided in the testicles, no one had the vaguest idea what it was.

The science of hormones, known today as endocrinology, was born in the quest for the essence of maleness. This quest began in prehistory when some proto-endocrinologist first noticed that men who had been castrated were quite different from ordinary men. As the quotation above from the Roman physician Aretaeus suggests, humankind has long posited the existence of a male essence that appeared to dwell in the testicles. Remove these structures, and maleness seems to rapidly melt away.

If some "essence of maleness" does reside in the testicles, it's not too great a leap to think that you might be able to transfer that essence to another person who might be in relative lack of it. From about 1000 A.D. on, the Chinese were regularly processing urine from young men (and women) to produce an extract which they used for treating impotence, prostate enlargement, and infertility.[1] By 1400 A.D., an Indian doctor named Susruta was recommending that impotent men add testicles (presumably from animals) to their diet.[2]

While this idea was intriguing, it took another 3 to 4 centuries for anyone to take it seriously enough to test it out. During the late 18th and 19th centuries, researchers began conducting legitimate scientific experiments in which they transplanted testicles (usually from roosters) into other animals that had no testicles, like capons (castrated roosters) and hens.

Paul de Kruif, in his wonderful 1945 book, *The Male Hormone*, pinpoints the birth of hormone science (endocrinology) to one such experiment conducted in 1849 by a German physiologist named Arnold Berthold. (The great Scottish physician John Hunter is also reported to have performed similar experiments in

# The Day of the Eunuch

**E**unuchs — **men lacking testicles** — have had a long and glorious history, especially in ancient China, Rome, and the Middle East. Because they lacked both the means and usually the desire to engage in sexual activity, kings, emperors, and lesser nobility, trusted eunuchs to safeguard the chastity of the women living in their harems. Eunuchs also functioned as chamberlains to these powerful men.

A few eunuchs even used their position of trust and closeness to powerful men to gather great power for themselves. One Chinese eunuch, named Wei Zhongxian, is considered to be the most powerful of them all. Wei rose from being a butler in the Emperor's household to completely dominate his teenaged Emperor and soon the entire Chinese government. Between 1624 and 1627, he controlled the palace with a division of eunuch troops, while ruthlessly exploiting and terrorizing the population. When the emperor died unexpectedly in 1627, Wei quickly fell from power and ended up hanging himself to avoid prosecution.

At various times during early Christian history, it became fashionable for religious zealots to demonstrate their purity of spirit and servitude to God by castrating themselves. As recently as the late 1800s, it was still a practice in Italy for parents to have their prepubertal boys castrated in order to train them to be adult singers but with a child's soprano voice. The voices of *castrati*, as these singers were called, were treasured for their eerie, otherworldly, high-pitched purity that resulted from an adult diaphragm and lungs driving air through a prepubertal larynx.

London during the late 1700s, but he never published his results, thus abandoning his claim to scientific immortality.) Berthold first removed the testicles from four roosters, turning them into capons. He then restored the testicles to the abdomens of two of the birds. As de Kruif describes it, "While the two caponized birds who'd got no testicle grafts became fat pacifists, these other two with the grafted testicles remained every inch roosters. They crowed. They battled. They chased hens enthusiastically. Their bright red combs and wattles kept growing."[2]

With Berthold's remarkable success, visions of returning youth began appearing in the minds of other scientists of the day. One of these was the eminent French physiologist Charles-Edouard Brown-Séquard, who at the age of 72, was feeling the need for rejuvenation, and saw in Berthold's roosters, one last chance to restore his own long-lost youth. In 1889, Brown-Séquard set about removing the testicles from dogs and guinea pigs, grinding them up, brewing them into a soup with salt water, and then injecting the soup under his skin. Before long, he announced to the scientific world in an article published in the premiere medical journal of the day, *The Lancet*, the miraculous return of his energy, physical endurance, muscular strength, and mental agility.[3]

Brown-Séquard's results took the scientific world by storm. Here was one of the world's most respected biomedical researchers, the disciple of the great Claude Bernard, and the man who had earlier discovered the significance of the adrenal glands, now proclaiming that he had apparently uncovered the long-sought pathway to extended, if not eternal youth.

Unfortunately for poor old Brown-Séquard, his return to youth quickly proved to be an illusion, leaving him the butt of endless jokes and derision. When he died a few years later, his reputation as one the leading scientific minds of the 19th century lay in ruins.

Even more unfortunately, while research on other newly discovered hormones, including those produced by the thyroid, adrenals, pituitary, and pancreas, burgeoned, further work on testicle extracts became the "cold fusion" of the day. No scientist who valued his reputation dared go near it, lest he be tarred with the same brush that did in Brown-Séquard. Another 30 to 40 years would pass before anyone made a serious attempt.

That courageous man was a University of Chicago organic chemist by the name of Fred C. Koch, who dared to resurrect the work of Berthold during the 1920s. Koch was the beneficiary of two fortunate circumstances. The first was his proximity to the Chicago stockyards, a ready and inexpensive source of bull's testicles. The second was a medical student, Lemuel C. McGee, who was willing to endlessly distill and extract the contents of those testicles in search of the elusive male hormone.

Eventually, their persistence paid off. From about 40 pounds of bulls' balls, Koch and McGee found that they could produce a tiny amount — 20 mg — of a substance, which when injected into capons over a period of weeks, could restore the birds' roosterhood, at least temporarily. Even more remarkable, their testicular extract worked not just in capons, but in castrated guinea pigs and rats as well.

In the years that followed, other scientists further isolated the active hormone, now called *testosterone*, defined its chemical structure, and actually produced crystals of it. A major breakthrough occurred in 1935, when a Yugoslav scientist named Leopold Ruzicka, who worked for a pharmaceutical company in Zurich, recognized that, although the testes *produced* testosterone, they really contained very little of it. The reason is that almost as soon as testosterone gets produced, it exits its glandular birthplace, hitches a ride on the nearby blood stream, and takes off for various parts of the body, some of them, like the brain, a substantial distance away. There are no testosterone reserves stored in the testes to tap into, as earlier scientists had assumed.

Rather than extracting these minuscule amounts of hormone from testicular tissue, Ruzicka, who was eventually awarded the Nobel Prize for his work with testosterone, discovered that it was possible to produce testosterone *de novo* from a much more abundant substance, **cholesterol**. In fact, that's basically how the body does it. The testosterone Ruzicka produced from cholesterol was identical to that which the body produces.

Ruzicka's discovery opened the door to large scale testosterone research. The ready availability of high quality natural testosterone seemed to promise answers to questions about masculinity, youth, longevity, and sexuality that had haunted humankind since the dawn of time. The only problem was that this natural testosterone was difficult to administer in amounts that would produce a physiological effect. Whether taken by mouth or injected, it would be quickly neutralized by the body's normal metabolic processes, in exactly the same way that endogenous testosterone is metabolized. (In order to promote their patentable and highly profitable synthetic "testosterones," drug companies – until very recently – emphasized this "drawback" to the use of natural testosterone.)

Nevertheless, it appeared that the curse of Brown-Séquard had been banished for good. As they began to awaken to the possible profits to be made from this newly discovered male hormone, pharmaceutical companies, as they are prone to do, set out to try "improve" on nature. Thus were born a long line of drugs, like testosterone esters – testosterone *propionate*, testosterone *cypionate*, testosterone *enanthate*, and testosterone *undecanoate*. A class of drugs known as oral *anabolic steroids*, of which *methyltestosterone* is the most notorious example, were particularly attractive because they could be taken by mouth. All but one of the testosterone esters required an injection.

This is a vital point that we will come back to time and again in this book: the distinction between **natural hormones** and **synthetic/patentable hormone-like drugs**:

- **Natural hormones** are identical in molecular structure to those the body produces. Even though they may be synthesized in a laboratory, sometimes from vegetable sources, the natural hormone molecules so produced cannot be distinguished from the inborn hormone, and the body treats them as such. Like other naturally occurring substances, such as air, water, and vitamins, natural hormones cannot be patented. Anyone can synthesize them and sell them.

- *Synthetic, patentable drugs* that masquerade as natural hormones are similar in molecular structure, but are never exactly the same as the natural molecule. By altering the natural molecule in some way, pharmaceutical company chemists attempt to improve on nature by making a drug that is more potent, longer-lasting, easier to administer, and patentable. Unfortunately, because drug molecules are necessarily different from natural molecules, the body treats them differently, which usually leads to adverse and even dangerous side effects.

## Research Explosion

Following Ruzicka's discovery research exploded, most of it testing the new testosterone-like drugs, rather than natural testosterone, which enjoyed only a brief moment on the scientific stage of the day. Beginning in the early 1940s, scores of studies and clinical observations were published demonstrating the potential value of "testosterone" replacement in patients with angina pectoris (chest pain caused by partially occluded coronary arteries, often a precursor to heart attacks), hypertension (high blood pressure), age-related muscle and bone atrophy, and prostate enlargement. They also appeared quite promising for treating men whose testicular function was impaired due to a congenital anomaly, illness, or castration. A few studies even reported positive effects of "testosterone" replacement in men going through male menopause, known in those days as "male climacteric."

In one such study, published in 1942, 24 menopausal men were treated with injections of 10 or 25 mg of testosterone propionate every other day (except Sunday). The men, whose complaints included fatigue, memory loss, lack of confidence, depression, insomnia, irritability, and various circulatory disturbances, all reportedly felt "greatly improved," sometimes after only a week or two of treatment.[4]

Granted that these early studies were often poorly controlled, generally included relatively few subjects, and utilized synthetic "testosterone" at wildly unphysiological doses, still their results suggested that "testosterone" replacement (if not *testosterone* replacement, using the natural hormone) could have important clinical benefits. Interestingly, this was decades before "hormone" replacement therapy (HRT utilizing patentable rather than natural estrogen) became commonplace for menopausal women.

It didn't take long before the early bubble of hope and expectation burst, however. This time, the reason was toxicity. The widespread use of the synthetic testosterone-like drugs, particularly, methyltestosterone and related drugs, resulted in an alarming number of cases of liver disease, including jaundice, hepatitis, and hepatic cancer, many of which were fatal. Beginning in the 1960s, the irresponsible use by athletes and body builders of anabolic steroid drugs to build muscle strength appeared to confirm the dangers of "testosterone" replacement. Despite unequivocal demonstrations of health benefits for many men when testosterone replacement was used responsibly, research in the area once again fell on hard times.

These unhappy circumstances still haunt the practice of medicine today, yet interest in testosterone replacement therapy for men has been undergoing a welcome renaissance of late. This has resulted from the confluence of several important trends:

- A growing acceptance by the medical community of the reality of a hormonally based male menopause.

- The ready availability of high quality, inexpensive *natural* testosterone, biosynthesized from plant precursor sources (such as soy and Mexican yam), but molecularly identical to that produced by the human body.

- The increasing realization that testosterone replacement offers important health benefits, ranging from relief of menopausal symptoms like insomnia, mood disorders, memory loss, to restoration of libido and protection against heart disease, muscle and bone wasting, cognitive deterioration, and prostate enlargement, with relatively little risk.

- The development of testosterone delivery systems, such as creams, gels, patches, and sublingual (under the tongue) tablets, that permit the easy and safe administration of physiologic doses of natural testosterone on a close-to-natural timetable.

- The recognition by many physicians that the natural testosterone formulations available today are far better, safer, and more convenient than those used by earlier generations.

# References

1. Needham J. *Science and Civilization in China (Vol. 5)*. Cambridge: Cambridge University Press; 1983.

2. de Kruif P. *The Male Hormone*. New York: Harcourt, Brace and Company; 1945.

3. Brown-Séquard C. The effects produced on man by subcutaneous injections of a liquid obtained from the testicles of animals. *Lancet*. 1889;2:105-107.

4. Werner A. *J Urol*. 1942;49:872.

# Chapter 3

# Testosterone: Hormone ... Steroid ... Androgen

W e've been talking about testosterone in rather general terms so far. Now it's time to get a bit more specific. Like other substances in the body, testosterone maintains various identities. By definition, testosterone is a *hormone*. In terms of its molecular structure, it is a member of the *steroid* family. In terms of its function, it is considered an *androgen*. What do these terms mean?

There is so much misinformation and misuse of terms like "hormone," "steroid," and "androgen" dispensed both by the lay and medical media, that it's hard, even for the most well-informed to keep the true meanings straight. To avoid being misled when discussing hormone replacement regimens, it is vitally important to understand what these terms actually mean and how they can be and are misapplied.

## Testosterone Is a Hormone (Drugs Are Not)

According to *Dorland's Illustrated Medical Dictionary*, the classical definition of a hormone is "a chemical substance, *produced in the body* by an organ or cells of a certain organ, which has a specific regulatory effect on the activity of a certain organ." Most hormones are produced in organs called *endocrine glands*, which secrete their product directly into the blood stream. In addition to testosterone, other familiar hormones include *adrenalin* (also called *epinephrine*), which is secreted by the inner part (medulla) of the adrenal glands; *cortisone*, from the outer part (cortex) of the adrenals; *thyroid hormone*, from the thyroid gland; *insulin*, from the pancreas; the *estrogens — estriol, estrone,* and *estradiol —* and *progesterone*, which are produced primarily by the ovaries in females (and to a lesser extent, by the adrenals and testes in men and by the adrenals in women), and several others.

In men, testosterone is produced primarily in glands called the ***testes*** from which it spills into the local blood supply. A small amount of testosterone is also produced in the adrenals. Carried by the blood stream, testosterone – or its metabolite, *dihydrotestosterone* (DHT) – binds to specific *target cells* all over the body, where it can exert a variety of effects, depending on the target tissue. These effects fall into three broad categories: ***masculinization***, ***anabolism*** (tissue building), and ***sexual arousal.*** Although testosterone is generally considered to be a "male hormone," it can and does produce all these effects in both men and women.

*Dorland's* goes on to point out that the definition of hormone has been loosened in recent years (by some) to apply to any substance that may *act* like a hormone, even though it may not be produced in the body by the specialized glands that normally produce and secrete hormones. In other words, substances that act like hormones in some ways (but not necessarily in others) may still be referred to as "hormones," and most people — medically learned or otherwise — will not give it a second thought. Typically, these pseudo-hormones are patented drugs designed to function like hormones.

Since the early 1900s, the pharmaceutical industry has worked very hard to promote this expanded definition of hormone, because it allows them to sell enormously profitable patentable substances under the "hormone" label. Suffice it to say, this strategy has been wildly successful. Do a quick scan of the scientific literature, and you'll find hundreds of articles that seem to describe the use of "testosterone" or other "androgens." Look closely, though, and you'll almost always find that identical-to-human testosterone or other androgen was not used, but rather a synthetic drug, like methyltestosterone or testosterone propionate. Yet, so infused with the company line are most medical researchers and physicians, that the various drug names and testosterone/androgen have become virtually interchangeable.

The same thing is true on the female side, where to most physicians, Premarin® *is* estrogen. In fact, Premarin® (known generically as *conjugated equine estrogens*) has evolved over billions of years to fit the unique needs of the female horse. It is quite different in structure and function from the estrogen produced by a human female's ovaries. When placed in a woman's body, Premarin® accomplishes many of the functions of natural human estrogen, but it also becomes a potentially dangerous drug with a high propensity to cause a variety of unwanted adverse effects up to and including endometrial (uterine) and breast cancer.[1]

While this cavalier attitude toward the subtle complexities of the human physiology has resulted in billions in profits for the pharmaceutical industry, it has also led to some unfortunate consequences for many of the people who have used these drugs under the mistaken impression that they were, in fact, *natural human hormones*.

Call them what you will, hormone-like drugs are most definitely not hormones, and they *never* work exactly like natural hormones. While the differences may sometimes be subtle, they can all too often be deadly. Women first learned this lesson even before men, when physicians encouraged them to take a synthetic "estrogen" called *diethylstilbestrol (DES)* during the late 1930s and early 1940s as a means of preventing miscarriages and alleviating menopausal symptoms. The DES experiment was an unmitigated disaster, causing cancer not only in the unfortunate women who took it, but also in their soon-to-be-born daughters.

Unbelievable as it sounds, a few years after the unfortunate experience with anabolic steroids in men, menopausal women were forced to relearn the same lesson all over again (because prescribing physicians and the pharmaceutical industry had obviously *failed* to learn it), when they were encouraged to use "estrogen" replacement. This time conventional medicine chose not to pre-scribe a synthetic drug, but instead "estrogen" that was promoted as "natural" but was natural only for female *horses* (i.e., Premarin®).

It took a several years of "estrogen" replacement therapy (ERT) before physicians started noticing that an alarming number of their patients were developing endometrial cancer. Their response was (and continues to be) to add another hormone-mimicking drug — usually medroxyprogesterone (Provera®), which is promoted as being equivalent to natural progesterone — to "oppose" the car-cinogenic effects of horse estrogen. While this combination, known misleadingly as "hormone" replacement therapy (HRT), can reduce the risk of endometrial cancer due to Premarin®, it has so many other unpleasant and dangerous side effects, that it's no wonder that as many as half the women who start on HRT discontinue treatment. Since natural estrogens, progesterone, and testosterone work better than these drugs and with far less risk of dangerous or unpleasant adverse effects, the logic of these drug therapies makes sense only if their main goal is not improved health for their users but enhanced profits for their manufacturers.

## Testosterone Is a Steroid

Steroids are a large group of lipids (fat-like substances) that play vital roles in many different biological systems. Among the best known steroids, in addition to testosterone, are *dihydrotestosterone (DHT)*, *progesterone*, *cortisone*, the *estrogens*, *pregnenolone*, *androstenedione*, and *dehydroepiandrosterone (DHEA)*. The moth-er of all steroids is a substance well-known to most people these days: ***cholesterol.*** * Figure 3-1 illustrates in a simplified way how

---

* Although cholesterol has developed a rather unsavory reputation in recent years due to its alleged connection with atherosclerosis, it is an absolutely essential ingredient to good health. For example, without cholesterol, we would be inca-pable of producing steroid hormones. A growing body of evidence suggests that diets and drugs that drastically reduce the level of cholesterol in the body may actually be doing more harm than good, in part because they limit the raw mate-rials from which steroids can be produced.

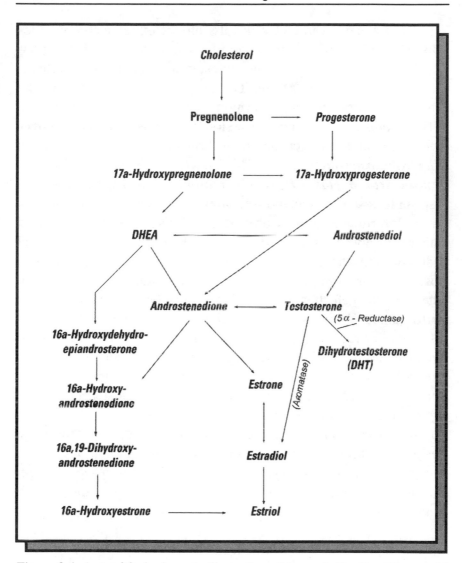

**Figure 3-1**. *A simplified schematic illustration of the anabolic side of the steroid family tree, showing the relationship of testosterone and the estrogens. Words in parentheses are enzymes required to convert testosterone to either estradiol or DHT. Note that all steroid hormones descend from cholesterol.*

some of the major steroids descend from cholesterol and are related to each other.

There is no need go too deeply into the extreme complexities of steroid biochemistry, but a couple of points should be emphasized. First is the fact that some testosterone is metabolized (chemically converted) to *estradiol*. The enzyme that accomplishes the feat of changing the male hormone into the female hormone is called *aromatase*, and the conversion process is called *aromatization*. Second is the fact that some testosterone is metabolized to *dihydrotestosterone* (*DHT*). This conversion is controlled by the enzyme *5α-reductase*. We will be returning to these two important steps in testosterone metabolism often in the pages that follow.

Unfortunately, the word "steroid" also gets tossed around rather loosely by the medical profession, the pharmaceutical industry, and the media, causing its true meaning to become obscured. For example, we frequently hear about athletes taking "steroids" to help them build bigger muscles and enhance their performance. Which steroids are they taking? Certainly not cholesterol or estradiol. In this instance, the "steroids" are usually not even true hormones but rather one of the many different synthetic "anabolic steroid" drugs. Developed mostly during the late 1940s and 1950s as attempts to produce synthetic "testosterone," these drugs were based on the molecular structure of natural testosterone but are, in fact, quite different. As the name suggests, they were designed to mimic the muscle- and bone-building (anabolic) property of natural testosterone. Unlike natural testosterone, though, they can be extremely toxic, especially at high doses and/or with long term use.*

---

* So concerned are government regulators about abuse of anabolic steroids that they have passed the Anabolic Steroids Control Act which classifies them as Schedule III drugs (along with other potentially dangerous drugs, such as codeine, hydrocodone, and some barbiturates). Curiously, *natural* testosterone, which is virtually never used by athletes in this way and has rarely, if ever, been shown to cause the toxic side effects associated with anabolic steroid drugs when used at physiologic doses, has nevertheless been caught up in the same government net as the synthetics. This makes testosterone the only hormone occurring naturally in the human body to be so restricted by the government.

We also hear about *steroids* being used to treat various inflammatory diseases, ranging from severe asthma and arthritis to simple itching. In these cases, the steroids being used are usually one of many synthetic drugs designed to mimic some of the normal actions of the steroid hormone *cortisone*, a natural anti-inflammatory hormone produced by the cortex of the adrenal glands. If a physician prescribes "cortisone," you can be virtually certain it's not a natural hormonal product, but instead a powerful synthetic drug (eg, triamcinolone, prednisone) based on the natural cortisone molecule but modified to enhance its potency or other properties and, of course, to make it patentable.

## Testosterone Is an Androgen

Androgens are steroid hormones that promote masculinization (also called virilization) and growth (anabolic effects). In humans, the major androgen is testosterone. Other important androgens are *DHT*, *androstenedione*, and *DHEA*.

- **DHT**. When the enzyme 5α-reductase acts on testosterone, DHT is formed. In many androgen-sensitive tissues, DHT can bind to androgen receptors about 10 times more tightly than testosterone, giving it far greater androgenic potency. DHT is believed to be responsible for such androgenic effects as facial and body hair, acne, male-pattern baldness, and prostate enlargement, although there's increasing evidence that DHT may not be solely responsible for the last two.

- **Androstenedione**. Androstenedione is considered a weak androgen. It is a precursor of testosterone, which means that the body makes testosterone from androstenedione. Some testosterone is also converted back into androstenedione. There is evidence that taking supplementary androstenedione may help increase testosterone levels naturally.

- **DHEA**. Once considered a mere intermediary steroid with no functions of its own, DHEA is coming to be recognized as having a wide range of important functions in the body. One reason DHEA, which is produced in the adrenal glands, turns out to be so important is that it occupies a central position in the steroid hierarchy (Fig. 3-1). Produced from cholesterol by way of pregnenolone, DHEA is metabolized to form androstenedione, which is converted directly to testosterone. Like testosterone, estrogen (in women), and other hormones, DHEA levels peak in the second or third decade of life and then begin a long decline. In men, about half of DHEA is lost by age 40; by age 80, only about 15% of youthful levels remain. Reduced levels of DHEA can translate into reductions in androstenedione, testosterone, DHT, and estradiol. Although it is metabolized to produce other steroid hormones, evidence is accumulating that DHEA by itself has numerous important health benefits.[2]

Although androgens are generally thought of as "male hormones," they are also present in females, albeit in smaller amounts than in males. Similarly, the "female" hormones, estriol, estrone,

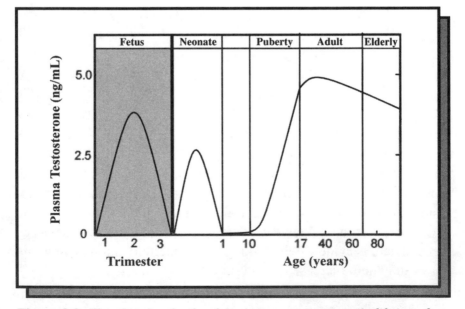

**Figure 3-2.** *The changing levels of testosterone over a man's lifetime, from conception to old age.*

and estradiol (the estrogens), are also found in males, again in smaller quantities than in females. In fact, in males (as well as females) estradiol is produced (in part) directly from testosterone (Fig. 3-1).

We should emphasize again that androgens are *natural* hormones, having specifically evolved to fit seamlessly into the complex jigsaw puzzle that is the human physiology. Although many physicians and medical researchers routinely refer to various drugs as androgens (or estrogens) because they act in some ways like their natural counterparts, this practice is incorrect, misleading, and ultimately hazardous. Like pieces designed for another puzzle, these drugs *never* fit perfectly into the human physiology. To the degree that they stick out, they can cause unwanted, unpleasant, and possibly dangerous side effects. It is doubtful that a natural androgen, administered in doses and on a schedule that mimics the body's normal physiology, would have such adverse effects.

## Testosterone Through the Ages of Man

About 95% of the testosterone in the male body is produced in the *testes* by *Leydig cells* (also called interstitial cells). The remainder is produced in the adrenal glands. (In females, both the ovaries and adrenals produce a small amount of testosterone.)

The concentration of testosterone rises and falls during three distinct periods of a man's life (Fig. 3-2). During gestation, it peaks during the second trimester, at which time it causes the fetus to differentiate into a male rather than a female. It rises again shortly after birth and then falls back to near zero, where it remains until puberty. Beginning at age 10 or 11, an accelerating increase in testosterone production stimulates the development of secondary sexual characteristics, such as facial and body hair, enlarged penis, prostate, and scrotum, deepening voice, and sperm production. Testosterone is also responsible for a post-pubertal growth spurt and, of course, an appreciation for the wonders of the female sex.

In the large majority of men, testosterone levels remain functionally normal until about age 50 or 60, at which point they begin

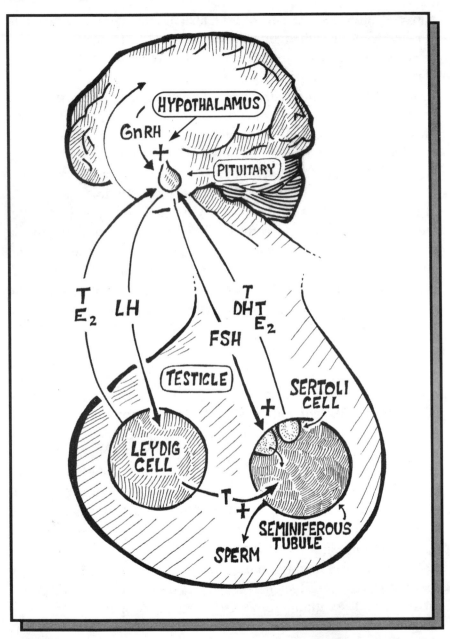

**Figure 3-3.** *The release and feedback of testosterone and other hormones in the hypothalamus-pituitary-testicular axis. T=testosterone; DHT=dihydrotestosterone; $E_2$=estradiol; LH=luteinizing hormone; FSH=follicle stimulating hormone; GnRH=gonadotropin-releasing hormone.*

a gradual final decline. As we discuss later, this age-related decline is responsible for a wide range of bodily changes that are coming to be recognized as elements of "male menopause."

No hormone works by itself. Testosterone is secreted by the testes in response to a signal that originates in the brain, as shown in Figure 3-3:

- Specifically, a region near the base of the brain called the *hypothalamus* releases a substance called *gonadotropin-releasing hormone (GnRH)*, which is carried to the nearby *pituitary* gland. The pituitary is regarded as the body's master gland because it releases so many different hormones and other substances that affect the function of all the other endocrine glands.

- The arrival of GnRH in the pituitary serves as a signal for the master gland to release two other hormones — *luteinizing hormone (LH)* and *follicle stimulating hormone (FSH)* — into the general circulation.[*]

- When LH reaches the Leydig cells of the testes, it initiates a series of biochemical steps that culminates in the synthesis and secretion of testosterone into the blood stream.

This complex hormonal system regulates itself, in part, via a negative feedback loop:

- Testosterone can be metabolized via any one of three primary pathways (Fig. 3-1), to form either *androstenedione* (a weak androgen), *DHT* (a very strong androgen), or *estradiol* (the "female hormone").

- When molecules of *estradiol*, and to a lesser extent *DHT*, reach the hypothalamus, they inhibit the release of GnRH – initiating a classic negative feedback loop.

---

[*] These two hormones exist in both males and females, but their names reflect their function only in females.

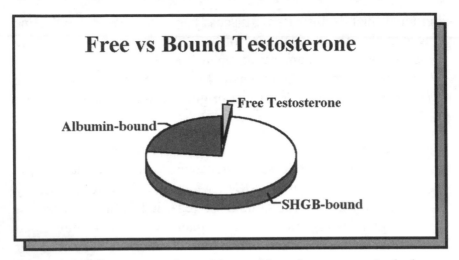

**Figure 3-4.** *Relative proportions of free and bound testosterone in the human blood stream.*

- The reduced amount of GnRH reaching the pituitary results in a reduction in the release of LH and FSH, and consequently, a slowdown in the production and release of testosterone from the testes.

- As men age and their testes begin to slow the production of testosterone (in part due to the loss of Leydig cells), the pituitary senses this slowdown (because less estradiol and DHT are produced to inhibit the release of LH) and increases its secretion of LH in order to compensate.

The production of sperm in the testes is closely tied to this hormonal cycle. FSH released from the pituitary binds to specific receptors in another part of the testes, called the *Sertoli cells,* which are located in the *seminiferous tubules,* the structure that comprises about 80 to 90% of the mass of the testicles. By stimulating the production of a protein that binds androgens, FSH promotes a higher concentration of testosterone in this region, which stimulates the maturation of sperm cells (*spermatogenesis*). Each day from puberty to death, the testes produce about 30 million new sperm.

# Testosterone: Free or Bound?

Testosterone circulates in the blood in two different forms: *free* and *bound* (Fig. 3-4). About 70 to 80% of circulating testosterone is bound to a protein named *sex hormone binding globulin (SHBG)*. Testosterone bound to SHBG is essentially out of action. It is locked up and can have no physiological effect on tissues. Another 20% or more of circulating testosterone is bound to another protein, *albumin*. Testosterone bound to albumin may be biologically available under certain conditions. Finally, only about 1 to 3% of circulating testosterone is *free*, which means it is completely biologically available and potentially active at testosterone target cells.

When referring to testosterone levels, it is extremely important to distinguish between the free and bound varieties. Here's why.

# The Decline and Fall of Testosterone

One reason for the historic confusion regarding the reality of a testosterone-related male menopause has been the assumption that testosterone levels do not decline very much with advancing years. Indeed, if you consider only *total testosterone* levels, this may seem to be a safe assumption, because many studies have found little or no change in total testosterone with age. How can such a small decline in total testosterone translate into the profound changes attributed to male menopause, the reasoning goes. But since the only testosterone that really matters in terms of biological activity in the human body is *free testosterone*, total testosterone can be a misleading measure.

The best way to document a decline in testosterone levels would be to follow a group of men from youth (or at least middle age) to old age and test them at regular intervals along the way. This would be a "longitudinal" study. Unfortunately, longitudinal studies are extremely expensive and difficult to run, so not surprisingly, only one major longitudinal study of testosterone levels in men has ever been carried out.[3] It followed 66 men, aged 41 to 61 years (at the start of the study), for 13 years. Among the many important

findings of this study was a small but significant gradual decline in
*total* testosterone levels with advancing age. Free testosterone was
not measured. (See Chapter 7 for further discussion of this important epidemiologic study.)

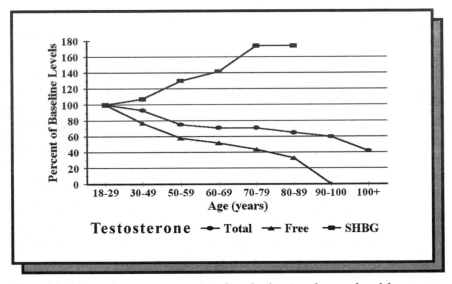

**Figure 3-5.** *Data from a cross-sectional study showing that total and free testosterone both decline with age, while SHBG rises. (Adapted from Vermeulen, 1993)*

Several cross-sectional studies measuring testosterone levels
have been done. In a cross-sectional study, a group of men of varying ages is identified and their testosterone levels are recorded and
grouped according to age. This is a less satisfactory solution than a
longitudinal design, because it measures testosterone at only a single point in time (albeit in men of a wide range of ages). A cross-
sectional study provides a kind of snapshot of the hormone levels
of the men in that group, which can then be extrapolated to the long
term for a given individual. With the proper controls and careful
interpretation of the data, however, cross-sectional studies can often
provide a fairly accurate picture, especially when the results are
supported by longitudinal studies, such as the one mentioned
above.

In one cross-sectional study, the eminent Belgian andrologist, Prof. Alex Vermeulen found that both total testosterone and free testosterone levels declined with age, while SHBG, which binds testosterone, rendering it permanently unavailable for biological uses, increased.[4] Free testosterone declined farther and at a faster rate than total testosterone (Fig. 3-5).

In another cross-sectional study — the Massachusetts Male Aging Study — the investigators evaluated hormone levels in a large group of men between the ages of 39 and 70. Overall, they found that in healthy men, free testosterone declined at a rate of 1.2% per year, and albumin-bound testosterone fell at 1.0% per year. At the same time, the levels of SHBG — along with SHBG-bound testosterone — *rose* at a rate of 1.2%. The net effect of all these changes was a very small decline in total testosterone of only 0.4% per year.[5] If you subtract out the SHBG-bound testosterone, which is inactive, the decline in testosterone appears much greater.

These same researchers found that the proportion of men aged 55 and older who could be classified as "testosterone deficient" (or "hypogonadal") depended on whether one measured

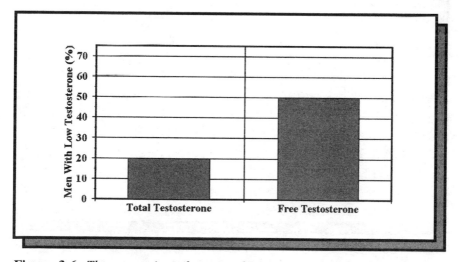

**Figure 3-6.** *The proportion of men with testosteone deficiency depends on whether total or free testosterone is measured. (Tenover, 1997)*

their total or free  testosterone. When they looked at total testosterone levels, only 20% were deemed testosterone-deficient. But
when they looked at free testosterone — the only testosterone that
really matters — they found 50% of this same group of men to be
deficient[6] (Fig. 3-6).

## The Daily Rhythm

The secretion of estrogen and progesterone in women rises and falls
on a familiar monthly cycle until they reach menopause. In men,
however, testosterone production is fairly steady, with no comparable cyclical changes. Within a given day, though, the levels do fluc-
tuate depending on the time of day. Figure 3-7 shows the results of
a small study conducted in New Zealand in which the serum levels
of total testosterone, free testosterone, and non-SHBG-bound

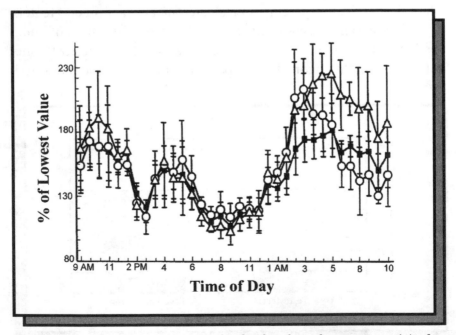

**Figure 3-7.** *Diurnal variation in the levels of total testosteone (■), free
testosterone (△), and non-SHBG-bound testosterone (○) in five healthy males
(aged 26-45 years). Levels are expressed as the mean percent of their respective
values at the point when testosterone was lowest. (Cooke et al, 1993)*

testosterone were measured every 45 minutes for 25.5 hours. Notice that the levels all peak at midmorning, late afternoon, and again between 3 and 5 AM.[7] There is some evidence that this circadian rhythmicity may break down in elderly men, such that the morning peak does not occur.[8]

As we will discuss later, it seems to make intuitive sense that a testosterone replacement regimen should attempt to mimic this natural circadian rhythm. Unfortunately, this has not typically been a priority among those who design or prescribe testosterone replacement regimens, at least until recently.

## Testosterone Replacement: What Are the Options?

It was not long after scientists discovered the structure of the testosterone molecule in the mid-1930s that they set about trying to "improve" upon it. The problem was that when natural testosterone (produced in the laboratory, but identical to the molecule the body produces) is injected into the body, it is metabolized very rapidly. This is as it should be, because that is how the body handles the testosterone it makes itself. It represents an "inconvenience" for drug manufacturers who want a product that is both effective and easy to use, however.

A natural testosterone pill was found to be less than optimal because hormonal testosterone taken by mouth and swallowed passes directly into the blood vessels that supply the liver, where it is inactivated to varying degrees. As a result, unpredictable amounts survive to enter the general circulation. Injections of natural hormonal testosterone fare only slightly better. Intramuscular implantation of natural testosterone crystals has enjoyed a limited degree of success, but this method of administration is extremely inconvenient and not always reliable, because the implants have a habit of working themselves out.

Thus, scientists (especially those working for pharmaceutical companies) in the 1930s and 1940s set out to develop ways to make

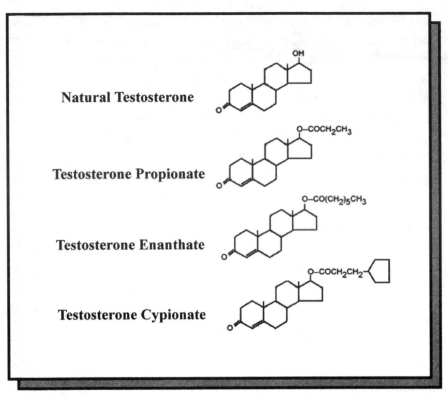

**Natural Testosterone**

**Testosterone Propionate**

**Testosterone Enanthate**

**Testosterone Cypionate**

**Figure 3-8.** *Differences in chemical structure between natural testosterone and various longer lasting injectable testosterone esters.*

the testosterone molecule more resistant to degradation by liver enzymes. They settled on two major methods:

- **Esterification of the testosterone molecule.** By substituting a chemical "side chain" called an *ester* for the OH (hydroxyl group) on the testosterone molecule, scientists found they could make the now modified testosterone molecule less soluble in water (Fig. 3-8). Thus, when dissolved in oil and injected into a muscle, it tends to diffuse out from its oily "depot" into the rest of the body at a far slower rate than injections of natural testosterone, significantly extending its duration of action. The longer the ester side chain they added, the longer the molecule would last. Thus, testosterone propi-

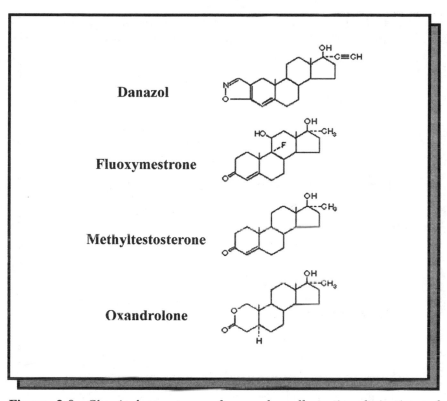

**Figure 3-9.** *Chemical structures of several orally active derivatives of testosterone.*

onate injections could be given two to three times a week, and testosterone enanthate and cypionate need be given only every two to four weeks to produce a comparable effect.

The body metabolizes these "esterified" versions of testosterone in a manner that is fairly consistent with the way it handles natural testostcrone, and most of the early research demonstrating clinical benefits of "testosterone" used these drugs. There are significant problems with them, however.

First, although testosterone esters are converted to free testosterone, which is metabolized in the same way as endogenous free testosteronc, various other unaltered compounds, metabolites, and conjugates are formed which have no business in the body and have never been metabolized by human bodies before.* (It is this last aspect which makes them more dangerous.)

Second, use of these drugs usually requires the individual to come to his doctor's office on a regular basis (from a two to three times a week to twice a month, depending on the drug) for intramuscular injections, which can be unpleasant, inconvenient, and, of course, expensive.

Third, and most importantly, the route of administration is decidedly unphysiological. Remember that the body normally puts out small amounts of testosterone on a more or less constant basis according to a diurnal pattern that includes regular peaks and valleys (Fig. 7). When these drugs are injected, "testosterone" levels rise sharply during the first 24 hours to the high normal or even supraphysiological range (hundreds of times higher than normal) and then gradually fall back into the hypogonadal (testosterone deficient) range until the next injection is due. Thus, the men who elect to take these injections are essentially boarding a roller coaster of changes in mood, sexual desire and activity, and energy level.[9] Moreover, the highs and lows in testosterone are reflected in highs and lows of the other hormones with which testosterone is normally involved, including estradiol, DHT, LH, FSH, androstenedione, and others.

- **17α-alkylation.** The attempts to create an orally active form of testosterone ran into even more trouble than the injectables. These products required even greater modifications of the testosterone molecule to make them resistant to degradation by the liver (Fig. 3-9). These are among the drugs that are typically referred to as oral "anabolic steroids." The major problem with these drugs is that they can be extremely toxic

---

* At least some of these byproducts are typically excreted in the urine and feces, which makes it easy to detect when an athlete has been using a synthetic form of testosterone to "bulk up."

to the liver. Harmful as they are, though, methyltestosterone remains the only oral form of testosterone approved by the FDA for use in the United States. Many menopausal women still take methyltestosterone, usually in combination with Premarin® (Estratest®), a particularly unhappy combination.

- **Testosterone undecanoate.** This testosterone ester is the only one that can be taken orally and still avoid first-pass metabolism in the liver. It must be taken two to three times a day and results in highly variable levels of testosterone in the blood. Testosterone undecanoate, which is probably safer than methyltestosterone, is used in Europe, Canada, and other countries, but it has never been approved for use in the U.S.

# Natural Testosterone Alternatives

The current trend in testosterone replacement therapy is the application of natural testosterone to the skin (***transdermal administration***). The fact that these products employ *natural* testosterone, rather than synthetic drugs derived from testosterone, is a step in the right direction and makes them clearly superior to any of the testosterone-like drugs that have been the standard conventional medical treatment for the last half century.

There are several variations of transdermal administration. Some are patented, high-tech, expensive products, while others are far simpler, nonpatented, and consequently, less costly to use. In the transdermal administration of testosterone, as in many other areas of life, simpler may be better.

- **The scrotal patch.** This high-tech product (Testoderm®) is an adhesive patch with a film containing natural testosterone that is derived from a vegetable source (Mexican yam or soy). When the patch is applied to the skin of the scrotum* once a day (typically in the morning) and left on for 22 to 24 hours,

---

* Scrotal skin was chosen because it is thin and at least five times more permeable to testosterone than other skin sites.

it results in a rise in serum testosterone levels over the next 4 to 8 hours to the mid-normal range, followed by a gradual decline over the remainder of the day. Clinical studies conducted by the manufacturer (ALZA Corp.) found a significant increase in sexual activity and an improvement in mood in 72 hypogonadal men using the scrotal patch for 12 weeks. It is not stated whether the improvement in sexuality was a result of the improved mood or an independent effect. Total cholesterol levels declined, but so did high-density lipoprotein (HDL) cholesterol (the "good" cholesterol).

Although these results are generally positive, and no serious unwanted effects have been reported  (except for the slight drop in HDL), the scrotal patch has some important drawbacks. First, it is terribly inconvenient. To assure good adhesion, the scrotal skin must be dry shaved at least once a week, which is likely to be an unpleasant prospect for most men. Daily application of the patch to the same location, which may be irritated by shaving, raises the possibility that the patch may cause further irritation. This raises the very real possibility that men may decide not to apply it on some days, which could result in mood swings, changes in sexuality from one day to the next, and probably other undesirable effects due to unnatural variations in testosterone levels. Second, while the scrotal patch produces levels of testosterone within the physiologic range *on average*, the normal diurnal variation (i.e., the three daily peaks) is lost, with the exception of the initial peak a few hours after the patch is applied. Third, dosing options are limited. Testosterone replacement needs can vary considerably from one man to the next, but the scrotal patch comes in only two dosages, 4 mg/day and 6 mg/day. The latter patch, which is 60 cm$^2$ in area, may be too large for some men, even though they may require that dose. No other options are available if higher or lower doses are required. Fourth, because the testosterone is absorbed directly into the scrotum, a location rich in the enzyme 5α-reductase, the scrotal patch causes a substantial — and unphysiological —

increase in the potent androgen DHT in the area of the prostate. The long-term effects of such high levels of DHT are unknown. Finally, as a high-tech, patented pharmaceutical product, the scrotal patch can be quite expensive, costing about $100 per month.

Because of all these problems, it appears that the scrotal patch is not long for this world. Even its manufacturer has recently come out with a non-scrotal patch (Testoderm TTS®) which seems certain to replace it. It's hard to imagine any man preferring a scrotal patch over a patch he could place on a more convenient part of his anatomy.

- **The (almost) anywhere patch.** Like the scrotal patch, the (almost) anywhere patch (Androderm®, Testoderm TTS®) is a high-tech vehicle for transdermal administration of natural testosterone. Unlike the scrotal patch, these products can be applied anywhere on the body except the scrotum and bony areas. Androderm's manufacturer (SmithKlineBeecham) reports that 12 months of use resulted in significant improvements in fatigue, mood, and sexual function.

These patches have several important advantages, compared with scrotal patches. First, and most obviously, they eliminate the inconvenience and discomforts associated with scrotal application, making it more likely that men will use the product daily. Also, since they can (and should) rotate the application sites, they minimize the risk of localized skin irritation. Despite this, though, skin irritation is quite common with these products and is a primary reason that many men quit therapy. Second, these patches permit a little more dosing flexibility. Since each Androderm patch contains enough testosterone to provide 2.5 mg per day, men can apply one, two, or three patches at a time, depending on their individual need. Third, testosterone is distributed throughout the body, rather than being concentrated in the scrotum, where it results in extraordinarily high local levels of DHT.

Where serum testosterone levels rise quite rapidly after application of the scrotal patch, reaching a maximum concentration within 2 to 4 hours, the (almost) anywhere patch causes
a much more gradual rise. Thus, the manufacturer of
Androderm® recommends applying the patch (or patches)
before bedtime in order to reproduce the normal morning
peak 8 to 12 hours later. Like the scrotal patch, though, the
complete circadian rhythm, with includes peaks in the late
afternoon and early morning (Fig. 3-7), is not duplicated. The
monthly cost of these patches is about $125.

- **Testosterone creams and gels.** The same natural testosterone used in the high-tech patches can also be formulated
into simple creams and gels that are available from a compounding pharmacist with a physician's prescription at a fraction of the cost. After being rubbed into the skin, the testosterone passes into the blood stream in much the same way
that the testosterone from the patches does. One of the major
advantages of these formulations is dosing flexibility. Instead
of being limited to one or two dosage strengths, the pharmacist can easily formulate a cream or gel at any strength the
prescribing physician determines is required to restore an
individual's youthful testosterone levels. Moreover, the
patient can apply the gel up to two or three times a day to
closely reproduce the natural circadian rhythm. Finally, the
cost of testosterone creams and gels is quite reasonable.
Depending on the dose, a month's worth might cost as little
as $35 to $45.

- **Sublingual (under the tongue) testosterone tablets.** If
testosterone is swallowed, it is immediately and almost completely metabolized in the liver, leaving virtually nothing that
is biologically active. If a testosterone tablet is allowed to dissolve under the tongue, though, the hormone will be absorbed
directly into the blood stream, bypassing the liver and pro-
viding a useful amount of biologically active hormone.
Compounding pharmacists can formulate testosterone into

sublingual tablets, which can function as a convenient, effective, and inexpensive delivery system.

Why have pharmaceutical companies elected to go the high-tech route if simple creams, gels, and sublingual tablets will work just as well? The answer can be summed up in one word: *patentability*. As a natural substance, testosterone itself cannot be patented, and *anyone* can sell it. Pharmaceutical companies, which are in business to maximize profits, prefer to sell products that are exclusively theirs. While testosterone is not patentable, a sophisticated patch delivery system containing testosterone is.

# References

1.  Wright J, Morgenthaler J. *Natural Hormone Replacement for Women Over 45.* Petaluma, CA: Smart Publications; 1997.

2.  Regelson W, Colman C. *The Superhormone Promise.* New York: Simon & Schuster; 1996.

3.  Zmuda J, Cauley J, Kriska A, Glynn N, Gutai J, Kuller L. Longitudinal relation between endogenous testosterone and cardiovascular disease risk factors in middle-aged men. *Am J Epidemiol.* 1997;146:609-617.

4.  Vermeulen A. The male climacterium. *Ann Med.* 1993;25:531-534.

5.  Gray A, Feldman HA, McKinlay JB, Longcope C. Age, disease, and changing sex hormone levels in middle-aged men: results of the Massachusetts Male Aging Study. *J Clin Endocrinol Metab.* 1991;73:1016-25.

6.  Tenover JL. Testosterone and the aging male. *J Androl.* 1997;18:103-6.

7.  Cooke R, McIntosh J, McIntosh R. Circadian variation in serum free and non-SHBG- bound testosterone in normal men: measurements, and simulation using a mass action model. *Clin Endocrinol.* 1993;39:163-171.

8.  Bremner WJ, Vitiello MV, Prinz PN. Loss of circadian rhythmicity in blood testosterone levels with aging in normal men. *J Clin Endocrinol Metab.* 1983;56:1278-81.

9.  Bhasin S, Bremner W. Emerging issues in androgen replacement therapy. *J Clin Endocrinol Metab.* 1997;82:3-8.

# Chapter 4

# The Ups and Downs of Male Sexual Arousal

**M**ale menopause isn't only about sex. Still, the first questions many middle aged men raise when the subject comes up are almost always about sex. Will I become impotent? Will I continue to enjoy sex? Will I even care? In his experience with more than 1,000 menopausal men, the British andrologist Malcolm Carruthers, M.D., found that 92% of his male menopausal patients were dissatisfied with their sex life.[1]

These fears are very real. Erectile dysfunction in aging men is more widespread than anyone (except perhaps the Viagra® marketing team) ever imagined. The Massachusetts Male Aging Study of 1,290 men (aged 40-70 years) found that the prevalence of impotence tripled from age 40 to 70. Overall, 52% of the participants had at least some degree of impotence. It was rated mild in 17%, moderate in 25%, and complete in 10%. Nor was complete impotence limited to the very old; 5% of the 40-year-olds reported that they had completely lost the ability to have an erection.[2]

Although men have faced the loss of their sexuality since the dawn of time, only within the last few years have they been able to ask, "What can I do about it?" and expect a real solution. That men are eager for such a solution was made evident by the recent Viagra® explosion. But while Viagra® has certainly garnered more attention as a remedy for failing masculine prowess than anything since Brown-Séquard began injecting himself with ground up dog and guinea pig testicles more than a century ago, it is not the ultimate solution to the problem. In fact, like most synthetic pharmaceutical products, it represents a highly focused, *symptomatic* approach to a problem that can often be better handled by *natural* or herbal substances that focus more on the underlying causes.

The ebbing of male sexuality, like sexuality itself, is an extraordinarily complex affair. In addition to declining testosterone (and other hormones), one has to consider a wide range of factors that might cause a man to lose interest in sex and/or to find his sexual ability slowly shrinking away. These factors include mood, especially depression, general health, stress, energy level, alcohol or tobacco use, serious illnesses like diabetes, atherosclerosis, heart disease, and prostate cancer, not to mention use of a wide range of common prescription and nonprescription drugs. In most cases, an interaction of two or more of these factors is probably at work.

In this chapter, we are going to go "behind the scenes" of male sexual arousal. We will describe what is happening at the hormonal, physiological, and anatomical level when a man becomes sexually aroused, how his penis becomes erect, and what goes wrong when it doesn't.

# How Testosterone Affects Sexuality

As a general rule, high testosterone levels are associated with high levels of sexual interest and activity, and low testosterone levels with less sexual interest and activity. Of course, things are never as simple as they seem, and the relationship between testosterone and sexuality, which is moderated by the complex interplay of cerebral, hormonal, and physiological events, is no exception.

Consider the complexity of sexuality itself. At its most basic level, you need a *sex drive*, what sex researchers have long called a *libido*. Libido is what turns a seemingly ordinary woman into an object of fantasy and desire and a target of sexual advances. Libido

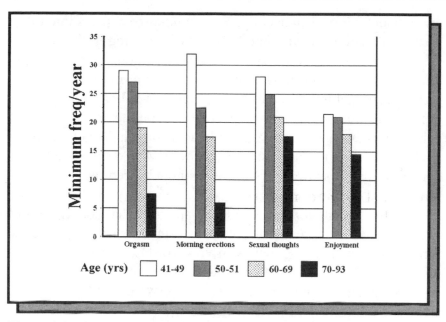

**Figure 4-1.** *The growing libido-potency gap. This graph shows the results of a study in men aged 41 to 93. Note that orgasm and morning/nocturnal erections (minimum freq/yr) decline far more than sexual thoughts and enjoyment with increasing age. (Adapted from Davidson et al, 1983)*

is what transforms a casual hug into an embrace of passion. Libido is the engine of sexuality; it needs to be running before anything else can happen.

*The "libido-potency gap."* The fuel the libido runs on is testosterone. While too much natural testosterone probably won't transform an ordinary man into a sexual predator, too little will most likely lead him toward a less active sex life. As men enter their menopausal years, the decline in libido they may experience usually closely parallels the gradual decline in free testosterone.

It is far from a simple relationship, though, because a man's interest in and desire for sex declines at a much slower rate than his ability to perform sexual acts. This leads to what some researchers have termed a "libido-potency gap" that widens as men age. The libido-potency gap is a classic example of the spirit being willing, but the flesh being weak (Fig. 4-1). In one study, for example, while more than 50% of men over age 80 continued to express interest in sexual intercourse, fewer than 15% were still doing it.[3, 4]

The most important cause of the libido-potency gap is *erectile failure*, also known as erectile dysfunction, impotence, impotency, "can't get it up" and/or "can't keep it up." Testosterone plays a fundamental role in producing erections, but again, it is not the whole story. A man can have trouble achieving and/or maintaining erections despite normal testosterone levels. And even when testosterone levels are extremely low, as in prepubescent boys and castrated men, erections can occur.

*Hormone of fantasy.* Evidence suggests that some types of erections may be more dependent on testosterone than others. In one small study, eight young men with very low testosterone levels due to injury or disease were either shown erotic films or asked to imagine a sexually exciting scene (sexual fantasy) under two different conditions: with "testosterone" replacement (oral testosterone undecanoate) or without it. The researchers found that overall, whether the men were on "testosterone" or not, the maximum size of their erections (as measured by the diameter of their penis) and the time it took them to achieve an erection were essentially the same.

On the other hand, the source of the sexual stimulation did make a difference. When the men were off "testosterone" replacement (i.e., testosterone deficient), their erections in response to their own sexual fantasies were significantly smaller and took longer to achieve compared with when they were on "testosterone." There was no difference, however, in their response to the erotic films.[5] Other studies have found that spontaneous erections, such as those that occur during sleep, are also highly dependent on testosterone level.[6, 7] Thus, while erections, per se, seem to be independent of testosterone, arousal related to sexual fantasy is testosterone-dependent.

## How to Make an Erection

A penile erection is a marvel of biological engineering, biomechanics, hydraulics, blood flow, and nervous control. Although it begins in the brain with an erotic stimulus, either external (e.g., an attractive woman or man) or internal (e.g., a fantasy of an attractive woman or man), and culminates with the rush of blood into the penis, it may be easier to understand how it works if we start at the penis and work backwards.

The hemodynamics of erection resemble a tire with a slow leak. As long as the amount of air flowing into the tire exceeds the amount leaking out, the tire remains hard. Once you stop putting air into the tire under pressure, the air inside starts to leak out until the air pressure inside is the same as the air pressure outside.

***The penile blood supply.*** Where a tire consists of a single open cavity, the penis consists of three chambers or *corpora* composed of a spongy tissue — the ***corpus spongiosum*** and two ***corpora cavernosa*** (Fig. 4-2). Branches of the penile artery open directly into these chambers, allowing them to fill rapidly when arterial blood flow is high, as occurs during periods of sexual arousal.

Blood exits the penile chambers ("leaks" out) via a system of veins. During sexual arousal, blood flows very rapidly into the penile chambers, which begin to fill and enlarge, like a sponge soaking up a spill. If inflow is rapid enough (the rate of blood flow during sexual arousal can increase 6- to 10-fold above the resting rate), the enlarging spongy tissue compresses the veins that serve as the escape valve (or "leak"), slowing outflow to a trickle.

The event that makes an erection possible is the rapid rush of blood through the penile arteries. Like all arteries in the body, the amount of blood that can flow through the various branches of the penile arteries is controlled by smooth muscle tissue that surrounds the arteries. In their non-aroused state, these muscles maintain a degree of tone (gentle squeezing) that keeps the blood vessels moderately constricted. This restricts the arterial diameter, thus limiting the blood flow to a level insufficient to fill the spongy tissue and compress the drainage veins.

During sexual arousal, though, the arterial muscles relax their grip, expanding the arterial inner diameter (or lumen), and opening

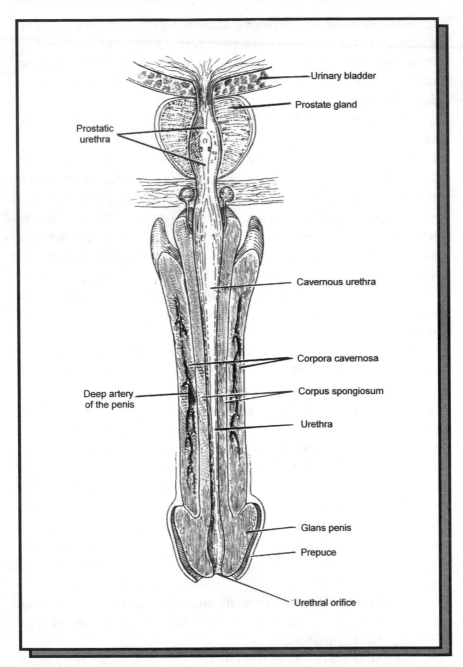

**Figure 4-2**. *Cross section of the penis.*

the penile sluice gates. Fast-flowing arterial blood rushes in, quickly filling the spongy tissue and compressing the drainage veins.*

Men with atherosclerosis or high blood pressure often lose their ability to have erections because the arteries that feed the penis become occluded and/or lose their ability to expand. In severe cases, blood may trickle in at a mere fraction of the rate required to fill the spongy tissue, leaving the penis permanently limp. In less severe cases, a moderate erection may be possible.

*Neural control.* Penile blood flow is at all times under the subtle control of a coordinated system of hormones, nerves, and neurotransmitters. Most erections begin in the brain, often with a conscious thought but sometimes without any obvious stimulus. No matter where they begin, though, they all end at the same place, the neurons (nerve cells) and arteries of the penis.

Various neurochemicals secreted by nerve cells and arterial endothelial cells contribute to the relaxation or contraction of the smooth muscle that surrounds the penile arteries. The major biochemicals that promote arterial smooth muscle relaxation/dilation are **nitric oxide (NO)** and **cyclic GMP (cGMP)**.

The neurotransmitter **noradrenaline** (also called **norepinephrine**) can cause arterial smooth muscle either to relax or contract, depending on which receptors it stimulates. Stimulation of α-adrenergic (alpha-adrenergic) receptors causes contraction, while stimulation of β-adrenergic (beta-adrenergic) receptors causes relaxation. Drugs that selectively block these receptors can affect the ability to have an erection. For example, a common class of anti-hypertensive (blood pressure lowering) medication is called β-blockers (beta blockers). As the name suggests, these drugs prevent stimulation of β-adrenergic receptors. While this action may help lower blood pressure, it is bad news for erections, which explains why these drugs are well-known to cause impotence.

---

* Although the behavior of many men may suggest otherwise, the contention that the large amount of blood shifted to the penis during an erection deprives the brain of sufficient blood to function effectively is without any scientific basis.

On the other hand, substances that block noradrenaline from stimulating α-adrenergic receptors can promote erections. As we will discuss in Chapter 5, one such substance is the ancient impotence cure *yohimbine*.

## Nitric Oxide: The Erection Builder

Nitric oxide (NO), which is produced by the endothelial cells that line the arterial lumen as well as by certain nerve fibers, is a potent vasodilator. NO acts like a kind of universal biochemical interpreter that translates chemical/electrical messages from one form to another. If you place a drop of NO on the muscles that encircle an artery, they instantly relax, allowing more blood to flow through them.

Once considered to be solely a toxic byproduct of certain chemical reactions that destroyed the ozone layer while causing acid rain and cancer, in the last decade, NO has come to be recognized as a vital component of human physiology in general and as a primary mediator of erection in particular.[8-10] In 1992, as evidence regarding the value of NO was becoming hard to ignore, the American Association for the Advancement of Science (AAAS) in its journal *Science,* named NO its "Molecule of the Year." "Like a squirt of some powerful perfume, a puff of nitric oxide spurs different cells into an array of different activities, from communication to defense to regulation," the *Science* authors wrote.[11] And in 1998, the scientists who began the new age of NO research were awarded the Nobel Prize.

Molecules of NO are generated when an enzyme called *NO synthase* (*NOS*), which is abundant in the nerve and muscle cells in and around the penis, strips away a nitrogen atom (N) from a passing molecule of the amino acid *L-arginine* (which comes from dietary sources) and combines it with an atom of oxygen (O).

NOS can be activated by a number of common substances released from nerves. Especially important in this regard is the neurotransmitter *acetylcholine* (*ACh*). Signals that begin in the brain centers that deal with sexual arousal travel to the penile arteries on neurons that transmit their messages using ACh.

Since NO molecules have a very brief life span (their half-life is only about 5 seconds), their site of activity has to be very close to home. NO formed in arterial endothelial cells and penile nerves passes directly into immediately adjacent smooth muscle cells that surround the penile arteries. This causes the arteries to relax and leads to a reduction in blood pressure. (A constant seepage of NO molecules is now recognized as being crucial for modulating blood pressure all over the body. The more NO that is present, the lower the blood pressure.)

Arthur L. Burnett, M.D., a urologist at Johns Hopkins University, says that NO acts as an essential chemical trigger in producing erections. "It's like turning on a light switch." Noting that all you need to light up a room are wires, lamps and light bulbs, he said, NO is "the switch that starts the process."[13]

*Testosterone and NO*. There appear to be two types of NOS. One type, called *constitutive* NOS is always available in cells to produce brief "puffs" of NO. The other type, called *inducible* NOS, is produced on demand by other chemical messengers. Although inducible NOS is produced more slowly than the constitutive variety, over a period of days it can produce at least 1,000 times more NO. One inducer of NOS may be testosterone. A study using laboratory rats found that testosterone stimulates the formation of NOS in penile nerve terminals, which was associated with an increase in erections.[12]

As we will discuss in Chapter 5, it is possible to raise NO levels naturally by ingesting supplements containing *L-arginine*. L-arginine supplements may thus help restore erections in some men with erectile dysfunction. They may also help enhance erections in men with normal erectile function.

## cGMP Delivers the Message

NO does not have a direct relaxing effect on arterial smooth muscle. Instead, NO works through a kind of biochemical "middle man" called *guanylate cyclase*, which is found inside arterial smooth muscle cells, to form a third compound, *cGMP*, which is considered to be a "second messenger." cGMP is what actually triggers muscle relaxation.

When injected directly into the penis, cGMP produces an erection that may last up to 40 minutes.[14] cGMP injections may not be necessary, however. The drug Viagra® promotes erections by slowing the normal metabolic degradation of cGMP. This results in an increase in the concentration of available cGMP in penile arterial smooth muscle, which causes it to relax. As we will show in Chapter 6, L-arginine accomplishes essentially the same result by creating more NO which stimulates more guanylate cyclase leading to the production of more cGMP.

# What Causes Erectile Failure?

The erection of the penis is a marvel of coordination among psychological, hormonal, neurological, and vascular factors. As long as they all work well together, the testes and penis respond to sexual stimuli as they were designed to. When something goes wrong with one or more of these factors, sexual function may suffer.

Experts in sexual medicine used to believe that if a man complained of erectile failure and did not have spontaneous erections during sleep, his impotence most likely had a *physiological* origin, i.e., it was caused by factors such as hormonal dysfunction, vascular or other disease, injury, or drugs. If he complained of impotence but still had erections in his sleep, though, it was thought the cause must be *psychological*, i.e., stress, "performance anxiety," or sexual partner- related.

This view of erectile failure is now considered to be oversimplified. The failure to achieve and maintain erections adequate for sexual intercourse is now known to have both physiological and psychological components, and in most cases, more than one factor is at work. As we described earlier in this chapter, low testosterone may be associated with a loss of spontaneous or nocturnal erections while erections in response to external sexual stimuli may still occur. Moreover, erections do occasionally occur in prepubescent boys and castrated men, both of which have little or no testosterone.

*Hormonal factors.* Low testosterone levels (known among medical types as *hypogonadism*) clearly play a role in the erectile response. Although testosterone is not essential for erections, it does appear to facilitate some types of erections.

As men age, their testosterone levels decline for a variety of reasons:

- *Their testosterone-producing Leydig cells begin to die off.* One study found the number of Leydig cells to be negatively correlated with age. The testes of older men had 44% fewer Leydig cells compared with those of younger men.[15] Fewer Leydig cells means less testosterone.

- *Sex hormone binding globulin (SHBG) increases with age.* SHBG permanently binds free testosterone, effectively reducing the amount of free testosterone available to produce the various androgenic effects.

- *Leydig cells may reduce their production of testosterone* in response to erroneous signals because of a disrupted feed-back system related to an excess of the "female hormone" *estradiol*. Recall that some testosterone is converted to estradiol by the enzyme *aromatase* (Fig. 3-1), and some of this estradiol feeds back to the pituitary to signal the master gland to slow its secretion of LH. With less LH reaching the testes, Leydig cells put the brakes on testosterone production.

- *Elevated estradiol levels* relative to testosterone may be an important factor in age-related hypogonadism leading to sexual dysfunction. Normally, testosterone and estradiol are in perfect balance, but too much estradiol in the system can significantly slow testosterone production. According to one hypothesis, with advancing age, the normal balance between testosterone and estradiol begins to tilt toward estradiol. At some point — a "biological point of no return" — the suppressive effects of estradiol on testosterone production begin to predominate, and testosterone levels fall to a new, lower level of equilibrium.[16]

If estradiol in the male body is a product of testosterone metabolism (aromatization), how is it possible for estradiol levels to increase with age while testosterone levels decrease? The explanation for this apparent paradox may lie in the changing composition of the body, specifically the increase in fatty tissue relative to lean muscle that typically occurs with advancing age. Fatty tissue contains lots of aromatase, compared with lean tissue. Thus, as fat accumulates in those beer bellies, love handles, and spare tires, more aromatase becomes available to grab up more testosterone and convert it to more estradiol. The fat also serves as a reservoir for storing extra estradiol. All that extra estradiol then feeds back to the pituitary, signaling the testes to slow down testosterone production by secreting less LH. As a result, estradiol levels go up relative to testosterone levels.[16]

- Elevations in the level of the hormone *prolactin* (usually due to a pituitary tumor), as well as too much — or too little — thyroid hormone, may occasionally cause sexual dysfunction.[17]

*Disease factors.* One of the most consistent findings in studies of age-related sexual dysfunction is that it always occurs more frequently and more severely in men who have certain serious, often chronic diseases or conditions. Among the most common disease states known to affect sexual function are:

- Diabetes mellitus
- Heart disease
- Hypertension (high blood pressure)
- Peripheral vascular disease, especially when the blood flow to and from the penis is impaired
- Neurologic damage, as may occur as a consequence of diabetes, prostatectomy, alcohol abuse, pelvic surgery, spinal

surgery or injury, and various chronic degenerative nerve diseases

* Peptic ulcer
* Arthritis
* Allergy
* Low plasma levels of HDL (the "good") cholesterol

*Drug use.* A variety of drugs, both legal and illegal, have been associated with as many as one case of impotence in four. The most important offending agents include:

* **Antidepressants,** especially monoamine oxidase (MAO) inhibitors and tricyclic anti- depressants, which are less commonly used these days, and the selective serotonin reuptake inhibitors (SSRIs), such as Prozac®, Zoloft®, and Paxil®, which are among the most prescribed drugs of all time. Depending on the drug and dose, unwanted effects such as decreased libido, erectile dysfunction, ejaculatory failure, and pain on ejaculation have been reported with these drugs.

* **Anti-anxiety drugs**, including diazepam (Valium®), alprazolam (Xanax®), and many others have been reported to interfere with orgasm and ejaculation.

* **Antipsychotic drugs.** Older drugs, such as chlorpromazine, thioridizine, and fluphenazine have been reported to decrease libido and impair ejaculation in as many as 25% to 60% of users.[18]

* **Antihypertensive drugs.** Among the most important drugs in this category are the thiazide diuretics (e.g., hydrochlorothiazide) and the β-blockers (e.g., Inderal®, Atenolol® and many others), ACE inhibitors (eg, Vasotec®, Capoten® and others), and calcium channel blockers (eg, Procardia®, Cardizem®, and others) which are well-known to diminish libido and impair erection and ejaculation.

* **Other cardiovascular drugs**, such as digoxin, drugs for normalizing heart rhythm (e.g., Calan®, Rhythmol®, and many

others), and drugs for reducing cholesterol (e.g., Zocor®, Pravachol®, and others), have been associated with loss of libido and impotence.

- **Anti-heartburn drugs**, especially Tagamet® and Zantac®, may cause loss of libido and erectile failure.

- **Opioids**, especially chronic use of legal (e.g., codeine, morphine) or illegal versions (e.g., heroin) are powerful inhibitors of libido and orgasm.

- **Cancer chemotherapeutic drugs** can cause a progressive decline in libido and erectile function during extended treatment.

- **Alcohol**. Although low doses of alcohol may enhance libido and remove inhibitions, higher doses quickly suppress sexual function, reduce libido, impair erection, and postpone ejaculation. About half of all chronic alcoholics may be impotent, with about half of these permanently disabled sexually.[18]

- **Tobacco**. Nicotine from cigarette smoke constricts the blood vessels that supply the penis, impeding erection.

*Psychogenic factors,* such as anxiety and relationship problems, are always important and often interact with other factors to reduce libido and adversely affect erectile function and ejaculation.

Now that we know how sexual arousal occurs and what can go wrong with it, in the next chapter, we will discuss how to restore a lagging libido and keep the erectile machinery running smoothly.

# References

1. Carruthers M. *Maximising Manhood*. London: HarperCollins Publishers; 1996.

2. Feldman HA, Goldstein I, Hatzichristou DG, Krane RJ, McKinlay JB. Impotence and its medical and psychosocial correlates: results of the Massachusetts Male Aging Study. *J Urol*. 1994;151:54-61.

3. Davidson J, Chen J, Crapo L, Gray G, Greenleaf W, Catania J. Hormonal changes and sexual function in aging men. *J Clin Endocrinol Metab*. 1983;57:71-77.

4. Mulligan T, Katz P. Erectile failure in the aged: evaluation and treatment. *J Am Geriatr Soc*. 1988;36:54-62.

5.  Bancroft J, Wu F. Changes in erectile responsiveness during androgen replacement therapy. *Arch Sexual Behav.* 1983;12:59-66.

6.  O'Carroll R, Shapiro C, Bancroft J. Androgens, behaviour and nocturnal erection in hypogonadal men: the effects of varying the replacement dose. *Clin Endocrinol (Oxf).* 1985;23:527-38.

7.  Kwan M, Greenleaf WJ, Mann J, Crapo L, Davidson JM. The nature of androgen action on male sexuality: a combined laboratory-self-report study on hypogonadal men. *J Clin Endocrinol Metab.* 1983;57:557-62.

8.  Burnett AL. Role of nitric oxide in the physiology of erection. *Biol Reprod.* 1995;52:485- 489.

9.  Argiolas A. Nitric oxide is a central mediator of penile erection. *Neuropharmacology* 1994;33:1339-1344.

10. Melis M, Argiolas A. Role of central nitric oxide in the control of penile erection and yawning. *Prog Neuro-Psychopharmacol Biol Psychiat.* 1997;21:899-922.

11. Culotta E, Koshland D, Jr. NO news is good news. *Science.* 1992;258:1862-1865.

12. Reilly C, Zamorano P, Stopper V, Mills T. Androgenic regulation of NO availability in rat penile erection. *J Andrology.* 1997;18:110-115.

13. Associated Press. Researchers find male sex trigger. *San Jose Mercury News.* San Jose, CA; 1992:2F.

14. Mirone V, Palmieri A, Nistico G. Intracavernous cyclic GMP produces penile erection in patients with erectile dysfunction [letter]. *Br J Urol.* 1993;71:365.

15. Neaves WB, Johnson L, Porter JC, Parker CR, Jr., Petty CS. Leydig cell numbers, daily sperm production, and serum gonadotropin levels in aging men. *J Clin Endocrinol Metab.* 1984;59:756-63.

16. Cohen P. The role of estradiol in the maintenance of secondary hypogonadism in males in erectile dysfunction. *Med Hypotheses.* 1998;50:331-333.

17. Rousseau P. Impotence in elderly men. *Postgrad Med.* 1988;83:212-219.

18. Deamer R. The role of medications in geriatric sexual function. *Clin Geriatr Med.* 1991;7:95-111.

# Chapter 5

# Re-Igniting the Sexual Fires: Testosterone

Menopausal men have dreamt about restoring their waning sexual powers for thousands of years. No sooner had a male hormonal extract been isolated in the late 1920s than researchers started giving it to men who had lost sexual function due to castration or disease. While it's easy to question the scientific ethics of some of these early human experiments, their results must have seemed startling and momentous to those who witnessed them first hand. Certainly, they could be poignant.

Soon after the University of Chicago chemist Fred Koch had found a way to extract a rather impure — but effective — mixture of male hormones from bulls' testicles, he found himself preparing increasing amounts of the stuff for other researchers who were finding ever more ways to test it out in lab animals like rats and capons. Koch's hormonal extraction process was tedious, smelly, costly, and inefficient, severely limiting the amount he could produce. To make 20 mg of active extract required cooking down more than 40 pounds of bulls' balls. There was no way he could ever make enough to sustain even a single human.

But then, one day Koch was approached by a Prof. A.T. Kenyon, who ran his own medical clinic. Kenyon wanted to know if Koch's brew would work on "eunichoid" men. Whether out of compassion or scientific curiosity, Koch agreed to give Kenyon what he needed. As Paul de Kruif tells the story:[1]

> Here in Professor Kenyon's clinic was a twenty-six-year-old man, or an almost-man, it would be more accurate to call him. At the age of fourteen he had developed a little pubic hair, but since that time he had made no manly progress. His voice was childish. Every two weeks, he pathetically shaved a bit of fuzz off his upper lip and his chin. He had experienced only the feeblest of sexual sensations, and these were very rare, and he had never had a discharge of sperm. The X rays showed that his long bones had not developed like

# A Note About Testosterone Research

In this chapter and those that follow, we describe a great deal of research about testosterone. Readers should be aware that, for reasons discussed in Chapters 2 and 3, the "testosterone" used in the vast majority of the early studies was not natural testosterone. Instead, most of the researchers used one of the injectable testosterone esters (e.g., testosterone propionate, testosterone cypionate, or testosterone enanthate), the orally active ester (testosterone undecanoate), or an orally active anabolic steroid (e.g., methyltestosterone).

Today, most knowledgeable physicians are coming to recognize that topical or sublingual (under the tongue) testosterone preparations employing natural (identical-to-human) testosterone provide a more physiologically normal experience that yields all the benefits associated with "testosterone" use but with far fewer adverse effects.

Although hundreds of studies were conducted using the inferior early "testosterone" preparations, well-controlled stud-

those of a grown-up. His testicles were tiny and his basal metabolism was low.

Koch, whether out of compassion or scientific curiosity, gave Kenyon all the testicular extract he had — enough for about 53 days of daily injections — making this patient the first human being ever to receive injections of male hormone.

As the injections continued, for the first time in his life, this boy, who could not seem to grow up, began to feel the hot surge of real sexual drive; and it was not in his mind only, but there was the most striking evidence of it physically, measurably, or, as the scientists say, objectively. During the period of

ies testing modern topical and sublingual preparations have only recently begun to appear, as the drug companies making testosterone patches and perhaps other natural testosterone products have increased their stake in the treatment of male menopause. So far these relatively few studies have supported the benefits of "testosterone" shown in the earlier studies, while producing fewer adverse effects.

As we discuss the benefits of testosterone replacement in the pages that follow, please keep in mind that our conclusions may be drawn, at least in part, from trials conducted using the older "testosterone" formulations. This requires a small leap of faith. You can't really know whether a natural version of testosterone taken via a skin cream, patch, or sublingual tablet is going to produce exactly the same benefits as a synthetic version of "testosterone" taken by depot injection or swallowed until you actually try it. Nevertheless, based on the few studies that have been done so far as well as on my own (JVW) clinical experience and that of my colleagues, we have every reason to believe that all the benefits evident in the early studies can be extrapolated to the use of modern topical/sublingual natural testosterone formulations in every respect without most of the adverse side effects.

these daily hormone injections, he became in a sexual sense like a strong and normal youth. For the first time in his life, he experienced, and repeatedly, the sexual climax of the ejaculation of semen.

Then the inevitable happened. Kenyon's hormone supply ran out. The 53-day supply had required the distillation of more than half a ton of bulls' balls. There was no way Koch could keep up with the demand. The experiment was over. "This human experimental animal who had been brought to the very threshold of a belated manhood, felt his borrowed virility fade away," wrote de Kruif. But we need not feel too sorry for the young man, he reminds us. "After all, when a man's testicles are off, they're off, and nature mercifully, maybe, made him forget how wonderful it had been when he still had them. This is observed by many physicians, questioning castrates. Their loss loses its first poignant tragedy."

## Restoring Sexual Function With Testosterone

The development of "testosterone"-like drugs, which began soon after Kenyon's heart-rending experiment, must have seemed like a godsend. After thousands of years of searching, physicians finally had ready supply of substances, that while not exactly like natural testosterone, appeared to function very much like the real thing.

Beginning in the late 1930s, it was common for researchers and physicians giving these formulations to men with testosterone deficiencies to observe a remarkable restoration of sexual arousal and activity. These formulations were often crude and tended to produce a very unphysiological, rapid, long-lasting increase in testosterone levels far above what the body was equipped to handle. Although the benefits were unmistakable, so were the unwanted effects and dangers.

Men living today are indeed fortunate in this regard. They are the first generation in the history of mankind to have available safe, reliable, and effective means of restoring lost sexual urges and erectile capacity. Key among these are natural testosterone supplements.

In men whose testosterone production has gone south, supplemental testostcrone may provide two important sexual benefits. It may reawaken their interest in and motivation for sex — their libido — making it easier for them to become sexually aroused. It may also help improve the quality and duration of their erections.

***Boosting a sagging libido.*** Sex begins in the head. To be sexually aroused is to be aroused *by* something — or someone — whether it is a living, breathing person of the opposite (or possibly the same) sex, a film or photo of a such a person, or simply a sexual fantasy existing solely in the imagination.

As testosterone levels fall with age, it may take more and more "effort" for a man to become aroused by sexual stimuli. First, the fantasies may go. Then he may find himself less and less aroused by images of attractive women. It is as though normally sexually arousing images pass through a kind of psychic "V-chip" that strips away all or most of their sexual aura. Whereas a male in his teens or 20s might get an erection at the mere thought of a sexual encounter, a menopausal male with a testosterone deficiency may find he needs considerable foreplay to reach a high enough level of arousal to achieve and maintain an erection.

Boosting testosterone levels can restore libido in men whose testosterone output is deficient. In one study conducted in Italy, 14 young men (mean age, 37 years) with low (<6.6 ng/mL) to low-normal (6.6-19.8 ng/mL) levels of free testosterone due to disease, injury, or genetic abnormality received either oral testosterone undecanoate or a placebo during two successive six-week periods. A double-blind design was employed so that neither the subjects nor the researchers knew who was getting which treatment until the study was over. The men were asked to rate their frequency of sexual thoughts and sexual desire weekly using four-point scales beginning prior to the start of treatment.

The results showed that "testosterone" replacement significantly increased both the frequency of sexual thoughts and sexual desire in the men with below normal free testosterone levels, but not in the men whose free testosterone levels were at the low end of the normal range (Figs. 5-1 and 5-2).[2]

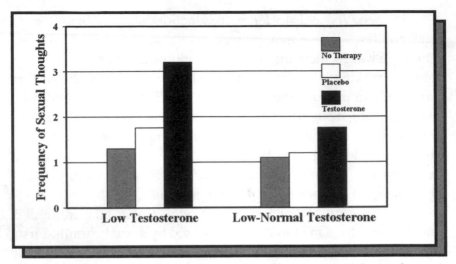

**Figure 5-1.** *Rating of frequency of sexual thoughts in men with low or low-normal levels of free testosterone. The men rated themselves using a 4-point scale (0 = no sexual thoughts, 4 = sexual thoughts several times a day). (Adapted from Carani et al, 1990)*

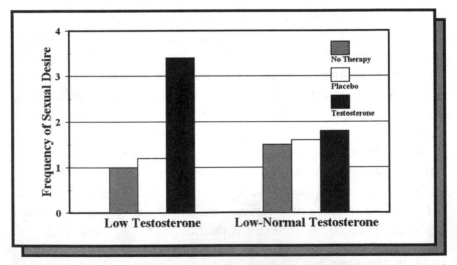

**Figure 5-2.** *Rating of frequency of sexual desire in men with low or low-normal levels of free testosterone. The investigators rated the men rated using a 4-point scale (0 = never achieves sexual excitement, 4 = achieves sexual excitement in the majority of occasions). (Adapted from Carani et al, 1990)*

Several other studies have shown similar increases in sexual interest, motivation, or arousability following intramuscular injections of testosterone enanthate or a time-release formulation of natural testosterone.[3-7]

Most recently, application of a natural testosterone patch (Androderm®) was shown to increase sexual desire to about the same level as that produced by testosterone enanthate injections. In this study, testosterone deficient men aged 21 to 65 rated their sexual desire, first during three weeks of testosterone enanthate injections, next during eight weeks of no treatment (androgen withdrawal), and finally during 12 months of testosterone patch use. The results (Fig. 5-3) showed that during the period of androgen withdrawal, sexual arousal and desire declined significantly. With daily application of the testosterone patch, libido returned and remained elevated throughout the 12-month test period.[8]

***Restoring erectile ability.*** A typical response of many men (and physicians) to erectile failure is to blame themselves (or their sexual partner) for their problem. Once a source of pleasurable anticipation, sexual encounters that occur under the cloud of problematic erections can quickly turn into a source of anxiety,

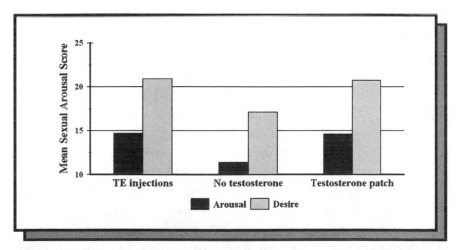

**Figure 5-3.** *Comparison of the effects of testosterone enanthate (TE) injections, androgen withdrawal (no testosterone), and a testosterone patch on libido in testosterone deficient men. (Adapted from Arver et al, 1996)*

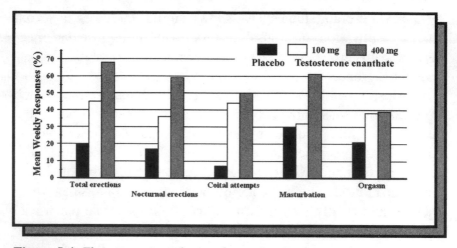

**Figure 5-4.** *The restoration of normal sexual activity in six hypogonadal men receiving either of two doses of testosterone enanthate or placebo. (Adapted from Davidson et al, 1979)*

stress, and relationship difficulties. Ever try to have an erection when you're scared, anxious, or worried? It's a sure fire recipe for failure.

Not long ago, experts in sexual medicine believed that virtually all cases of impotence were due primarily to some type of psychological "performance anxiety." Physiological etiologies and treatments were typically given short shrift, while behavioral sex therapy techniques were the treatment of choice. Today, the pendulum has swung almost completely to the opposite extreme. Most cases of erectile dysfunction are now thought to at least begin with a physiological problem, although the lens of the psyche is almost certain to magnify the problem.

When erectile difficulties are associated with a testosterone deficiency, testosterone replacement has usually been quite effective in restoring erections. Typical of the research in this area was a small study in which either testosterone enanthate (100 mg or 400 mg) or a placebo was given to six adult hypogonadal men (aged 32-65 years) once every four weeks over a period of five months. Neither the men nor the investigators knew from one month to the next who was getting "testosterone" and who was getting placebo.

Throughout the course of the study, the men recorded their sexual activity and experiences in a daily log. As shown in Fig. 5-4, "testosterone" injections resulted in large, dose-dependent increases in total erections, nocturnal (sleep) erections, coital attempts, masturbation, and orgasms. The authors were impressed with the "rapidity with which the administration of testosterone was followed by the stimulation of sexual activity...the latency being measured in days rather than weeks."[3]

In a study employing a slow-release form of natural testosterone, the sexual function of seven of eight hypogonadal men returned to normal within three weeks.[5]

Of particular interest are the recent studies employing one of the natural testosterone patches. In one such study, the mean number of erections per week increased from 2.3 during an androgen withdrawal period to 7.8 during testosterone treatment.[8] Significant increases were also seen in the duration and rigidity of erections, as well as in the *erectile index*, a measure of average penile rigidity (calculated by multiplying the total number of erections per hour by

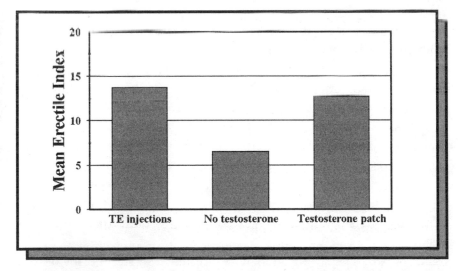

**Figure 5-5.** *Changes in penile erectile index (average rigidity) in 37 testosterone deficient men treated with testosterone enanthate (TE) injections (10 days) followed by no testosterone/androgen withdrawal (7 weeks) followed by a natural testosterone patch (12 months). (Adapted from Arver et al, 1996)*

the mean duration of an erection by the mean degree of rigidity) (Fig. 5-5).

In a trial of the scrotal patch, four of five men reported improved sexual function within one to two weeks after starting treatment with a low-dose patch. The fifth man improved when he was switched to a higher-dose patch.[9]

## Testosterone Replacement in Menopausal Men

Although there is no doubt that testosterone replacement can restore sexual arousal, desire, and activity in younger men with a testicular deficiency, what about menopausal men whose testosterone levels have declined with age? Few well-controlled studies have been published to answer this important question.

The first systematic confirmation that testosterone could be effective in restoring sexuality in menopausal men came in 1944.[10] The authors, Carl G. Heller, Ph.D., and Gordon B. Myers, M.D., measured testosterone levels in 38 men complaining of typical menopausal symptoms, including impotence, which was present in 32 of the men. They found normal hormone levels in 15 of the men and reduced testosterone in 23. They then began a series of injections of testosterone propionate.

Of the 20 men with low testosterone levels who were treated (three men were not treated), "testosterone" replacement resulted in the "complete abolition of all vasomotor, psychic, constitutional and urinary symptoms" in 17. Sexual potency was restored to normal in all but two of the men. When they increased the "testosterone" dose, "the sexual vigor of both refractory cases exceeded that of normal men," Heller and Myers wrote. Discontinuation of "testosterone" replacement resulted in the return of menopausal symptoms and the loss of sexual potency until treatment was restarted.

Treatment of nine men with normal testosterone levels did not yield any significant improvement either in menopausal symptoms or sexuality. This suggested to the authors that, although these men appeared to be menopausal, their symptoms were not due to testicular failure.

During the early 1960s, a German physician named Tiberius Reiter, who practiced in London, published the results of his 12 years of experience gathered from the intramuscular implantation of various doses of testosterone crystals in 240 men (aged 40-75 years) complaining of menopausal symptoms, including impotence, depression, urinary disturbance, and thyroid-related disturbances (He called this the "I.D.U.T. syndrome.").[11] Dr. Reiter had each man rate his degree of impotence on a 12-point scale (0 = his potency at age 25, 12 = complete impotence lasting two years) prior to the start of testosterone replacement and again at two and four months.

Dr. Reiter observed an improvement in erectile ability that appeared to be dose-dependent (Fig. 5-6). Although this study did not contain the usual controls (e.g., placebo, subject/investigator blinding, etc.), the large number of subjects, the consistency of the results, and the fact that the higher doses appeared to work better all combine to suggest that Dr. Reiter's data be taken seriously.

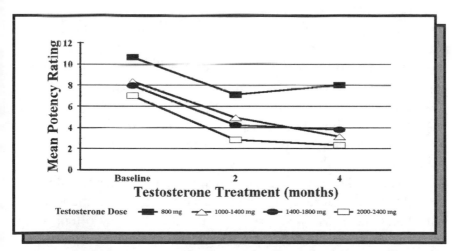

**Figure 5-6.** *Improvement in erectile ability in menopausal men receiving four different doses of testosterone via intramuscular implantation. Erectile ability was rated by the men on a 12-point scale (see text). (Adapted from Reiter, 1963)*

The British andrologist Malcolm Carruthers, M.D., has conducted what is perhaps the largest uncontrolled trial of "testosterone" replacement by giving menopausal men in his practice various formulations of "testosterone" over the last 10 years.[12] In addition to such typical symptoms of male menopause as fatigue, depression, irritability, aches, pains, stiffness, and night sweats, Dr. Carruthers found sexual problems, including loss of libido and erectile problems, in 90% of the men. He has prescribed "testosterone" — usually oral testosterone undecanoate, a few oral anabolic steroids, or implantable testosterone crystals — to more than 1,000 of his patients, ranging in age from 31 to 80 years (mean age, 54).

He reports that all the men treated with "testosterone" have experienced "an overall feeling of increased vitality and well-being," less depression and irritability, and increases in "drive and assertiveness." In terms of sexuality, some of Dr. Carruthers's patients reported "penile enlargement and increased genital sensitivity" and statistically significant increases in total sexual activity, including both intercourse and masturbation. Overall, he writes, "A statistically highly significant improvement in erectile function occurred in 70 percent of my first 400 cases treated with a variety of different forms of testosterone."

Although it is impossible to exclude the chance that Dr. Carruthers's results might be due to a "placebo effect" (i.e., the power of suggestion), he argues, like Reiter, that the positive effects appeared only after he gave higher doses of "testosterone." In essence, then, the lower doses can be seen as functioning as a kind of placebo. Had the treatment, per se, been functioning as a placebo, it is likely that positive effects would have been seen at these lower doses as well.

While acknowledging that much remains to be learned about the role of testosterone in sexual arousal and performance, Dr. Carruthers states, "It is surprising but gratifying how often, when adequate testosterone therapy is given, all the symptoms of andropause disappear within a few weeks or months, including erectile difficulties, particularly when other factors contributing to its onset or continuation are dealt with."

Although sexuality was not a primary measure, a well-controlled study of testosterone replacement conducted by Dr. Joyce S. Tenover, of the University of Washington, yielded an interesting finding. Dr. Tenover administered "testosterone" (testosterone enanthate injections) or placebo to each of 13 healthy men, aged 57 to 76 years, who had low or borderline levels of total testosterone.[13] The men received either "testosterone" or placebo for three months at a time before being switched to the alternate treatment. Although the men were not supposed to know which treatment they were getting at any given time, 12 of the 13 were able to guess correctly when they were on "testosterone" based on increases in their libido, aggressiveness in business transactions, or a general increase in their sense of well-being.

# Who Can Benefit From Testosterone Replacement?

As with many medical questions, there's no "one-size-fits-all" answer. Personal and family health history, present physical and mental condition, and laboratory tests all need to be taken into consideration. Sometimes even then a clear-cut answer can't be given, and a "clinical trial" (a fancy way of saying "let's try it and see what happens") is the best available route. Let's go through these factors one at a time:

*Personal history.* Is there a definite decline in libido? Is there a decline in ability to achieve and sustain erections? Any change in rate of beard growth? Any lessening in body hair? What about muscle size and strength, and ability to work hard before muscle fatigue sets in? What about that hard-to-define area sometimes called "mental edge," being "sharp" mentally?

Of course, answers to these and other questions are conditioned not only by the level of a man's testosterone, but many other factors, too, both physical and emotional. For example, tobacco smoking is known to simultaneously increase the risk of atherosclerotic small blood vessel occlusion (narrowing, which can influence erections) and increase the risk of prostate cancer.

*Family health history.* Have any older male relatives become "feeble old men," stooped, bent over, weak, "just getting through," but without any particular disease or illness to explain it? Have any older male relatives become senile or developed Alzheimer's disease? How many have had heart attacks or other forms of atherosclerotic disease, especially at age 60 and older? How about diabetes, or osteoporosis?

Just as importantly, have any male relatives had enlarged prostates? What about prostate cancer in the family?

*Present physical and mental condition.* During a thorough health history and physical examination with possible "hormone replacement" in mind, a doctor will make an estimation (based on his or her experience) of a man's mental/emotional condition. It's likely that muscle size and strength, as well as hair growth and distribution will be checked. The prostate gland, penis, and testicles will all be examined. Although there's no consensus about this, some physicians also take into consideration the condition of the skin and immediately underlying tissues. Each individual physician will likely check individual areas he or she believes to be important.

*Laboratory evaluations.* Certainly testosterone levels will be checked, and it's likely "free testosterone" levels will be checked, too. LH (see Chapter 3) may be checked. Estrogens may be checked, as its becoming more apparent that the estrogen/testosterone ratio and the effect of estrogen "feedback" on LH (see Fig. 3-3) must be taken into consideration. Since hormone replacement is under consideration, the PSA (prostate specific antigen) test or the newly developed cPSA test will very likely be done to evaluate the risk of prostate cancer. Hormone checking will probably be done along with routine testing of blood count, cholesterol, and so on. (Although laboratory testing is one of the most important advances in 20th century medicine, physicians of all types are still carefully taught in medical school that it should NEVER be the only factor considered.)

Once all of this has been done, only then should the physician and the man involved go over all the relevant factors before arriving at a decision about testosterone replacement. Sometimes the decision is clear-cut. But as noted above, sometimes a "clinical trial" with careful follow-up (especially of prostate health) is the only way to go.

# References

1. de Kruif P. *The Male Hormone*. New York: Harcourt, Brace and Company; 1945.

2. Carani C, Zini D, Baldini A, Della Casa L, Ghizzani A, Marrama P. Effects of androgen treatment in impotent men with normal and low levels of free testosterone. *Arch Sexual Behav*. 1990;19:223-234.

3. Davidson JM, Camargo CA, Smith ER. Effects of androgen on sexual behavior in hypogonadal men. *J Clin Endocrinol Metab*. 1979;48:955-958.

4. Anderson RA, Bancroft J, Wu FC. The effects of exogenous testosterone on sexuality and mood of normal men. *J Clin Endocrinol Metab*. 1992;75:1503-1507.

5. Burris A, Ewing L, Sherins R. Initial trial of slow-release testosterone microspheres in hypogonadal men. *Fertil Steril*. 1988;50:493-496.

6. Salmimies P, Kockott G, Pirke K, Vogt H, Schill W. Effects of testosterone replacement on sexual behavior in hypogonadal men. *Arch Sexual Behav*. 1982;11:345-353.

7. Kwan M, Greenleaf WJ, Mann J, Crapo L, Davidson JM. The nature of androgen action on male sexuality: a combined laboratory-self-report study on hypogonadal men. *J Clin Endocrinol Metab*. 1983;57:557-562.

8. Arver S, Dobs A, Meikle A, Allen R, Sanders S, Mazer N. Improvement of sexual function in testosterone deficient men treated for 1 year with a permeation enhanced testosterone transdermal system. *J Urol*. 1996;155:1604-1608.

9. Ahmed S, Boucher A, Manni A, Santen R, Bartholomew M, Demers L. Transdermal testosterone therapy in the treatment of male hypogonadism. *J Clin Endocrinol Metab*. 1988;66:546-551.

10. Heller C, Myers G. The male climacteric and its symptomatology, diagnosis and treatment. *JAMA*. 1944;126:472-477.

11. Reiter T. Testosterone implantation: A clinical study of 240 implantations in ageing males. *J Am Geriatrics Soc*. 1963;11:540-550.

12. Carruthers M. *Maximising Manhood*. London: HarperCollins Publishers; 1996.

13. Tenover JS. Effects of testosterone supplementation in the aging male. *J Clin Endocrinol Metab*. 1992;75:1092-1098.

# Chapter 6
# Re-Igniting the Sexual Fires: Beyond Viagra®

A lthough Viagra® gets all the headlines these days (thanks to millions in pharmaceutical company public relations and advertising), there are several natural treatments that appear to be equally effective in restoring erectile ability, are probably far safer, and certainly less expensive. Some of these, like *ginseng, muira puama,* and *ginkgo biloba,* are ancient herbal remedies that have recently received scientific support. Others, like the steroid hormone/testosterone precursor *androstenedione* and the amino acid *L-arginine,* have well-documented modes of action and increasing bodies of research to support their use in men with erectile disorders. Before a man goes down the Viagra® road, we strongly suggest giving one or more of these natural options a serious try.

## Androstenedione: The Natural Testosterone Booster

*Androstenedione* (pronounced ANDRO-STEEN-*DYE*-OWN) is an androgenic hormone and a metabolic precursor of testosterone. The male body produces androstenedione in the testes and adrenal cortex from either 17-hydroxyprogesterone or DHEA and quickly turns it primarily into testosterone and, to a lesser extent, estrone and estriol (see Fig. 3-1). Androstenedione also occurs naturally in meat and in the pollen of the Scotch pine tree.* Preliminary evidence suggests that taking androstenedione supplements made from these external sources may be a natural and safe way of increasing testosterone levels.

Androstenedione was first synthesized during the 1930s by the same researchers who first synthesized testosterone.[1] Shortly thereafter, it was discovered that, like testosterone, androstenedione had both masculinizing and anabolic properties in dogs.[2] Nevertheless, androstenedione was dismissed as a mere intermediate steroid and promptly forgotten until the 1960s, when researchers found that it could elevate testosterone levels in *women* by as much as three-fold above normal.[3]

Of particular interest in this investigation was the fact that the testosterone boost caused by androstenedione was transient. The peak level lasted only a few minutes, and testosterone levels returned to normal within a few hours, which is generally what happens with the body's own internally produced androstenedione.

According to a German patent for an orally active form of androstenedione, a 50-mg dose can raise plasma testosterone levels in men from 140% to 183% above normal. East German researchers became particularly enamored of androstenedione nasal spray during the 1960s and 1970s as an adjunct to anabolic steroid drugs in athletes because of its ability to elevate testosterone levels while going largely undetected by standard steroid testing regimens.

A recent small study by Gary Rheinschild, M.D., a California urologic surgeon, clearly demonstrated that a sublingual (under the tongue) androstenedione spray could significantly elevate testosterone levels for a short time. Dr. Rheinschild measured baseline testosterone levels in four men and then administered androstene-

---

* Because it occurs naturally in plants and the human body, androstenedione is legally classified as a "dietary supplement" and can, therefore, be sold "over the counter" without FDA approval.

# Androstenedione and Media Distortions

As Mark McGwire was making his epic surge toward the Major League Baseball home run record in the summer of 1998, his admission that he was taking androstenedione thrust this previously obscure steroid hormone into the media spotlight, amidst the usual distortions and misinformation. In many reports, *natural* androstenedione was depicted as an "anabolic steroid drug," with little or no effort made to distinguish it from truly dangerous anabolic steroid *drugs*, such as methyltestosterone.

These media reports generally gave the impression that the well-known problems related to the use of these drugs (and by implication, androstenedione) were related to their anabolic (tissue building) properties. This is simply not true. If these drugs cause problems, it is because they are *unnatural* substances for which the body lacks the resources (such as enzymes and cofactors) to properly metabolize them. As a result, they form toxic metabolic byproducts which may cause liver disease, cancer, and other very serious health problems. None of these problems are related to the drugs' anabolic or masculinizing properties, per se.

As a naturally occurring hormone, supplements of androstenedione, when taken at reasonable doses, are metabolized in exactly the same way that the androstenedione produced in the body is metabolized. No excessive anabolic or masculinizing effects have ever been reported; nor are any toxic byproducts formed that might cause liver disease or cancer. The only products formed from the metabolism of androstenedione supplements are testosterone and estrone.

dione. He measured plasma levels of testosterone every 30 minutes for up to 3 hours. The results (Fig. 6-1) showed a rapid rise in testosterone for all four subjects ranging from 22% to 52%. The increase in testosterone even occurred in a 54-year-old man (a body builder), despite the fact that he was also taking testosterone injections on his own. Overall, the hormonal changes were accompanied by feelings of increased energy, strength, and well-being. Although the effects of androstenedione on sexuality were not assessed, it is a reasonable assumption that elevating testosterone levels in men who are testosterone deficient should be beneficial.

**Figure 6-1**. *Change in blood levels of free testosterone in four men following use of androstenedione sublingual spray. Data are presented as percent change from baseline (0) at 30, 90, and 150-180 minutes after administration of androstenedione.(Source: Gary Rheinschild, MD, and Vitamin Research Products)*

# L-Arginine: Just Say Yes to NO

Among the most important findings in the study of human sexuality in the last half century was the discovery in the early 1990s that the messenger molecule *nitric oxide* (*NO*) is the primary physiologic mediator of penile erections.[4] As we discussed in Chapter 4, NO produced by nerve stimulation originating in the brain diffuses to arterial smooth muscle and penile muscular tissue where it causes these muscles to relax, thereby facilitating increased blood flow to and engorgement of the penis; in other words, an erection.

Many different avenues of research have demonstrated that increasing the amount of NO in the arteries that serve the genital region enhances penile erection. Some drugs, known as NO donors, are extremely potent erection producers. Among these drugs are nitroglycerin, sodium nitroprusside, and isoamyl nitrate. None of these drugs is suitable for inducing erections, however, because they are all potent vasodilators – some used for treating serious heart conditions – and can be difficult to use and even very danger-ous for some people.[5] Some require injection of the drug directly into the penis shortly before intercourse. More importantly for most people, though, the erections they produce are artificially hard and long-lasting, having no connection at all with sexual arousal.

On the other hand, it is possible to raise NO levels safely and naturally, enabling normal erections during sexual stimulation, by taking supplements of the conditionally essential amino acid **L-arginine**, one of the building blocks of proteins in the body. When we say that L-arginine is "conditionally essential," we mean that the body sometimes cannot manufacture sufficient amounts from other substances the way it does some other (nonessential) amino acids. To maintain your supply of arginine at a reasonably high level, it is important that you either consume foods containing this nutrient (e.g., dairy products, nuts, chicken, turkey, and other fowl) or take L-arginine supplements.

Until about 20 years ago, L-arginine was largely ignored, except in its very limited protein-building role. Arginine has now been identified as the main source of the primary molecule respon-sible for penile erections, **nitric oxide (NO)**. Quite simply, L-arginine supplies the nitrogen – N – that the body uses to build NO from nitrogen and oxygen – O.

Can consuming L-arginine supplements improve a man's ability to have an erection? Yes. Studies in both animals and humans have shown that L-arginine supplements can lower blood pressure in general by enhancing dilation of arteries.[6-11] Injection of L-arginine directly into the cavernosal (spongy) tissue of the penis

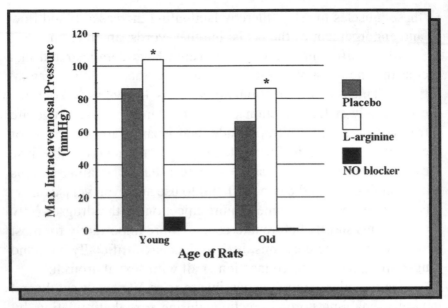

**Figure 6-2.** *Significantly increased erections (as measured by maximum intra-cavernosal blood pressure) in young and old rats before (placebo) and after ingesting L-arginine for 8 weeks. Administration of a drug that blocks the formation of NO completely prevented erections. (\* p <0.05) (Adapted from Moody et al, 1997)*

can induce erections in lab animals by the same means, arterial relaxation.[\*5]

Of particular significance was a recent study in which groups of young and old rats drank water to which L-arginine had been added for eight weeks. The animals' erectile ability (in response to a mild electrical stimulus) was evaluated by measuring the blood pressure inside their penile cavernous spaces (the higher the maximum intracavernosal pressure, or MIP, the bigger and harder the erection).[12] In the younger rats (aged five months), MIP increased 21% over their control level (no L-arginine supplementation). In the older rats (aged 20 months), it increased by 30% (Fig. 6-2).

---

\*   This ability makes arginine an excellent – but unfortunately rarely used – treatment for high blood pressure. Unlike most anti-hypertensive drugs, which can cause impotence, arginine actually promotes erections as it lowers blood pressure.

To hammer home the point that NO made from L-arginine was indeed responsible for the animals' erectile enhancement, the researchers then gave them a substance called L-NAME,* which functions as a kind of "anti-arginine" by blocking the formation of NO by NOS. As shown in Figure 6-2, the NO blocker obliterated the erections in these animals, making them completely impotent. Although the authors cautioned against humans running out and taking high doses of L-arginine, they were hopeful, concluding, "These data support the possible use of dietary supplements with L-arginine for treatment of erectile dysfunction."

The first (and so far, only) human trial of L-arginine's effects on erectile ability was actually conducted several years earlier by two urologists, Adrian Zorgniotti, M.D., of New York University School of Medicine, and Eli F. Lizza, M.D., of the University of Medicine and Dentistry of New Jersey. Although it was a small trial that lacked some important controls, its results were extremely promising.

Dr. Zorgniotti was no newcomer to creative solutions for genital and urinary disorders. Earlier in his career, among other innovations, he had developed a jockstrap-like device designed to improve fertility by lowering the temperature of the scrotum, and an impotence treatment featuring buccal (inside the cheek)/sublingual (under the tongue) administration of the anti-hypertensive drug, phentolamine.[13] Well-respected by his colleagues all over the world, he founded the International Society for Impotence Research (ISIR) in 1978, which has met every other year since to discuss advances in impotence research, and which publishes the *International Journal of Impotence Research*.

Drs. Zorgniotti and Lizza began by giving 15 impotent[†] men a placebo for two weeks to establish a baseline for sexual function. (The men did not know they were taking inactive "dummy pills"

---

* L-NAME is shorthand for N-Ω-nitro-L-arginine methyl ester.

† Their impotence was due to atherosclerosis in the penile arteries.

during this phase of the experiment.) During this control period, the men also began keeping a daily journal in which they recorded how they felt, with a particular focus on their sexual function. Then for the next four weeks, they were secretly switched to oral L-arginine supplements (2.8 grams per day).

Not much happened during the first two weeks of L-arginine treatment. The next two weeks were another story, though. Six of the men (40%) began recording marked improvements in their ability to achieve and maintain erections. They noted in their diaries that their erections were harder and longer-lasting than they had been just a few weeks earlier. Some men wrote that, once again, vaginal penetration was possible. As in Tenover's study of the effects of testosterone enanthate,[14] many of the men were quite aware of feeling different during the L-arginine treatment, compared with the placebo.

Zorgniotti and Lizza also found that age was a factor in determining which subjects responded. The mean age of responders was 37.5 years, compared with 55.4 years for non-responders. The authors had no firm explanation for why the older men were generally less responsive to L-arginine, but it is possible that their atherosclerosis was farther advanced, thus inhibiting normal blood flow to the penis.[15]

What can we make of these results? Do they *prove* that L-arginine supplements can help restore sexual ability? No, they probably don't. This was never intended to be more than a pilot study, designed to point the way to the next stage of research. Unfortunately, Dr. Zorgniotti died shortly after completing the study, and no one has since followed up.

Clearly, though, given L-arginine's known mechanism of action and the results of animal studies, not to mention years of anecdotal reports from L-arginine users, plenty of room for optimism exists. Even though the two urologists described the 2.8-gram-per-day dose of L-arginine as being "large," many people take much higher doses of L-arginine – double or triple the amount or more – in order to obtain other benefits from this amino acid, including sexual enhancement, growth hormone release,[16,17] more rapid wound healing,[18] and enhanced immune function.[19-23] If 2.8 grams per day can restore sexual function in 40% of users, it is entirely possible that higher doses would have a greater effect.

*A **natural alternative** to Viagra®?* If you think (or have been told by your physician) that you need Viagra®, you may want to try L-arginine first, because both substances accomplish the same end – elevation of cGMP leading to vascular muscle relaxation – by slightly different routes. Recall that Viagra® works by inhibiting the enzyme phosphodiesterase type 5 ($PDE_5$), which normally breaks down cGMP, the substance that actually causes arterial smooth muscle to relax. Preventing the metabolic breakdown of cGMP allows more of it to accumulate, thus allowing more arterial relaxation and more blood to flow into the penis. The more cGMP, the more the penile blood vessels relax, the better the erection.

Under normal circumstances, NO (produced from dietary L-arginine) binds to the enzyme guanylate cyclase, forming new cGMP.[24] Increasing the amount of L-arginine increases the amount of NO formed. Thus, by enhancing NO formation, L-arginine supplements also increase cGMP levels, but they do so in a more physiologic way. In other words, more L-arginine means more NO, which means more cGMP and better erections, naturally.

What's wrong with the way Viagra® does it? Viagra® is a *synthetic* substance, designed in a laboratory specifically to inhibit $PDE_5$. Unlike L-arginine, the body has not evolved any enzymes over the millennia to metabolize Viagra® into other useful and/or harmless substances. As a result, like all other synthetic drugs, it can and will cause unwanted effects. Among these effects is an interaction with vasodilating drugs known as nitrates (e.g., nitroglycerin) which can be fatal. Less serious side effects include an alteration in headache, stomach upset, flushing, and color vision.[25] The Federal Aviation Administration (FAA) was so alarmed by this last side effect that it has forbidden airline pilots from flying within eight hours of taking Viagra®.

Although Viagra® was initially portrayed in the media as a very safe drug, in August 1998, only five months after it was launched, the FDA confirmed that 69 men using Viagra® had died. Forty-six of these deaths were related to cardiovascular disease (e.g., stroke, heart attack, cardiac arrest). In 21 cases, the cause of death was unknown. Did Viagra® kill these men? Perhaps they would have died anyway, even if they had not taken it. Perhaps, the vigorous sexual activity made possible by Viagra® was too much for their diseased cardiovascular systems. Given the high stakes involved, including the riots that would certainly ensue should the drug be recalled, neither the FDA nor Pfizer, Inc., Viagra's manufacturer, is willing to make the connection at this point.

Nevertheless, the evidence keeps building. A month later, the September 3, 1998 issue of the *New England Journal of Medicine* contained a series of letters from physicians reporting instances of cardiac arrhythmia and lung hemorrhage in men with a history of heart disease who had been taking Viagra®. In one letter, the writers pointed out that, since sexual activity in men with a history of heart disease is often associated with arrhythmias, and since sexual activity facilitated by Viagra® increases the risk of a serious adverse event in men with pre-existing cardiovascular disease, physicians would do well to subject these men to a stress test before prescribing this drug for them.[26]

Clearly, any man with cardiovascular disease may be increasing his risk of a heart attack or stroke by engaging in sexual activity, with or without Viagra®. To the degree that L-arginine and testosterone increase sexual activity, they too may be increasing that risk. The advantage of these natural substances over a synthetic solution like Viagra® is that they may actually reduce the risk in the long run. As we have mentioned earlier, L-arginine supplements have been shown to lower blood pressure, inhibit atherosclerosis, and strengthen weakened heart muscles, even when these indicators of cardiovascular disease become serious enough to cause symptoms of congestive heart failure.[27-29]

Testosterone replacement has also been associated with improved cardiovascular health, a fact that is just now coming to be recognized by many physicians in this country, although it has been known in Europe for some time. We will discuss this important aspect of testosterone replacement in the next chapter.

*Safety considerations.* L-arginine is generally considered to be safe and nontoxic, even at the higher doses that may be required for sexual enhancement (6 grams per day or more). However, there are some people who should consult their physician before using it. These include pregnant women and people with diabetes, cancer, or herpes infections, especially herpes infections of the eye or brain.

Individuals with more common recurrent outbreaks of herpes in the oral or genital regions can usually take advantage of L-arginine if they also supplement with sufficient selenium (which specifically inhibits herpes viruses). They can also offset the potential herpes stimulatory effects of L-arginine by taking an equivalent amount (or more) of the amino acid L-lysine, which has an effect opposite to L-arginine on these viruses.

Although it's wisest to work with a physician who is skilled and knowledgeable in nutritional therapies, many of the men with whom I (JVW) work have found 500 μg of selenium (along with L-lysine equivalent to or greater than the quantity of L-arginine) safe and effective. As a "side benefit," selenium is being found in recent research to protect against various cancers, including prostate cancer. (See Chapter 8.)

## Yohimbine: The Ancient Prosexual Remedy

The inner bark of the tree known as *Pausinytalia yohimbe* has long held a special place in the life and rituals of the people of West Africa. When brewed into a tea and consumed, it was said to enhance virility and sexual prowess.[30] For the last 70 or 80 years, an extract of this bark, known as *yohimbine*, has been used in the United States to treat sexual problems in both men and women.[31] In fact, until Viagra® came along, yohimbine was the only medication approved by the FDA for treating impotence. Although considerable controversy exists within medical circles regarding the actual therapeutic value of yohimbine, there seems to be little doubt that it has at least a moderate effect in restoring libido and erectile function in some men.

Yohimbine probably works because it prevents noradrenaline from stimulating $\alpha_2$-adrenergic receptor sites, but it is not clear whether it exerts its primary prosexual effect in the brain or in the penile arteries.[31] When injected into male rats, yohimbine has been shown to enhance sexual behavior as measured by decreases in the time it takes males to mount females and ejaculate. It also increases the frequency of penile erections.[32, 33] Yohimbine has even been shown to stimulate copulating behavior in rats that have been castrated (i.e., no testosterone) or have had their genitals anesthetized.[34, 35]

Of particular interest was a study that compared the effects of yohimbine in young and old male rats. In a mounting test designed to assess sexual arousal or motivation, yohimbine significantly increased the mounting frequency of the older rats. In a mating test, yohimbine also increased the number of older rats that actually copulated and ejaculated. In neither test, though, did the older rats quite reach the level of sexual activity of the younger rats.[36]

Most trials of yohimbine in human males have been criticized for various methodologic inadequacies.[31] The results of these trials have generally shown that yohimbine can provide a therapeutic effect in many men with sexual dysfunctions, although the improvement may not always be enough to qualify for statistical significance. The best of these studies have employed a placebo-controlled, double-blind, crossover design, in which two groups of men received either yohimbine or placebo. After a predetermined period, the men were switched (crossed over) to the opposite treatment.

In one such study, 48 men diagnosed with "psychogenic" impotence, took either yohimbine (6 mg, 3 times a day) or placebo. After 10 weeks, 62% of the men treated with yohimbine reported some improvement in sexual function, compared with 16% of the placebo group. This difference was statistically significant.[37] In another trial involving 100 men diagnosed with impotence due to organic causes, 43% of the yohimbine-treated

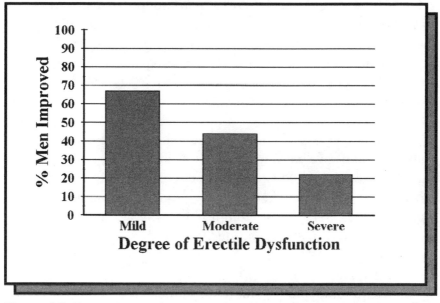

**Figure 6-3.** *Percent improvement in men with three degrees of erectile dysfunction following yohimbine treatment. (Adapted from Susset et al, 1989)*

men and 28% of the placebo-treated men were reporting improved sexual function after 10 weeks, although this difference was not statistically significant.[38]

In what is perhaps the most extensive evaluation of yohimbine so far, Dr. Jacques Susset of the Brown University Medical School asked impotent men to take either yohimbine (21-42 mg per day) or placebo using a crossover design. After four weeks of treatment, 14% of the men felt that their erectile ability had been fully restored, 20% reported a partial response, and 65% reported no improvement, for an overall response rate of 34%. Upon further analysis, the investigators found that yohimbine worked best in men who had the mildest degree of erectile dysfunction for the shortest duration, the best penile blood flow, and the highest levels of testosterone (Fig. 6-3).

The most recent (1997) well-controlled study of yohimbine was conducted in Germany. A total of 83 men diagnosed with either organic or psychogenic erectile dysfunction were asked to take yohimbine (10 mg, 3 times a day) or placebo for 8 weeks. The over-all response rate was 71% for yohimbine and 45% for placebo, a statistically significant difference.[39]

The doses of yohimbine most commonly reported to be safe and effective range from 18 mg to 100 mg per day, usually divided into three to four doses. One study evaluating a single daily 100-mg dose found no benefit.[40]

Yohimbine is available over the counter in a variety of for-mulations and by prescription in 5.4-mg tablets (yohimbine hydrochloride, USP). Most researchers consider it to be generally safe and well-tolerated when used according to recommended dos-ing guidelines. The most commonly reported adverse effects include anxiety, dizziness, headache, nausea, urinary frequency, insomnia, and increased blood pressure. Heart arrhythmias have also occasionally been seen.

***Who should/should not use yohimbine?*** Men who have known high blood pressure are generally advised not to take yohim-bine. In cases where it is prescribed despite pre-existing high blood pressure, very close monitoring is necessary. Yohimbine should be stopped if it is associated with any further blood pressure increas-es. Men with a family history of high blood pressure also should be monitored if they are taking yohimbine.

# Other Vitamin, Herbal, and Botanical Prosexual Products

Folklore is filled with substances that are supposed to enhance sex-uality. It is beyond the scope of this book to discuss all of these, but three stand out because at least some scientific research has sug-gested that they might indeed have some value.

***Ginseng.*** *Panax Ginseng* has been one of the most widely used plant products in Asian medicine for at least 2,000 years. Long regarded as a stimulant for sexual activity and fertility, ginseng has been shown in recent scientific studies to also be potentially valu-able for a wide variety of uses, including reducing blood pressure, lowering cholesterol, preventing abnormal heart rhythms, blocking inflammation, stimulating healing, enhancing resistance to infection, preventing oxidative damage (antioxidant action), and enhancing fertility.[41]

Worthy of special note is research demonstrating possible physiologic mechanisms for ginseng's legendary prosexual properties. In a study in lab rats, 5% ginseng added to the animals' diet for 60 days resulted in a 163% increase in serum testosterone levels.[42] Other studies have demonstrated that ginseng may improve blood flow to the penis (as well as the brain, heart and other vital organs) by releasing NO from arterial endothelial cells.[43-45]

*Muira puama.* This folk medicine, derived from a shrub that grows in the Amazon region of Brazil, is also called *marapuama* and *potency wood.* Biologists know it as *Ptychopetalum olacoides,* *P. uncinatum,* or *P. guyanna.* In South American folklore, it is considered to be an aphrodisiac and a treatment for impotence.

A study conducted by Dr. Jacques Waynberg from the Institute of Sexology in Paris, France, suggests that there may be substance to this traditional use.[46] He asked 262 men complaining of lack of sexual desire and inability to attain or maintain an erection to take Muira puama (1-1.5 grams per day). Within two weeks, 62% of the men with low libido reported an increase in their sexual desire, and 51% of the men with erectile dysfunction reported improvement. It is unclear how much of these benefits were due to a placebo effect since there apparently was no placebo control in this study. Nevertheless, if further studies confirm this benefit, Muira puama could turn out to be an important natural treatment for some men with sexual disorders.

*Ginkgo biloba.* Another botanical remedy prominent in Asian medicine, ginkgo biloba is widely advertised in the West as an aid to maintaining mental alertness and memory as we grow older. Many research studies have also shown ginkgo to be a major aid in improving small vessel blood flow, a purpose for which it is widely used in European countries.

According to the results of one study, ginkgo may also be able to improve blood flow through penile arteries. In this study, which was conducted in Germany, 60 men with "proven arterial erectile dysfunction" (unresponsive to injections of the vasodilating drug papaverine) were asked to take ginkgo biloba extract, 60 mg daily, for 12 to 18 months. Penile arterial blood flow was evaluated by technological means every four weeks. The first signs of improvement were seen after six to eight weeks. After six months, 30 of the 60 the men had regained erectile function. In 12 men, papaverine, which had previously been unsuccessful, now worked. Fifteen of the men had improved penile blood flow but still did not respond to papaverine. Only three men had no measurable improvement at all.[47]

# References

1.  Ruzicka L, Wettstein A. The crystalline production of the testicle hormone testosterone (androsten-3-ol-17-ol). *Helvetica Chimica Acta*. 1936;18:1264-1275.

2.  Kochakian C, Murlin J. The relationship a synthetic male hormone androstenedione to the protein and energy metabolism of castrated dogs and the protein metabolism of a normal dog. *Am J Physiol*. 1936;117:642-657.

3.  Mahesh V, Greenblatt R. The in-vivo conversion of dehydroepiandrosterone and androstenedione to testosterone in the human. *Acta Endocrinol*. 1962;41:400-406.

4.  Burnett AL. Role of nitric oxide in the physiology of erection. *Biol Reprod*. 1995;52:485- 489.

5.  Melis M, Argiolas A. Role of central nitric oxide in the control of penile erection and yawning. *Prog Neuro-Psychopharmacol Biol Psychia*. 1997;21:899-922.

6.  Clarkson P, Adams M, Powe A, et al. Oral L-arginine improves endothelium-dependent dilation in hypercholesterolemic young adults. *J Clin Invest*. 1996;97:1989-1994.

7.  Amezcua JL, Palmer RM, de Souza BM, Moncada S. Nitric oxide synthesized from L-arginine regulates vascular tone in the coronary circulation of the rabbit. *Br J Pharmacol*. 1989;97:1119-1124.

8.  Chester AH, O'Neil GS, Tadjkarimi S, Palmer RM, Moncada S, Yacoub MH. The role of nitric oxide in mediating endothelium dependent relaxations in the human epicardial coronary artery. *Int J Cardiol*. 1990;29:305-309.

9.  Moncada S. The first Robert Furchgott lecture: from endothelium-dependent relaxation to the L-arginine:NO pathway. *Blood Vessels*. 1990;27:208-217.

10. Palmer RM, Ashton DS, Moncada S. Vascular endothelial cells synthesize nitric oxide from L-arginine. *Nature*. 1988;333:664-666.

11. Vallance P, Collier J, Moncada S. Nitric oxide synthesised from L-arginine mediates endothelium dependent dilatation in human veins in vivo. *Cardiovasc Res.* 1989;23:1053-1057.

12. Moody J, Vernet D, Laidlaw S, Rajfer J, Gonzalez-Cadavid N. Effects of long-term oral administration of L-arginine on the rat erectile response. *J Urol.* 1997;158:942-947.

13. Zorgniotti AW. Experience with buccal phentolamine mesylate for impotence. *Int J Impot Res.* 1994;6:37-41.

14. Tenover JS. Effects of testosterone supplementation in the aging male. *J Clin Endocrinol Metab.* 1992;75:1092-1098.

15. Freundlich N. Much ado about NO. *Harvard Health Letter.* 1993;18:6-8.

16. Merimee TJ, Rabinowitz D, Fineberg SE. Arginine-initiated release of human growth hormone. Factors modifying the response in normal man. *N Engl J Med.* 1969;280:1434- 1438.

17. Knopf R, Conn J, Floyd JJ, et al. The normal endocrine response to ingestion of protein and infusions of amino acids. Sequential secretion of insulin and growth hormone. *Trans Assoc Am Physicians.* 1966;79:312-321.

18. Daly JM, Reynolds J, Thom A, et al. Immune and metabolic effects of arginine in the surgical patient. *Ann Surg.* 1988;208:512-523.

19. Alexander JW, Peck MD. Future prospects for adjunctive therapy: pharmacologic and nutritional approaches to immune system modulation. *Crit Care Med.* 1990;18:S159- S164.

20. Alexander JW, Gottschlich MM. Nutritional immunomodulation in burn patients. *Crit Care Med.* 1990;18:S149-S153.

21. Alexander JW. Immunoenhancement via enteral nutrition. *Arch Surg.* 1993;128:1242- 1245.

22. Alexander JW. Specific nutrients and the immune response. *Nutrition.* 1995;11:229-232.

23. Alexander JW, Ogle CK, Nelson JL. Diets and infection: composition and consequences. *World J Surg.* 1998;22:209-212.

24. Pickard R, Powell P, Zar M. Nitric oxide and cyclic GMP formation following relaxant nerve stimulation in isolated human corpus cavernosum. *Br J Urol.* 1995;75:516-522.

25. Morales A, Gingell C, Collins M, Wicker P, Osterloh I. Clinical safety of oral sildenafil citrate (Viagra™) in the treatment of erectile dysfunction. *Int J Impotence Res.* 1998;10:69-74.

26. Schwartz I, McCarthy D. Sildenafil in the treatment of erectile dysfunction (letter). *N Eng J Med.* 1998;339.

27. Bode-Boger SM, Boger RH, Creutzig A, et al. L-arginine infusion decreases peripheral arterial resistance and inhibits platelet aggregation in healthy subjects. *Clin Sci (Colch)*. 1994;87:303-310.

28. Bode-Boger SM, Boger RH, Alfke H, et al. L-arginine induces nitric oxide-dependent vasodilation in patients with critical limb ischemia. A randomized, controlled study. *Circulation*. 1996;93:85-90.

29. Rossitch E, Jr., Alexander Ed, Black PM, Cooke JP. L-arginine normalizes endothelial function in cerebral vessels from hypercholesterolemic rabbits. *J Clin Invest*. 1991;87:1295-1299.

30. Morgenthaler J, Joy D. *Better Sex Through Chemistry*. Petaluma, CA: Smart Publications; 1994.

31. Riley AJ. Yohimbine in the treatment of erectile disorder. *Br J Clin Pract*. 1994;48:133- 136.

32. Smith E, Lee R, Schnur S, Davidson J. Alpha 2-adrenoceptor antagonists and male sexual behavior: II. Erectile and ejaculatory reflexes. *Physiol Behav*. 1987;41:15-19.

33. Smith ER, Lee RL, Schnur SL, Davidson JM. Alpha 2-adrenoceptor antagonists and male sexual behavior: I. Mating behavior. *Physiol Behav*. 1987;41:7-14.

34. Clark JT, Smith ER, Davidson JM. Testosterone is not required for the enhancement of sexual motivation by yohimbine. *Physiol Behav*. 1985;35:517-521.

35. Clark JT, Smith ER, Davidson JM. Enhancement of sexual motivation in male rats by yohimbine. *Science*. 1984;225:847-849.

36. Smith E, Davidson J. Yohimbine attenuates aging-induced sexual deficiencies in male rats. *Physiol Behav*. 1990;47:631-534.

37. Reid K, Surridge D, Morales A, et al. Double-blind trial of yohimbine in treatment of psychogenic impotence. *Lancet*. 1987;2:421-423.

38. Morales A, Condra M, Owen J, Surridge D, Fenemore J, Harris C. Is yohimbine effective in the treatment of organic impotence? Results of a controlled trial. *J Urol*. 1987;137:1168-1172.

39. Vogt H, Brandl P, Kockott G, et al. Double-blind, placebo-controlled safety and efficacy trial with yohimbine hydrochloride in the treatment of nonorganic erectile dysfunction. *Int J Impot Res*. 1997;9:155-161.

40. Teloken C, Rhoden E, Sogari P, Dambros M, Souto C. Therapeutic effects of high dose yohimbine hydrochloride on organic erectile dysfunction. *J Urol*. 1998;159:122-124.

41. Salvati G, Genovesi G, Marcellini L, et al. Effects of Panax Ginseng C.A. Meyer saponins on male fertility. *Panminerva Med*. 1996;38:249-254.

42. Fahim MS, Fahim Z, Harman JM, Clevenger TE, Mullins W, Hafez ES. Effect of Panax ginseng on testosterone level and prostate in male rats. *Arch Androl.* 1982;8:261-263.

43. Chen X, Lee TJ. Ginsenosides-induced nitric oxide-mediated relaxation of the rabbit corpus cavernosum. *Br J Pharmacol.* 1995;115:15-18.

44. Chen X. Cardiovascular protection by ginsenosides and their nitric oxide releasing action. *Clin Exp Pharmacol Physiol.* 1996;23:728-732.

45. Chen X, Salwinski S, Lee TJ. Extracts of Ginkgo biloba and ginsenosides exert cerebral vasorelaxation via a nitric oxide pathway. *Clin Exp Pharmacol Physiol.* 1997;24:958-959.

46. Waynberg J. Aphrodisiacs: Contribution to the clinical validation of the traditional use of Ptychopetalum guyanna. *First International Congress on Ethnopharmacology.* Strasbourg, France; June 5-9, 1990.

47. Sikora R, Sohn M, Friedrich J, Rohrmann D, Schafer W, Anchen F. Ginkgo biloba extract in the therapy of erectile dysfunction. *J Urol.* 1989;141:188A.

# Chapter 7
# Hormone of the Heart

D iseases of the heart and blood vessels kill about half a million men (along with half a million women) in the United States each year. Everyone recognizes that the risk of developing one of these diseases grows with age, but the fact that the increased risk may be tied to male menopause and the reduction in androgens has not yet completely penetrated the walls of conventional medicine. This is a very sad situation because there is unmistakable evidence, some of it dating back more than half a century, that:

- Testosterone is a primary factor in the health of the heart and blood vessels.
- Testosterone levels decline with age.
- Restoring testosterone (and DHEA) to youthful levels can yield significant health benefits, including protection against the various manifestations of atherosclerotic disease.

This is not to say that testosterone replacement can cure or prevent all heart disease. Nevertheless, there is good reason to believe that declining testosterone levels may lay the groundwork for some of the destructive changes that ultimately lead up to a heart attack or stroke.

## Keeping the Blood Flowing

The most common form of cardiovascular disease is *atherosclerosis* – the accumulation of fatty plaque deposits in arteries all over the body. Narrowing of arteries caused by plaque restricts the flow of blood to such vital organs as the heart, brain, kidneys, and penis, as well as to the limbs, fingers and toes. Blood, of course, supplies these organs with life-giving oxygen and nutrients, while it carts away metabolic products and other substances for excretion or recycling elsewhere in the body. Restricting the flow of blood to these locations can only be detrimental to health.

Depending on the location of the restriction, atherosclerosis can manifest in a variety of ways. A blockage in one or more of the coronary arteries that supply the heart muscle is called *coronary atherosclerosis*; if the blockage is complete, it will cause a *heart attack*. If the blockage is not quickly removed, the muscle that depends on that artery may die (*myocardial infarction,* or *MI*). A blockage in the arteries supplying the brain is called a *cerebrovascular occlusion*; if the occlusion is not rapidly cleared away, it will cause a *stroke*, in which the brain tissue served by the blocked (occluded) blood vessel dies. Restricted blood flow in the legs, known as *claudication*, interferes with the ability to walk and can cause pain and disability. When the restriction or blockage is complete, infection and gangrene may follow, often leading to amputation of the toes, feet, and even parts of the legs. Restricted or blocked arteries in the penis can cause *impotence*. Fortunately for us men, the entire organ doesn't die and require amputation!

The chest pain of *angina pectoris* is a signal that too little blood is getting through narrowed coronary arteries to meet the heart's current needs, especially during physical or emotional stress. Angina is often treated with drugs, such as nitroglycerin, which rapidly, but temporarily, dilate coronary arteries, allowing more blood through to the starving heart muscle.*

Surgical methods of treating angina are also quite popular these days. These methods include *balloon angioplasty* (inserting a deflated balloon on the end of a long flexible tube into the coronary arteries, inflating it at the appropriate location, which literally flattens the plaque). At best, this tends to be a temporary solution, since these arteries often close up again, sometimes within a few months. Considering the short-term benefit, the risks of balloon angioplasty are quite high.

Another risky, costly, and temporary – yet extremely common – "solution" to coronary heart disease (CHD) is *coronary artery bypass graft surgery* (*CABG*). In this procedure, a length of vein is removed from the patient's leg and transplanted (grafted) into the heart to replace a length of diseased coronary artery. Like angioplasty and vasodilating drugs, bypass grafts often become occluded again, requiring further surgery. Despite a (media-influenced) widespread favorable impression of CABG surgery, no well-researched scientific evidence shows that CABG surgery saves more lives than less drastic procedures. In the long run, the only people who seem to benefit from CABG procedures are the surgeons who perform them.†

Preventing atherosclerosis in the first place is obviously a better solution than any of the above. Thus, we are urged to give up smoking and start taking expensive drugs to lower cholesterol and reduce high blood pressure. Physicians and public health agencies remind us incessantly to eat more fiber, fruits, vegetables, and oats, and less red meat and fat, and, of course, to exercise. If a physician

---

* Nitroglycerin works because it "donates" molecules of nitric oxide (NO), which functions as a potent vasodilator. See Chapter 6 for more about the importance of NO.

† At $50,000 or more per procedure, it may be with good reason that heart surgeons commonly pronounce the abbreviation CABG as "cabbage!"

is really current with biomedical research, he or she may also recommend taking antioxidant supplements, including vitamins C and
E, and B-vitamins, especially vitamins B6, B12, and folic acid, all
of which have been clearly shown to significantly reduce the risk of
having a heart attack or stroke.[1-10] While some of this is good
advice, some of it – like cholesterol lowering drugs and margarine
(e.g., hydrogenated fats) – may do more harm than good.

Most physicians practicing in this country today completely
ignore the role of testosterone and other hormones in maintaining
men's cardiovascular health. In fact, it was only until relatively
recently that most physicians believed that elevated testosterone
was actually dangerous for the heart. This view seems to be based
on two misconceptions. First, elevated testosterone levels in *women*
can be dangerous. This may be true, but women are not men, and
there is no logical reason why both sexes should react to testosterone in precisely the same way. Second, careless use of anabolic
steroid *drugs*, such as the especially dangerous methyltestosterone
– but not physiological amounts of *natural* testosterone – by some
athletes and bodybuilders has been associated with serious heart
disease.

## How Testosterone Protects the Heart

Evidence that testosterone might be good for the circulation goes
back to World War I. At that time, a Danish surgeon named
Thorkild Rovsing encountered a young soldier who had died a sud-
den and violent death. His testicles were intact, however, and Dr.
Rovsing decided to transplant them into the body of an old man suffering from gangrene in one of his limbs. Remarkably, the man's
gangrene healed completely.[11]

In the years leading up to World War II, most work on testosterone was conducted in Germany. Researchers showed, for example, that "testosterone" treatment (primarily using testosterone
esters) could normalize faulty glucose metabolism (a major coexisting condition with cardiovascular disease), relieve angina, and
improve leg pain in men suffering from intermittent claudication.[11]

In 1939, Edward A. Edwards, M.D., a surgeon at the Tufts College Medical School in Boston, Massachusetts, published a pre-liminary report in the *New England Journal of Medicine* suggesting circulatory benefits of testosterone.[12] During his treatment of cas-trated men, Dr. Edwards had noticed that the skin of these men seemed to not be getting enough blood. On the contrary, blood seemed to be collecting in lower portions of the men's bodies, like the legs and lower abdomen. Was this poor circulation related to their lack of testosterone? Treatment of these men with "testos-terone" (testosterone propionate) injections led to impressive improvement. "After treatment with testosterone propionate, there was an increase in "arterialization" and blood volume in those regions normally containing many arteries, such as the head, palms of the hands, and soles of the feet," Edwards reported. Would "testosterone" produce similar results in men with intact testes but who have poor circulation due to age-related diseases such as ath-erosclerosis or other organic vascular disease?

Based on the first seven such patients Edwards treated, the answer was clearly, "Yes." Not only did "testosterone" restore arte-rial circulation to the skin, it appeared to normalize blood pressure in two cases, heal or improve two cases of gangrene, relieve leg pain in two patients, and improve walking ability in all seven patients. "Subjectively, the patients reported an increased activity and feeling of optimism," Edwards wrote, noting also that these results were similar to those reported by other researchers treating patients with male hormone.

A leading testosterone researcher during the 1940s was Maurice A. Lesser, M.D., of the Boston University School of Medicine. In 1946, Dr. Lesser published the results of 100 consec-utive angina pectoris patients (92 men and 8 women, aged 34-77 years) treated with "testosterone" (testosterone propionate) for as long as four or five months.[13] Prior to treatment, all patients had a "clearly established" diagnosis of angina pectoris based on a histo-ry of chest pain precipitated by physical exertion or emotion and relieved by rest or nitroglycerin treatment. The results were strik-ing, with 91 of 100 patients showing improvement (Fig. 7-1):

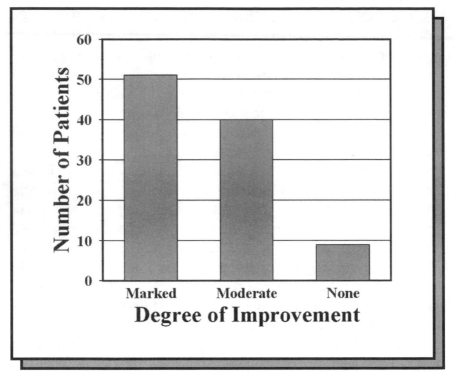

**Figure 7-1.** *Number of angina pectoris patients reporting improvement following treatment with "testosterone." (Adapted from Lesser, 1946)*

- 51 patients showed "marked improvement," which was defined as the ability to increase physical activity without precipitating an anginal attack for up to two months after discontinuing "testosterone" therapy.

- 40 patients showed "moderate improvement," defined as a reduction by at least 50% in the number of anginal attacks compared with the pre-treatment rate.

Dr. Lesser was aware that a placebo effect might be at work here, thus rendering any conclusions regarding the clinical value of testosterone invalid. To discount that possibility, prior to starting them on "testosterone" treatment, he gave six consecutive injections of sesame oil (the vehicle in which testosterone propionate

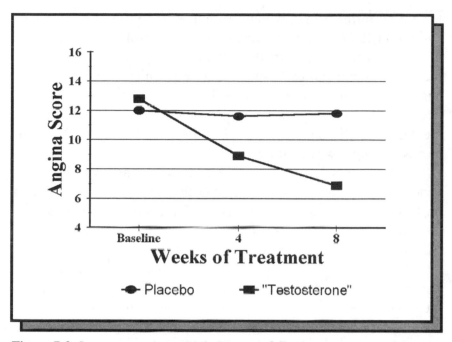

**Figure 7-2.** *Improvement in anginal symptoms following treatment with "testosterone" (testosterone cypionate). The anginal score was based on the sum of ST segment depression in four different ECG leads. (Adapted from Jaffee, 1977)*

was dissolved) to five different patients – without their awareness. None of these patients showed any improvement during the placebo phase, but once switched to "testosterone," they all began showing progressive improvement.

Dr. Lesser pointed out that the relief provided by testosterone propionate was "not instantaneous," in contrast to nitroglycerin, the only other successful treatment of angina at the time. In fact, it took a mean of 28 days to achieve "definite" improvement with "testosterone" treatment, and 43 days for "marked" improvement. On the other hand, relief could be long-lasting, ranging from two to 34 months after discontinuation of treatment. Treatment with nitroglycerin lasts only as long as the drug levels remain at an active level.

These results can be questioned due to their lack of adequate experimental controls and objective measures; not so a study by

Martin D. Jaffee, M.D., which was published in the *British Heart Journal* in 1977.[14] Using a randomized, double-blind, placebo-controlled design, Dr. Jaffee treated 50 men with post-exercise ST segment depression (an early electrocardiographic – EKG – sign of angina) with either weekly injections of "testosterone" (testosterone cypionate) or placebo. While attached to an EKG recorder, the men took an exercise stress test at baseline and again after four weeks and eight weeks of treatment.

The results left no doubt that "testosterone" was having a beneficial effect. As shown in Fig. 7-2, the placebo had no effect on post-exercise ST segment depression. By contrast, "testosterone" treatment resulted in highly significant decreases of 32% after four weeks and 51% after eight weeks.

A Chinese study also found that "testosterone" (testosterone undecanoate) treatment could benefit cardiac function in elderly men diagnosed with coronary heart disease.[15] Of the 62 men who participated, 60 had had a heart attack between three months and five years prior to the study. The other two had had complete occlusion of at least one major coronary artery. At the start of the study, the 62 patients had significantly lower testosterone levels compared with 50 age-matched controls. The researchers used a crossover design, in which the men took either "testosterone" or placebo for a period of time and then were switched to the opposite treatment.

During the two and a half months the men were taking "testosterone," their angina was markedly relieved. Self-reported anginal symptoms were reduced by 77% in the "testosterone" group, compared with 7% in the placebo group. Objective measures supported the patients' perceptions. EKG recordings both in the laboratory and in the "real" world (as measured by a portable EKG monitor) indicated significant improvement: 69% vs 8% on EKG, and 75% vs 8% on the portable monitor, respectively. The authors reported no obvious unwanted effects of the treatment.

Despite all these encouraging results, though, no one had ever confirmed that low testosterone could actually lead to atherosclerosis and/or coronary heart disease. It was still considered possible, for example, that the low testosterone levels sometimes (but not

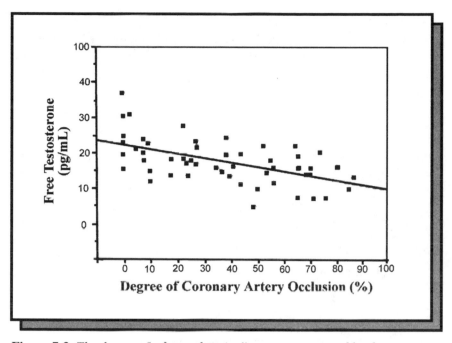

**Figure 7-3.** *The degree of atherosclerotic disease, as measured by the mean per-cent coronary artery occlusion, increased significantly with declining levels of free testosterone. This graph shows the correlations between free testosterone levels and degree of coronary artery occlusion for 55 men undergoing coronary anglography because of symptoms of coronary heart disease. Each point represents a different man. (Adapted from Phillips et al, 1994)*

always) found in men who had suffered a heart attack were a *result* of the disease, not a *cause* of it.

This connection was finally made in 1994 in a study by Gerald B. Phillips, M.D., and his colleagues at Columbia University College of Physicians and Surgeons.[16] Dr. Phillips conducted what amounted to a cross-sectional study of 55 consecutive men (mean age, about 61 years) who were undergoing coronary angiography[*] because they had chest pain and/or an abnormal stress test. None of the men had ever had a heart attack or stroke. At the

---

[*] A very common diagnostic test in which a radiopaque dye injected into a patient's coronary arteries makes those arteries visible on X-ray.

# Testosterone and Heart Disease Risk

*Men with low testosterone levels also tend to have these heart disease risk factors:*

- Angina pectoris
- Atherosclerosis
- Diabetes
- High blood glucose
- High blood cholesterol
- High blood triglycerides
- High blood pressure
- High body mass index (obesity)
- High waist-to-hip ratio
- High levels of blood clotting factors
- Low levels of blood clotting inhibitors

time of the angiography, the researchers took blood samples from the men, which they later analyzed for the levels of hormones, lipids (fatty substances, like cholesterol and triglycerides), clotting factors, and other clues to the men's health.

Phillips found a clear *inverse* relationship between testosterone levels and the degree of coronary artery disease. The lower the testosterone, the more occluded the men's arteries were. When they looked only at the level of free testosterone, the relationship was even more dramatic (Fig. 7-3).

Phillips found that testosterone levels also correlated with several important risk factors for heart attack. Men with low testosterone had a greater tendency for their blood to clot,* higher insulin

---

* Due to lower levels of the clot inhibitor PAI-1 (plasminogen activator inhibitor-1) and higher levels of the clot promoter fibrinogen.

levels, a sign of insulin resistance and abnormal glucose metabolism, and lower levels of HDL ("good") cholesterol. In previous studies, Phillips had found that, in men who had not yet had a heart attack, low testosterone was associated with such risk factors as diabetes, high blood levels of glucose, cholesterol, and triglycerides, high blood pressure, obesity, an increased waist-to-hip ratio (the "love handle/spare-tire syndrome"), and increased blood clotting factors.[17]

Based on these results, Phillips suggested that low levels of testosterone – especially free testosterone – could lead to atherosclerosis and might be an early sign of impending heart attack. Moreover, he proposed that the converse was also true, that testosterone may protect against atherosclerosis in men.[16]

## Decreasing Risk Factors

A number of studies have demonstrated that testosterone minimizes several important risk factors for heart attack, including:[11,18-22]

- Reducing cholesterol and triglycerides
- Reducing blood glucose levels
- Decreasing visceral fat mass
- Normalizing blood clotting

Of these, the two that have probably received the most study are blood clotting and cholesterol.

*Reduced tendency of blood to clot.* The tendency of blood to clot increases as men age.[23] Could this be due to the age-related decline in testosterone? Quite possibly, and here's why.

Blood contains some factors that promote clotting and others that inhibit it. In a highly oversimplified sketch of the extremely complex clotting process, blood clots form when an insoluble protein – *fibrin* – is formed from *fibrinogen*, with the help of many different substances. Fibrin forms the essential portion of all blood clots.

Modulating blood clotting is a process called *fibrinolysis* (-*lysis* , from the Greek word for *dissolve*), which literally dissolves blood clots. Key among the blood's fibrinolytic factors is the enzyme *tissue plasminogen activator* (*t-PA*), which promotes the rapid dissolution of fibrin. So potent is t-PA that it is now being produced by genetic engineering techniques and successfully used as a "clot-busting" drug. Typically, bioengineered t-PA is given to people in the early stages of a heart attack in order to dissolve the clot before it has a chance to do too much damage.

# The Trouble With Anabolic Steroid Drugs

Much of the hesitation to use natural testosterone to prevent or treat cardiovascular diseases arises from a fear that the hormone will actually *cause* heart problems, not cure them. Where does this fear come from? There's only one possible place – the misuse of anabolic steroid drugs.

Most studies show natural testosterone to be beneficial, or at worst, neutral with regard to cardiovascular health. Anabolic steroid drugs are a completely different story. Since they resemble the testosterone molecule in some ways but not in others, they work like testosterone in some ways but not in others. One of the ways they don't work like testosterone is in terms of toxicity. Although there are many such drugs, each with its own risk:benefit profile, it can generally be stated that those anabolic steroid drugs that do not also cause liver damage outright may be laying the foundation for a heart attack or stroke, even in young, well-conditioned athletes with no other risk factors. In addition to promoting blood clots, high dose anabolic steroids have also been found capable of *increasing* cholesterol levels.[24]

The release of endogenous t-PA into the circulation from the endothelial cells that line the inside of arteries is partly under the control of a substance identified as *plasminogen activator inhibitor (PAI 1)*. High levels of PAI 1 inhibit t-PA release, reducing fibrinolytic activity and increasing the risk of clot formation and decreasing the chances of surviving a heart attack.[24] Testosterone reduces PAI 1, allowing t-PA to function normally.[25] A study by researchers at the University of Cincinnati College of Medicine found that men with higher levels of endogenous testos-

*Promoting blood clotting.* Anabolic steroids have long been known to enhance the synthesis of both pro- and anti-clotting proteins, such as fibrinogen and plasminogen.[40] The clue to which predominates in a given individual may lie with the dose. At low doses, some anabolic steroid drugs have been shown to enhance fibrinolytic activity, much as testosterone itself does.[41-43] At high doses, however, they clearly promote clotting.

It appears that high doses of anabolic steroid drugs increase the tendency of certain blood cells – called *platelets* – to glue themselves together. This process, known as *platelet aggregation,* is a necessary step in the formation of blood clots. In a study of 28 weight lifters, high dose anabolic steroid drug use was associated with a greater tendency toward platelet aggregation.[44]

*Increasing cholesterol.* Anabolic steroid drugs, but not natural testosterone, can disrupt lipid levels. This was demonstrated in studies in which an anabolic steroid drug, such as stanozolol or methyltestosterone, caused large reductions in HDL cholesterol, as well as striking increases in LDL cholesterol and other pro-atherosclerotic factors. By contrast, "testosterone" (testosterone enanthate) decreased HDL by only by a small amount. Other studies have found no change in HDL and decreases in LDL following treatment with testosterone enanthate.[45-47]

terone also had higher levels of t-PA, as well as lower levels of PAI 1, fibrinogen, and triglycerides.[26]

Administration of testosterone has been shown to enhance fibrinolytic activity in men in a manner not that different from what estrogens do in women.[24] In one study, high doses of testosterone enanthate were given to a group of normal men. Within 16 weeks of treatment, their fibrinogen levels, (*ie*, blood clotting ability) had dropped by about 15%.[27]

***Normalization of blood lipids.*** Just 10 or 15 years ago, it was the conventional wisdom in medicine that testosterone and other androgens could increase a man's risk of heart disease, in part by disturbing the normal lipid balance, i.e., by increasing LDL ("bad") cholesterol and triglycerides and decreasing HDL ("good") cholesterol. While many physicians still believe this, it has since become apparent to anyone paying attention to the scientific literature that this is nonsense. It does not make sense physiologically: if high endogenous – natural, internally produced – testosterone levels promote heart disease, why does heart disease appear most often in older men whose testosterone levels have started to fall? It became clear in the late 1980s that instances of heart disease that *appeared* to be associated with testosterone were really caused by use of excessively high doses of anabolic steroid drugs, which are *not* natural testosterone. (See box.)

Most studies published throughout the 1980s repeatedly confirmed that endogenous testosterone was positively correlated with HDL ("good")-cholesterol and inversely correlated with triglycerides.[28-34] In a recent review of studies on the androgen-lipid relationship, one of the leading American medical "authorities" on this subject, Elizabeth Barrett-Connor, M.D., of the University of California, San Diego, reported that *every study that included at least 100 men had found a positive association between testosterone and HDL-cholesterol.* "Adult men with high normal concentrations of endogenous testosterone have more favorable levels of several major heart disease risk factors, including HDL-cholesterol, a more suitable fat pattern, and lower glucose and insulin levels than do men with low testosterone concentrations," she concluded.[35]

Only a few small studies have examined the effects of testosterone supplementation on cholesterol levels.[20, 36-38] In reviewing these trials, Dr. Barrett-Connor also noted, "Exogenous testosterone given parenterally [administered in a way that avoids digestion, e.g. via IV or injection] in physiologic doses to middle-aged men does not lower HDL-cholesterol and may reduce visceral adiposity ['spare tire' or 'love handle' syndrome], glycemia [elevated blood glucose], and insulin resistance [a sign of diabetes and a precursor to coronary heart disease]."[35]

Another leading voice in testosterone research, J. Lisa Tenover, M.D., of the Emory University School of Medicine, Atlanta, appears to agree. In a recent review of research on testosterone replacement in men, Dr. Tenover wrote, "Uniformly, such studies have shown either a decrease or no change in serum total cholesterol and low-density lipoprotein (LDL) cholesterol, while only one of five studies demonstrated a decline in high-density lipoprotein (HDL) cholesterol levels."[39]

## Keeping Testosterone and Estrogen in Balance

In Chapter 4, we suggested that there might be a "biological point of no return" where the normal balance between testosterone and estradiol (the most abundant and most potent human estrogen) starts tilting toward estradiol. When this happens, estradiol's suppressive effects on testosterone production (via decreased LH release) begin to predominate, causing testosterone levels to drop to a new, lower level of equilibrium.[48]

Both low testosterone and high estradiol levels have been linked to cardiovascular disease. Indeed, there is good reason to believe that what is important to a man's health is not necessarily the absolute values of each hormone but rather the *testosterone:estradiol ratio*. In one study, Norwegian researchers analyzed the blood of 42 healthy, middle-aged men judged to be at risk for coronary heart disease. They found a highly significant correlation between a low testosterone:estradiol ratio and impaired fibrinolytic capacity.[49]

There has been some confusion about the role of these hormones, in part because some studies have shown correlations with heart disease while others have not. In Phillips' angiographic study of 55 men, for example, estradiol concentration was not related to coronary artery disease, despite the fact that other studies that have shown high estrogen levels were clearly associated with the risk of myocardial infarction in men – the opposite of what occurs in women.[50-52]

The connection between estrogen levels and the risk of MI was first demonstrated during the 1970s when Phillips compared 15 men (aged 32-42 years) who had had a heart attack with 15 matched healthy controls. He found that estrogen levels were significantly higher in the heart attack patients and that they had been elevated prior to the attack.[51] He also found that an elevation in the estrogen:testosterone ratio caused a form of "mild diabetes" that was commonly associated with MI. Dr. Phillips concluded from these data that "an alteration in the sex hormone milieu is the major predisposing factor for myocardial infarction."[53, 54]

How can high estrogen be a risk factor for MI but not for atherosclerosis, while low testosterone seems to increase the risk of both? Dr. Phillips reasons that low testosterone increases the risk of atherosclerosis *and* thrombosis (blood clot formation), but high estrogen only increases the risk of thrombosis and spasms of the coronary arteries.[16]

In women, the hormone balance goes the other way. High estrogen levels protect women against heart disease. Most women do not begin to develop serious heart disease until after menopause, when their ovaries have ceased producing estrogens. Taking supplemental estrogens (and sometimes small amounts of testosterone) after menopause significantly cuts their risk of developing heart disease during the postmenopausal years.

# The Remarkable Dr. Møller

One of the most important, yet least appreciated, advocates of the use of testosterone in the treatment of cardiovascular diseases was the Danish physician Jens Møller, M.D., who lived from 1904 to 1989. According Dr. Møller's long-time colleague, Malcolm Carruthers, M.D.,[55] medicine was actually his second career. Until the end of World War II, Møller was a successful entrepreneur with offices in London, Paris, and Berlin. It was not until after the War, when he was 45 and looking for more meaning in his life, that Møller turned to medicine. Wasting no time, he qualified for medical school in just three months, a quarter of the usual time, and began practicing just five years later.

Purely by chance, Møller found a job working with a Danish physician named Tvedegaard. Dr. Tvedegaard had already developed a controversial reputation based on his use of testosterone for treating severe arterial disease, a practice he had learned from German physicians before the war.*

*Amazing results.* Like the Germans before him, Dr. Tvedegaard was achieving "amazing results" in patients with severe cases of "intermittent claudication," painful leg cramps due to impaired circulation – usually from atherosclerosis – in the lower limbs. As this disease progresses, the circulation may become so poor in some areas that local tissue starts to die. If the local blood supply is too feeble to permit significant access by protective elements of the immune system, infection and gangrene may set in. The usual treatment has always been amputation of the gangrenous digit or limb.

Yet here was Dr. Tvedegaard apparently stopping and sometimes even reversing the otherwise inexorable progress of this ter-

---

* Germany, Møller pointed out, was the "cradle of hormones." Nearly all the important research on testosterone and other hormones, from Berthold's capons to the synthesis of testosterone in the 1930s, had originated in Germany. He believed that the intervention of WW II, combined with prejudice against all things German in the years afterward, probably delayed the acceptance of testosterone as a treatment for cardiovascular disease.[11]

rible disease. "Night cramps would...go, which greatly improved the quality of sleep. Cold, blue, painful feet and legs would become pink and comfortable as the circulation mysteriously improved. Even gangrene would heal without surgery," writes Dr. Carruthers, who witnessed many of these remarkable recoveries.[55]

Not surprisingly, the medical orthodoxy of Denmark, which had suffered mightily under the Nazi occupation just a few years earlier, looked with extreme suspicion on this unusual *German* therapy. Tvedegaard had to raise funds to support his research, often calling on his patients for help. Danish medical journals repeatedly rejected his papers, and he was denied the opportunity to speak at medical conferences. Given the lack of *published* support for his claims, it was easy to reject them as "unsupported," "untested," or simply, "quackery." (This, incidentally, is exactly the same line of reasoning used today by the medical establishment in the U.S. and elsewhere to disparage and suppress natural, nutritional, and other patented non-pharmaceutical treatments.)

One day in 1957, the bureaucrats at the Danish Health Service decided that they had finally had enough of Drs. Tvedegaard and Møller. Bypassing their usual procedures for disciplining physicians who dared step out of line, they arranged to have the state police pay the two physicians a visit. They were accused of bilking the state by prescribing (and thus forcing the government to reimburse part of the cost of) testosterone for uses for which it was not "approved" (i.e., circulatory problems).

Tvedegaard and Møller were up against powerful odds and unscrupulous prosecutors who tried to seize their patient records (depriving them of the very evidence they needed to defend themselves), and who concocted false stories about supposed patient maltreatment. During a two year struggle, Møller seized the gauntlet from the old and ailing Tvedegaard, carrying the battle not only to the courts, but to the medical community and the general public as well.

Møller was a worthy opponent for the regressive Danish medical establishment. Not only was he a creative thinker, he was also a master of medical theater. At one point, after gathering the latest research on testosterone along with the support of the leading German endocrinologists of the day, he organized a public meeting of 1,500 patients and relatives of patients in order to raise funds to continue his research. Somehow, he managed to have a group of physicians from the Danish Health Service sit in the front row, where he confronted them with the latest research on testosterone and dared them to contradict him. "They couldn't, and left the hall in a state of confusion and acute embarrassment," writes Malcolm Carruthers.[55]

In the end, though, it was not public relations but good medicine that won the day. As luck would have it, one of Møller's patients was a close relative of a Minister of Justice who happened to be on the State Medical Ethics Committee. When the Minister heard first hand how his relative had benefitted from their treatment, he had the court decisions against the two physicians overturned. Remarkably, Møller's fiercest opponent, the Director of the Danish Health Authority also had friends and relatives who were taking testosterone under Dr. Møller's care. When he saw how well they were doing, he too did a 180° turnabout and became director of an organization set up to *promote* the use of testosterone.

In 1976, Møller founded the European Organization for the Control of Circulatory Diseases (EOCCD), which continues to carry on his ideas. Right up until the time of his death, Møller continued to be an active researcher and vocal advocate for testosterone replacement therapy. Notes Carruthers, who worked closely with Møller in the last decade of his life, "It was difficult to keep up with him even when he entered his eighties, and it soon became apparent that he certainly took his own medicine, which was as effective for him as it was for his patients."[55]

***Decades ahead of his time.*** Having come to medicine so late in life, Møller brought with him the eye of the iconoclast. This made it easier for him to discount many of the conventional ideas that are typically spoon fed as fact to eager young doctors-to-be. Key among these was the nature and treatment of cardiovascular disease.

Over his 30+ year medical career, Dr. Møller reported having successfully treated thousands of patients with testosterone esters. He had seen "testosterone's" beneficial effects with his own eyes. He *knew* it worked. He had little patience with the medical profession's insistence on large, expensive double-blind, placebo-controlled trials before accepting the validity of a particular treatment. He pointed out, for example, that many patients taking "testosterone" require individualized treatment strategies that may not fit comfortably within the rigid methodological confines of such a study.

In addition, he had serious ethical concerns with withholding a treatment he knew worked from some patients (placebo controls) simply to satisfy a statistical requirement. "I do not wish to treat my patients and fellow human beings as if they were rats," he said. He made an analogy with insulin in diabetics. "Nobody in their right mind would dream of dividing diabetic patients into two groups, treating one with insulin and letting the other group perish, simply because insulin action and the pathogenesis of diabetes mellitus are not fully understood," wrote Møller.[11]

His clinical findings using "testosterone" replacement fell into three general categories:

- Complete healing of gangrene of the upper and lower extremities.

- Improvement of impaired carbohydrate metabolism.

- Milder and fewer angina pectoris attacks, as well as normalized EKG findings.

In one of the few studies that Møller published, he evaluated the effects on blood cholesterol levels of giving "testosterone" (testosterone enanthate) injections to 300 men (aged 41 to 82 years) with "recognizable circulatory diseases." The study, which was carried out at the State Hospital in Copenhagen, showed that cholesterol levels dropped in 83% of the patients during testosterone treatment. The average reduction in cholesterol concentration in these men was 26%.[11]

Møller's efforts to discover why "testosterone" replacement worked led him to a view of cardiovascular disease and its treatment that was radically different from what most physicians are taught. In Møller's view, conventional medicine sees cardiovascular disease (CVD) as primarily a plumbing problem. The aim is to keep the pipes clear and the pump working. The focus is on *symptoms* of the disease – high cholesterol, hypertension, atherosclerosis, thrombosis (clot formation), intermittent claudication, angina, and other familiar manifestations – but not on what is really causing them.

This attitude has given rise to scores of drugs that attack these symptoms – lowering cholesterol, reducing blood pressure, and dilating coronary arteries – as well as surgical procedures that essentially ream out or replace clogged arteries as though they were lengths of copper tubing. "The press and medical journals have repeatedly published articles claiming that arteries are pipes which get sooted up due to butter consumption and can be cleared by pipe cleaners and margarine," wrote Møller. "This theory does not have anything to do with the 'prevention and treatment' of CVD."[11]

Without getting too deeply into his complex theorizing, Møller viewed the normal condition of a living organism as a balance between **anabolic** (protein building) and **catabolic** (protein destroying) processes. The primary anabolic hormone is **testosterone**; the primary catabolic hormone is another steroid, **cortisol**. CVD results when catabolic influences come to predominate, leading to the accumulation of excess cholesterol, impaired carbohydrate metabolism, decreased fibrinolysis, and other well-known symptoms.

"Life unfolds in protein," wrote Møller. "Protein is the living, respiring substance that needs to be fueled and supplied with oxygen to sustain combustion and provide energy for the unique material that is life itself – performing physical activity, expressing itself in the actions of every enzyme, regulating every function of the body. Protein is the substance on which all the biochemical and physiological activity of life is based. And testosterone is the hormone whose major role is to build up this core substance."[22]

For physicians to treat high cholesterol or any of the other common symptoms and pretend that they are really treating CVD is not only foolish, it may even be dangerous, according to Møller. He argued, first, that cutting dietary cholesterol made no sense, pointing out that the daily cholesterol content in the diet has no appreciable effect on plasma cholesterol levels. Moreover, drastically reducing cholesterol levels, whether by a low-fat diet or drugs may cause more harm than good. "Organisms cannot exist without cholesterol, which takes part in all cell functions," Møller wrote. "If we interfere with this system, e.g., medically, the result may be that we decrease resistance to infection; we may even accelerate the aging process."[22]

Møller was particularly opposed to the use of drugs that lower cholesterol levels, which have since become very popular. Recall that testosterone itself (as well as all other steroid hormones) is derived from cholesterol. Cholesterol is also a vital component of cell membranes. He argued that many cholesterol-lowering drugs available at that time caused more cholesterol to be excreted than the body was able to synthesize. "The result is a negative cholesterol balance, which can lead to impotence and impaired cardiac function, resulting, for instance, in angina pectoris and other signs of serious cardiovascular disease such as claudication," he stated.[22]

Møller claimed that the occurrence of impotence in some men taking cholesterol-lowering drugs was a direct confirmation of his theory. "The cholesterol is wasted by going down the drain instead of building testosterone," he said. "Decreasing the cholesterol level alone may in fact result in a decrease in the production of testosterone, which plays an important role in maintaining normal circulation... It is totally incomprehensible to me how such a substance can be used by serious practitioners of medicine, who inflict CVD on their patients instead of curing it."[22]

## Dr. Møller's Legacy

A decade after his death, it's a safe bet that hardly any physicians in the United States have ever heard of Dr. Jens Møller or his theories about the nature and treatment of cardiovascular diseases. Yet, it is becoming increasingly apparent that Møller was right on target.

During the late 1980s, even before Møller died, medical scientists were starting to recognize that many seemingly independent biochemical abnormalities are actually symptoms of an underlying cause of much cardiovascular disease. It is now accepted as fact that many cases of atherosclerosis, along with its correlates and clinical consequences, are part of a syndrome that includes increased insulin resistance and insulin levels, poor blood sugar regulation, elevated cholesterol and triglyceride levels, high blood pressure, and abdominal obesity.[56] For lack of a better name – or understanding – of this syndrome, it has been labeled "Syndrome X" or "Metabolic Syndrome."

While scientists have known for decades that these symptoms occur together, or "cluster," in certain individuals, they tended to look at them as independent *risk factors* for the really serious diseases of the heart and blood vessels. The reality of "Syndrome X" suggests that much, if not most, coronary heart disease, intermittent claudication, diabetes, hypertension, along with blood lipid aberrations, clotting problems, obesity and so on, are all different manifestations – or *symptoms* – of the *same disease*.

If this all sounds familiar, it should, because Jens Møller said basically the same thing for 25 years. Møller was convinced that CVD is basically a *metabolic* disturbance, exactly what is implied by Syndrome X. If you compare the symptoms that comprise Syndrome X with those associated with low levels of testosterone (See page 128), you find an almost perfect correspondence. Not surprisingly, these are the same symptoms that respond to treatment with testosterone. Is testosterone the ideal treatment for Syndrome X?

We have no doubt that Møller would think so. The medical community, however, still has a ways to go to catch up with him. Current thinking regarding the cause of Syndrome X is leaning toward a defect – possibly inherited – in the body's ability to produce and process insulin. It's true that long term insulin resistance

and elevated insulin levels are associated with diabetes, hypertension, atherosclerosis, coronary heart disease, and all their blood
clotting and cholesterol disturbances. As yet, no consideration is
given to another metabolic step, a step involving testosterone.
Testosterone, as many studies have demonstrated, can affect all
these same processes *including insulin resistance.*

Because of its incomplete view of circulatory system diseases, conventional medicine continues to treat patients *sympto-
matically* – usually with drugs that lower cholesterol, reduce blood
pressure, normalize heart beat, dilate coronary arteries, and now,
help maintain insulin function. We are told to exercise and to lose
weight, and often we are offered more drugs to help accomplish the
latter.

Unfortunately, men are almost never offered testosterone to
prevent or treat heart disease associated with male menopause. The
patches being marketed today by pharmaceutical companies are
aimed primarily at men with low libido or impotence as a result of
a testosterone deficiency, not to treat or prevent heart disease. While
physicians are free to prescribe testosterone to any patient for any
reason, most are locked into the conventional treatment of cardiovascular disease, and few are aware how beneficial testosterone
might be for prevention or treatment.[*]

Awareness will grow as more and more men begin using the
new natural testosterone products that are becoming increasingly
available. It is only a matter of time before someone does the study
demonstrating that men who use them have less cardiovascular disease than those who do not. Already, the results of a major longitudinal epidemiologic study by Dr. Joseph M. Zmuda and colleagues
at the University of Pittsburgh and Wayne State University suggest
that Møller was on the right track.[47]

This study followed men enrolled in the large, long-running
Multiple Risk Factor Intervention Trial (MRFIT) for 13 years,
monitoring their testosterone levels as well as a wide range of other

---

[*] It is interesting that Tvedegaard and Møller were prosecuted for prescribing
testosterone for just such an "off-label" use.

health-related variables. The men were divided into two groups. One group received "special intervention" consisting of drug treatment for hypertension, counseling to help them stop smoking, if necessary, and dietary advice for lowering blood cholesterol. The other group received only their usual health care.

Zmuda and co-workers found that total testosterone levels decreased gradually over the 13 years of the study. Although various cross-sectional studies had suggested a decline in testosterone with advancing age, this was the first time it had been demonstrated in a longitudinal study. The average rate of decline was small but significant, about -0.2% per year.

The decline in testosterone levels was particularly marked in men who had a type A personality. Type A men are intense, hard-driving, competitive, in a hurry, and easily angered. Hormonally, they respond to stress or challenges with exaggerated increases in the adrenal steroid *cortisol*, the effects of which are primarily *catabolic*. As Møller theorized, cortisol suppresses testosterone levels, which may help explain why: 1) these men have lower

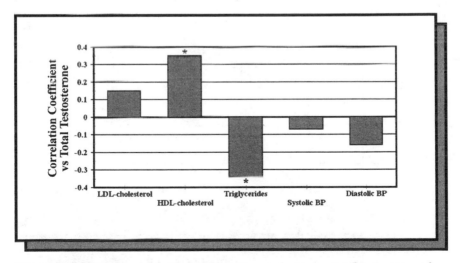

**Figure 7-4.** *Significant correlations between endogenous total testosterone levels and HDL-cholesterol and triglycerides in middle-aged men during a 13-year longitudinal study. * p <0.01 (Adapted from Zmuda et al 1997)*

testosterone levels, and 2) they are at much greater risk for coronary heart disease.

One of the most surprising results in this study was the finding that the men in the "special intervention" group experienced greater reductions in total testosterone than did the men in the usual care group. There were no differences between the two groups in cigarette smoking (which was also associated with lower testosterone), body weight at baseline, or weight change over the 13 years.

How did Zmuda et al explain this puzzling difference? (Jens Møller would not have been puzzled!) Apparently, drastically cutting fat intake, as these men were encouraged to do in accord with orthodox medical thinking, can be harmful. They wrote: "It is possible that this sustained reduction in dietary fat consumption contributed to a greater decrease in total testosterone levels during fol-

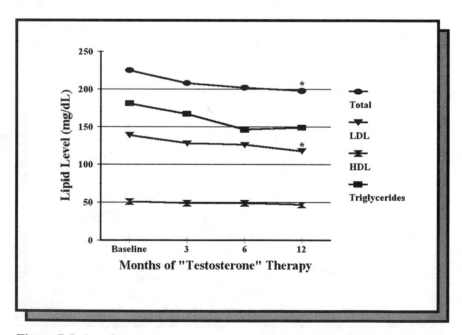

**Figure 7-5.** *Significant reductions in total and LDL-cholesterol and no change in HDL-cholesterol in elderly men with low endogenous testosterone levels during treatment with testosterone enanthate. * p <0.05 (Adapted from Zgliczynski et al 1996)*

low-up." They supported this conclusion by citing research done in the 1980s showing that a decrease in dietary fat consumption reduces levels of total testosterone, free testosterone, and androstenedione.[57]

Another important question Zmuda and his colleagues were attempting to answer was whether the increased incidence of atherosclerotic cardiovascular disease associated with aging is related to the decline in testosterone. Previous cross-sectional studies had clearly pointed in this direction.[18,35,58,59] Zmuda et al found that the decline in testosterone over 13 years was independently and significantly correlated with a decrease in HDL cholesterol and an increase in triglycerides, both of which are considered to be traditional "risk factors" for atherosclerosis and coronary heart disease (Fig.7-4). In other words, as testosterone levels fell, so did HDL, and triglyceride levels rose.

More importantly, replacing testosterone seems to have a beneficial effect on lipoproteins. In a 1992 study, Dr. Joyce S. Tenover assessed the effects of three months of "testosterone" (testosterone enanthate) therapy in 13 healthy men (aged, 57-76 years) who had low to borderline endogenous testosterone levels. "Testosterone" replacement resulted in significant declines in total cholesterol and LDL-cholesterol of about 11%. Dr. Tenover noted that these changes in lipoproteins "are in marked distinction to changes seen with oral anabolic steroids."[36]

A similar result was achieved by a group of Polish researchers. In a recent study, they gave "testosterone" (testosterone enanthate) to 11 healthy elderly men with low testosterone levels and monitored their cholesterol levels for 12 months. They found that "testosterone" supplementation caused a significant decline in total cholesterol and LDL-cholesterol, a non-significant decline in triglycerides, and no change in HDL-cholesterol (Fig. 7-5).[60]

## DHEA and the Heart

Although, we've been focusing primarily on testosterone, we cannot end this chapter without at least a brief mention of another androgen that has received a great deal of attention in recent years, particularly with respect to heart disease. That androgen is DHEA.

DHEA, which is produced mainly in the adrenal glands, lies at the heart of the steroid family. (See Fig. 3-1.) Descended from cholesterol by way of pregnenolone, DHEA is a direct precursor of androstenedione and androstenediol, both of which are metabolized to make testosterone.

Despite the fact that DHEA is abundant throughout the human body, it was, until just a few years ago, considered a "junk hormone," with no apparent purpose of its own. In fact, research on DHEA, which is still in its infancy, suggests that nothing could be farther from the truth. William Regelson, M.D., of the Medical College of Virginia, in his book *The Superhormone Promise*, calls DHEA "the superstar of superhormones" and "one of the most powerful tools" available for enhancing and extending life.[61]

Considering that DHEA an androgen, it should come as no surprise that DHEA has some very testosterone-like behavior. First, like testosterone, DHEA reaches its peak levels during a man's early 20s and then begins an inexorable decline. Unlike testosterone, the decline of DHEA is relatively rapid. By age 40, men have only about half the DHEA they had in their 20s, and the decline continues well into the ninth decade. By age 80, a man may have only 15% and by 90, only 5%.[61]

DHEA replacement has also been shown to be associated with such beneficial testosterone-like effects as:

- Feelings of energy and well-being[62]
- Improved insulin sensitivity and glucose tolerance[63]
- Reduced death from coronary heart disease[64]
- Lower obesity/waist-to-hip ratio[65]
- Slowed progression of atherosclerosis[66,67]
- Enhanced libido and erectile ability[61]
- Reduced depression and enhanced cognition[68]

DHEA may diverge from testosterone in the type of cardio-vascular protection it provides. While testosterone raises HDL-cholesterol slightly and lowers LDL-cholesterol and triglycerides, DHEA does not seem to affect blood lipids very much. Some research, however, suggests that DHEA prevents platelet aggregation (as does testosterone), and it may also have other actions that interfere with the formation and progression of atherosclerosis, including preventing the oxidation of LDL-cholesterol.[69]

# References

1.  Stephens N, Parsons A, Schofield P, et al. Randomized controlled trial of vitamin E in patients with coronary disease: Cambridge Heart Antioxidant Study (CHAOS). *The Lancet.* 1996;347:781-786.

2.  Axford-Gately R, Wilson G. Myocardial infarct size reduction by single high doses or repeated low dose vitamin E supplementation in rabbits. *Can J Cardiol.* 1993;9:94-98.

3.  DeMaio S, King Sd, Lembo N, et al. Vitamin E supplementation, plasma lipids and incidence of restenosis after percutaneous transluminal coronary angioplasty (PCTA). *J Am Coll Nutr.* 1992;11:68-73.

4.  Rapola J, Virtamo J, Haukka J, et al. Effect of vitamin E and beta carotene on the incidence of angina pectoris. *JAMA.* 1996;275:693-698.

5.  Steiner M. Influence of vitamin E on platelet function in humans. *J Am Coll Nutr.* 1991;10:466-473.

6.  Enstrom JE, Kanim LE, Klein MA. Vitamin C intake and mortality among a sample of the United States population. *Epidemiology.* 1992;3:194-202.

7.  McCully K. *The Homocysteine Revolution*: Keats Publishing, Inc.; 1997.

8.  McCully K. Homocysteine, folate, vitamin B6, and cardiovascular disease (Editorial). *JAMA.* 1998;279:392-393.

9.  Stampfer M, Malinow M, Willett W, et al. A prospective study of plasma homocyst(e)ine and risk of myocardial infarction in US physicians. *JAMA.* 1992;268:877-881.

10. Stampfer M, Malinow M. Can lowering homocysteine levels reduce cardiovascular risk? *N Engl J Med.* 1995;332:328-329.

11. Møller J, Einfeldt H. *Testosterone treatment of cardiovascular diseases.* Berlin: Springer-Verlag; 1984.

12. Edwards E, Hamilton J, Duntley S. Testosterone propionate as a therapeutic agent in patients with organic disease of the peripheral vessels. *N Engl J Med.* 1939;220:865.

13. Lesser M. Testosterone propionate therapy in one hundred cases of angina pectoris. *J Clin Endocrinol.* 1946;6:549-557.

14. Jaffee M. Effect of testosterone cypionate on postexercise ST segment depression. *Br Heart J.* 1977;39:1217-1222.

15. Wu SZ, Weng XZ. Therapeutic effects of an androgenic preparation on myocardial ischemia and cardiac function in 62 elderly male coronary heart disease patients. *Chin Med J (Engl).* 1993;106:415-8.

16. Phillips GB, Pinkernell BH, Jing TY. The association of hypotestosteronemia with coronary artery disease in men. *Arterioscler Thromb.* 1994;14:701-6.

17. Phillips GB. Relationship between serum sex hormones and the glucose-insulin-lipid defect in men with obesity. *Metabolism.* 1993;42:116-20.

18. Barrett-Connor E, Khaw KT. Endogenous sex hormones and cardiovascular disease in men. A prospective population-based study. *Circulation.* 1988;78:539-45.

19. Marin P. Testosterone and regional fat distribution. *Obes Res.* 1995;3 Suppl 4:609S- 612S.

20. Marin P, Holmang S, Jonsson L, et al. The effects of testosterone treatment on body composition and metabolism in middle-aged obese men. *Int J Obes Relat Metab Disord.* 1992;16:991-7.

21. Rebuffe-Scrive M, Marin P, Bjorntorp P. Effect of testosterone on abdominal adipose tissue in men. *Int J Obes.* 1991;15:791-5.

22. Møller J. *Cholesterol. Interactions with Testosterone and Cortisol in Cardiovascular Diseases.* Berlin: Springer-Verlag; 1987.

23. Bennet A, Sie P, Caron P, et al. Plasma fibrinolytic activity in a group of hypogonadic men. *Scand J Clin Lab Invest.* 1987;47:23-7.

24. Winkler U. Effects of androgens on haemostasis. *Maturitas.* 1996;24:147-155.

25. Caron P, Bennet A, Camare R, Louvet JP, Boneu B, Sie P. Plasminogen activator inhibitor in plasma is related to testosterone in men. *Metabolism.* 1989;38:1010-5.

26. Glueck C, Glueck H, Stroop D, Speiers J, Hamer T, Tracy T. Endogenous testosterone, fibrinolysis, and coronary heart disease risk in hyperlipidemic men. *J Lab Clin Med.* 1993;122:412-420.

27. Anderson RA, Ludlam CA, Wu FC. Haemostatic effects of supraphysiological levels of testosterone in normal men. *Thromb Haemost.* 1995;74:693-7.

28. Dai WS, Gutai JP, Kuller LH, Laporte RE, Falvo-Gerard L, Caggiula A. Relation between plasma high-density lipoprotein cholesterol and sex hormone concentrations in men. *Am J Cardiol.* 1984;53:1259-63.

29. Dai WS, Kuller LH, LaPorte RE, Gutai JP, Falvo-Gerard L, Caggiula A. The epidemiology of plasma testosterone levels in middle-aged men. *Am J Epidemiol.* 1981;114:804-16.

30. Gutai J, LaPorte R, Kuller L, Dai W, Falvo-Gerard L, Caggiula A. Plasma testosterone, high density lipoprotein cholesterol and other lipoprotein fractions. *Am J Cardiol.* 1981;48:897-902.

31. Heller RF, Wheeler MJ, Micallef J, Miller NE, Lewis B. Relationship of high density lipoprotein cholesterol with total and free testosterone and sex hormone binding globulin. *Acta Endocrinol (Copenh).* 1983;104:253-6.

32. Hamalainen E, Adlercreutz H, Ehnholm C, Puska P. Relationships of serum lipoproteins and apoproteins to sex hormones and to the binding capacity of sex hormone binding globulin in healthy Finnish men. *Metabolism.* 1986;35:535-41.

33. Khaw KT, Barrett-Connor E. Endogenous sex hormones, high density lipoprotein cholesterol, and other lipoprotein fractions in men. *Arterioscler Thromb.* 1991;11:489-94.

34. Lichtenstein MJ, Yarnell JW, Elwood PC, et al. Sex hormones, insulin, lipids, and prevalent ischemic heart disease. *Am J Epidemiol.* 1987;126:647-57.

35. Barrett-Connor EL. Testosterone and risk factors for cardiovascular disease in men. *Diabete Metab.* 1995;21:156-61.

36. Tenover JS. Effects of testosterone supplementation in the aging male. *J Clin Endocrinol Metab.* 1992;75:1092-1098.

37. Morley JE, Perry HMD, Kaiser FE, et al. Effects of testosterone replacement therapy in old hypogonadal males: a preliminary study. *J Am Geriatr Soc.* 1993;41:149-52.

38. Urban RJ, Bodenburg YH, Gilkison C, et al. Testosterone administration to elderly men increases skeletal muscle strength and protein synthesis. *Am J Physiol.* 1995;269:E820-6.

39. Tenover JL. Testosterone and the aging male. *J Androl.* 1997;18:103 6.

40. Barbosa J, Seal US, Doe RP. Effects of anabolic steroids on haptoglobin, orosomucoid, plasminogen, fibrinogen, transferrin, ceruloplasmin, alpha-1-antitrypsin, beta-glucuronidase and total serum proteins. *J Clin Endocrinol Metab.* 1971;33:388-98.

41. Kluft C, Preston FE, Malia RG, et al. Stanozolol-induced changes in fibrinolysis and coagulation in healthy adults. *Thromb Haemost.* 1984;51:157-64.

42. Kluft C, Bertina RM, Preston FE, et al. Protein C, an anticoagulant protein, is increased in healthy volunteers and surgical patients after treatment with stanozolol. *Thromb Res*. 1984;33:297-304.

43. Mannucci PM, Kluft C, Traas DW, Seveso P, D'Angelo A. Congenital plasminogen deficiency associated with venous thromboembolism: therapeutic trial with stanozolol. *Br J Haematol*. 1986;63:753-9.

44. Ferenchick G, Schwartz D, Ball M, Schwartz K. Androgenic-anabolic steroid abuse and platelet aggregation: a pilot study in weight lifters. *Am J Med Sci*. 1992;303:78-82.

45. Thompson PD, Cullinane EM, Sady SP, et al. Contrasting effects of testosterone and stanozolol on serum lipoprotein levels. *JAMA*. 1989;261:1165-8.

46. Friedl KE, Hannan CJ, Jr., Jones RE, Plymate SR. High-density lipoprotein cholesterol is not decreased if an aromatizable androgen is administered. *Metabolism*. 1990;39:69-74.

47. Zmuda JM, Fahrenbach MC, Younkin BT, et al. The effect of testosterone aromatization on high-density lipoprotein cholesterol level and postheparin lipolytic activity. *Metabolism*. 1993;42:446-50.

48. Cohen P. The role of estradiol in the maintenance of secondary hypogonadism in males in erectile dysfunction. *Med Hypotheses*. 1998;50:331-333.

49. Andersen P, Norman N, Hjermann I. Reduced fibrinolytic capacity associated with low ratio of serum testosterone to oestradiol in healthy coronary high-risk men. *Scand J Haematol*. 1983;30 (Suppl 39):53-57.

50. Phillips GB, Pinkernell BH, Jing TY. The association of hyperestrogenemia with coronary thrombosis in men. *Arterioscler Thromb Vasc Biol*. 1996;16:1383-7.

51. Phillips GB. Evidence for hyperoestrogenaemia as a risk factor for myocardial infarction in men. *Lancet*. 1976;2:14-8.

52. Phillips GB, Castelli WP, Abbott RD, McNamara PM. Association of hyperestrogenemia and coronary heart disease in men in the Framingham cohort. *Am J Med*. 1983;74:863-9.

53. Phillips GB. Evidence for hyperestrogenemia as the link between diabetes mellitus and myocardial infarction. *Am J Med*. 1984;76:1041-8.

54. Phillips GB. Relationship between serum sex hormones and glucose, insulin and lipid abnormalities in men with myocardial infarction. *Proc Natl Acad Sci U S A*. 1977;74:1729-33.

55. Carruthers M. *Maximising Manhood*. London: HarperCollins Publishers; 1996.

56. Reaven G. Role of insulin resistance in human disease. *Diabetes*. 1988;37:1595-1607.

57. Hamalainen E, Adlercreutz H, Puska P, Pietinen P. Diet and serum sex hormones in healthy men. *J Steroid Biochem.* 1984;20:459-64.

58. Phillips GB, Yano K, Stemmermann GN. Serum sex hormone levels and myocardial infarction in the Honolulu Heart Program. Pitfalls in prospective studies on sex hormones. *J Clin Epidemiol.* 1988;41:1151-6.

59. Yarnell JW, Beswick AD, Sweetnam PM, Riad-Fahmy D. Endogenous sex hormones and ischemic heart disease in men. The Caerphilly prospective study. *Arterioscler Thromb.* 1993;13:517-20.

60. Zglicznski S, Ossowski M, Slowinska-Srzednicka J, et al. Effect of testosterone replacement therapy on lipids and lipoproteins in hypogonadal and elderly men. *Atherosclerosis.* 1996;121:35-43.

61. Regelson W, Colman C. *The Superhormone Promise.* New York: Simon & Schuster; 1996.

62. Morales AJ, Nolan JJ, Nelson JC, Yen SS. Effects of replacement dose of dehydroepiandrosterone in men and women of advancing age. *J Clin Endocrinol Metab.* 1994;78:1360-7.

63. Bates C, Egerman R, Umstot E, Buster J, Casson P. DHEA attenuates study-induced declines in insulin sensitivity in postmenopausal women. *Ann NY Acad Sci.* 1995;774:291-293.

64. Barrett-Connor E, Khaw KT, Yen SS. A prospective study of dehydroepiandrosterone sulfate, mortality, and cardiovascular disease. *N Engl J Med.* 1986;315:1519-24.

65. Barrett-Connor E, Ferrara A. Dehydroepiandrosterone, dehydroepiandrosterone sulfate, obesity, waist-hip ratio, and noninsulin dependent diabetes in post menopausal women: the Rancho Bernardo Study. *J Clin Endocrinol Metab.* 1996;81:59-64.

66. Gordon GB, Bush DE, Weisman HF. Reduction of atherosclerosis by administration of dehydroepiandrosterone. A study in the hypercholesterolemic New Zealand white rabbit with aortic intimal injury. *J Clin Invest.* 1988;82:712-20.

67. Herrington DM. Dehydroepiandrosterone and coronary atherosclerosis. *Ann N Y Acad Sci.* 1995;774:271-80.

68. Wolkowitz OM, Reus VI, Roberts E, et al. Antidepressant and cognition-enhancing effects of DHEA in major depression. *Ann N Y Acad Sci.* 1995;774:337-9.

69. Alexandersen P, Haarbo J, Christiansen C. The relationship of natural androgens to coronary heart disease in males: a review. *Atherosclerosis.* 1996;125:1-13.

# Chapter 8

# Protecting the Prostate: The Role of Androgens

It's a safe bet that, by the time a man reaches middle age, he knows some other man who has experienced "prostate problems" – if he hasn't experienced them himself. Statistically speaking, if a man lives long enough in the U.S., prostate problems are almost inevitable.

Yet, most men probably know less about their prostate than they do about their testes. While they tend to become quite familiar with the size, feel, and location of their testes over the course of a lifetime, the prostate usually remains a mystery – at least until it starts acting up.

## Prostate Growth: Normal and Not So Normal

The prostate is a 20- to 25-gram (slightly less than 1 ounce) walnut-sized organ that sits astride the urethra at the base of the bladder. The urethra is the tube that conducts urine from the bladder and sperm-laden semen from the seminal vesicle through the penis and into the outside world (Fig. 8-1). During the first inch or so its journey, the urethra passes through the prostate.

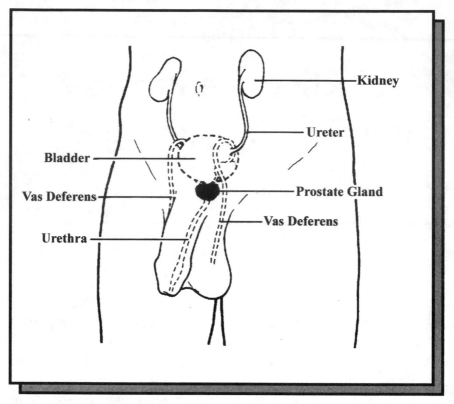

**Figure 8-1**. *Schematic illustration of the genitourinary system showing the relative position of the prostate, bladder, urethra, and other important organs.*

There are three general periods of prostate growth in a man's life:

1. From birth through puberty, a period of extremely low testosterone levels, the prostate forms, but remains tiny, weighing only 1 to 2 grams

2. As testosterone begins flooding the system during a male's teenage years, prostate growth erupts, finally leveling off at its adult plateau of 20 to 25 grams.

3. Around age 50, the prostate may begin to grow again, even as testosterone, which had heretofore stimulated growth, begins to decline. (If this sounds puzzling, you're right. Read on.)

In the U.S., the prostate is the most common site of cancer (317,000 new cases in 1996), and the second leading cause of cancer deaths in men. The prostate is also the most common site of non-cancerous excess tissue growth or enlargement, known as *benign prostatic hyperplasia*\* (or *hypertrophy*) – *BPH*, for short. BPH is far more common than prostate cancer. More than half of all men in this country above the age of 50 develop a significant degree of BPH, and if they survive into their 80s, 8 out of 10 will have it. Because of this, many medical practitioners have come to regard BPH as a "normal" part of aging. Just because it is so common, though, does not mean prostate hyperplasia cannot be prevented or reversed.

In the beginning, the symptoms of prostate cancer and BPH are fairly similar. Because the urethra is completely encased in the prostate as it exits the muscular urinary bladder, excessive growth of prostate tissue can compress the urethra, restricting the flow of urine. Imagine what happens when a garden hose becomes kinked or compressed. The high-pressure outflow from the nozzle end may slow to a trickle if the obstruction upstream is severe enough.

Physicians diagnose prostate enlargement via three general methods:

- **Digital examination.** The physician actually feels the prostate by inserting his gloved finger into the rectum. This method is crude at best, but still useful. Unfortunately, it may miss early changes.

- **PSA test.** PSA (prostate specific antigen) is a substance secreted by certain prostate cells. Elevated levels of PSA may be an early sign of prostate cancer, although the test is far from 100%-accurate. Improved versions of the PSA are just becoming available; one that looks very promising is the

---

\* Hyperplasia refers to an increase in the number of prostate cells; hypertrophy refers to increased growth of the prostate gland itself. The former is coming to be considered a more accurate description of the prostate enlargement.

cPSA. (Your doctor should know about the cPSA and other more accurate "PSA updates.")

- **Symptoms.** By the time a man begins experiencing symptoms of prostate enlargement, it is probably pretty far advanced. Yet, for many men, this is often the first indication that something is amiss.

## Symptoms of Prostate Enlargement

Men with mild prostate enlargement may not even notice any difference. It is likely at first that the bladder compensates for a slight obstruction by just squeezing a little harder. Eventually, though, compensation becomes impossible, and the man becomes aware that his urinary stream is noticeably weaker. Sometimes his bladder may not empty completely, a condition called *urinary retention*. When the bladder fails to empty completely, it is, of course, going to fill up faster. This translates into more trips to the bathroom, especially during the night, a condition we medical types like to call *frequency*.

Another familiar problem with enlarged prostates is *hesitancy*. This is the delay from the time a man steps up to the toilet or urinal and his bladder starts squeezing out its contents. Healthy men may sometimes experience a hesitancy delay in association with anxiety. With prostate enlargement, the delay can last up to several minutes. *Dribbling* also is common.

If BPH is allowed to progress, the bladder may completely lose its ability to empty its contents. This condition, known as *acute urinary retention* brings many men to hospital emergency rooms, where the only immediate relief may be catheterization. Prolonged, or *chronic* urinary retention can lead to kidney failure. The standard treatment for prostate enlargement that has gone this far may be a surgical procedure known as *TURP*, short for *transurethral resection of the prostate*. Think of TURP as a kind of Roto-Rooter® treatment, and you'll get the picture. A newer procedure, called *TUNA*, short for *transurethral needle ablation*, employs a heated needle and is supposed to minimize postoperative problems. It goes without saying that it's best to treat BPH before it gets this bad.

Prostate cancer can cause all the same symptoms as BPH, although it may start metastasizing – sending cancerous cells all over the body – before noticeable obstructions occur. This is a particularly dangerous turn of events because, once it starts metastasizing, prostate cancer can become a terminal illness. In advanced cases, castration is considered by most physicians in this country as the only viable therapeutic alternative.

## Science and the Conventional Medical Wisdom

Given the ubiquity of prostate disorders and the enormous resources that have been expended to understand and treat them, it is truly remarkable how little medical researchers really know about the prostate (and we can safely assume that most practicing physicians know even less). As the prostate expert Dr. John T. Isaacs of The Johns Hopkins School of Medicine has written, "Despite the major progress that has occurred in the biological sciences during the last 50 years, it is rather remarkable that we are about to enter the twenty-first century, and still the specific function of the prostate gland is unknown. Indeed, the prostate is the largest organ of unknown specific function in the human body."[1]

One particularly important area of controversy concerns the way steroid hormones affect the prostate. Everyone accepts that androgens are an important factor in prostate maintenance and growth, but it is not at all clear whether the androgens testosterone, dihydrotestosterone (DHT), and dehydroepiandrosterone (DHEA) *cause* excessive prostate growth or *inhibit* it. Enough evidence exists for each view to keep both sides well-armed.

Not surprisingly, when it comes to the best (and worst) treatments, confusion and contradiction reign. The specific therapy a physician offers a man with BPH or prostate cancer may depend to a large extent on which side of the Atlantic Ocean they both happen to be living at the time.

The conventional medical wisdom in the U.S. at the moment is that testosterone is bad and DHT is really bad for the prostate. Reflecting this view, virtually all "approved" therapeutic interventions focus on reducing the amount and/or influence of testosterone and DHT on prostate tissue. These treatments range from expensive high-tech drugs which are designed solely to block the conversion of testosterone to DHT, to the unkindest cut of all, complete castration, the last word in de-androgenization. Not only do you not have much excess growth after castration, you don't have much of a prostate either. Testosterone stimulates the growth of both normal and abnormal prostate cells. Remove it, and the prostate rapidly shrivels away.

On the other hand, a growing segment of physicians, especially in Europe but in this country as well, are beginning to wonder whether testosterone and DHT have been getting a bad rap all this time. They point to evidence, some of it dating back to the 1940s, that testosterone may actually be essential for keeping the aging prostate healthy. They question whether expensive drugs like *finasteride* (**Proscar®**), which are widely promoted by pharmaceutical companies and prescribed by most physicians, are really superior to natural and botanical therapies like *saw palmetto* (*serenoa repens*), *pygeum*, and others. Much of the evidence suggests that the limited benefits the pharmaceutical drugs provide may not be worth their high price or their unwanted adverse effects. This is especially true in light of the excellent efficacy and safety records associated with the natural products.

More and more men and physicians – often under pressure from their patients to offer them safer, more effective treatments – are starting to pay closer attention to the natural products as well as to diet and nutritional factors like fat intake (How much? What kinds?), zinc, essential fatty acids, antioxidants, including carotenoids (especially lycopene), selenium, and vitamin D, all of which are now known to affect prostate health. They do this at some risk because going against the conventional medical wisdom has been landing innovative physicians in hot water, both professionally and legally, for centuries.

## Androgens and the Prostate

This much is certain. When testosterone enters the cells that comprise the prostate, it undergoes a metabolic transformation to form other steroid hormones. More than 95% of the testosterone that enters the prostate gets converted by the enzyme *5α-reductase* into the very potent androgen DHT. DHT then binds to androgen receptors, stimulating the synthesis of specific proteins that cause the proliferation of new prostate cells, while postponing the death of some older prostate cells. Normally, there is sufficient testosterone (and DHT) to maintain a perfect balance between old cell death and new cell birth.

If too much DHT is causing prostate growth to get out of hand, then reducing the level of DHT should have some therapeutic value. Based on this reasoning, pharmaceutical company researchers have focused their efforts on developing drugs that interfere with the action of 5α-reductase. The best-known *5α-reductase inhibitor* is **Proscar®**, which is manufactured by Merck & Co. and is officially approved in the U.S. and many other countries for treating BPH.

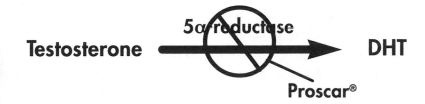

Does Proscar® work? Yes, but only up to a point. Double-blind, placebo-controlled studies (sponsored by Merck, of course) in men with BPH have demonstrated significant reductions in

DHT,[2] as well as decreases in prostate volume,[3] and improvements in urinary function.[4]

Despite these positive results, something is still very wrong with this picture. First, of course, there is the paradox mentioned earlier: BPH and prostate cancer hardly ever occur in teenagers and men below the age of 50, yet this is the age when testosterone levels reach their peak. If testosterone is the *cause* of excessive prostate growth, then why don't men start experiencing problems until testosterone levels start to *drop*? Why do the risks of BPH and prostate cancer continue to grow with age, even as testosterone levels continue to fall?

Also, Proscar® reduces the DHT concentration in the prostate by more than 80%, yet the prostate decreases in size by only about 18%, and only about 37% of men who take the drug for a year experience any improvement in their symptoms. Moreover, about 5% of Proscar® users suffer sexual side effects including decreased libido, impotence, and ejaculatory disorders.

Although the DHT theory would seem to dictate that Proscar® should be helpful in at least preventing prostate cancer,[5] clinical trials say otherwise. The 5α-reductase inhibitor seems to have no ability to prevent prostate cancer in men who are at high risk and may actually *increase* the risk for men with a certain type of malignancy. A recent study conducted by a University of Southern California team found that, of 27 high-risk men who took Proscar®, eight developed tumors within a year despite post-treatment levels of DHT 67% lower than baseline. By comparison, only one man out of the 25 who got no treatment at all developed cancer. Proscar® seemed particularly dangerous for men with a precancerous condition called *prostate intraepithelial neoplasia*, or *PIN*.[6]

Several other lines of evidence suggest that the testosterone-DHT-prostate picture is a lot cloudier than we have been led to believe. For example, when men are given the drug leuprolide, which suppresses the production of testosterone (and therefore, DHT as well), it has to reduce testosterone by 50-fold below normal in order to reduce prostate volume by only 30 to 40%.[7-9]

The testosterone-DHT theory assumes that DHT levels, at least, are elevated in men with enlarged prostates. While such elevations may occur in some patients, they may not be a necessary condition. Some studies have shown that prostatic DHT levels do not have to be elevated in men with BPH. One study compared tissue taken from healthy and hyperplastic prostates. No difference was found in steroid hormone levels. The DHT content of the healthy prostate tissue was 5.1 ng/g; for BPH tissue it was 5.0 ng/g.[10] In a Utah-based study, men whose brothers developed prostate cancer before age 62 had a fourfold higher risk of prostate cancer, compared with the general population of the State of Utah. When they examined the hormone levels of these men, the researchers found that *the highest risk was associated with families with the lowest plasma levels of androgens.*[11]

Recently, three studies from the U.S., Greece, and Sweden found no relationship between *circulating* DHT levels and the risk of developing a malignancy of men with prostate cancer. On the other hand, elevated *circulating* testosterone levels were associated with an increase in risk. *Intra-prostatic* androgen levels were not measured, however.[12-14] It is very possible that they might differ.

The ability of *saw palmetto* and *pygeum* to reduce symptoms of BPH also suggests that, while high DHT may be a factor, something else is clearly going on. We will discuss saw palmetto and pygeum in some depth in Chapter 9. For the moment, though, suffice it to say that they have little or no ability to inhibit 5α-reductase at therapeutic doses (a fact that is poorly recognized even by many who endorse its use), and yet can be very effective therapies, especially when used in combination.

## Treating BPH with Androgens

To most physicians in this country, treating BPH or prostate cancer with androgens seems just like throwing gasoline on a smoldering fire. In fact, though, there is good reason to believe that androgens may actually be therapeutic for the aging prostate.

The idea of using androgens as prostate treatment goes back at least as far as the 1940s. In one study published in 1944, for example, 86 men with BPH were given a series of testosterone propionate injections. After three to six weeks of injections, 69 of the men were described as "completely cured" of their urinary symptoms. Even after the "testosterone" injections were terminated, "complete clinical recovery" was reported to last for months or even years.[15]

Concern regarding the possibility that testosterone treatment might induce cancer has been around from the start. In a 1946 question-and-answer feature in the *Journal of the American Medical Association,* the author (presumably an editor of the journal) wrote: "Carcinoma of the prostate apparently occurs rarely in a patient who is receiving testosterone propionate; the medicament may be given when indicated without worrying about its carcinogenic properties." After warning physicians to make certain that patients do not have prostate cancer initially, they point out, "The likelihood of inducing it with testosterone propionate is evidently so slight that it may be disregarded."[16]

From the 1940s through the 1960s, Tiberius Reiter, M.D., whose pioneering work on androgens and sexual function was mentioned in Chapter 5, implanted high doses of pure crystalline testosterone into the muscle of hundreds of middle-aged men, achieving a kind of timed-release effect. The implant maintained elevated levels of testosterone in the body for six to seven months. (He also implanted a small pellet of estrogen.)

Dr. Reiter reported that, in more than 100 of these men over many years, he had never seen a case of prostate cancer. Although urinary symptoms sometimes appeared early in therapy, suggesting an initial degree of prostate enlargement, these vanished within a few weeks and never reappeared. "We have observed no other form of treatment able to reduce enlarged prostates to their normal size and consistency," he wrote, "and in our opinion, even advanced cases of prostate enlargement with the presence of residual urine [acute urinary retention syndrome] can be left, under observation, to testosterone implantation as the sole method of medical treatment."[17]

The British andrologist Dr. Malcolm Carruthers, who has treated more than 1,000 menopausal men with various forms of testosterone, also downplays the risk of prostate cancer. "Fifty years' treatment of hypogonadal patients with testosterone implants and 30 years of treatment with injections of testosterone enanthate do not show any rising incidence of prostate cancer or even of benign hypertrophy," he writes.[18]

The innovative French urologist, George Debled, M.D., also claims remarkable success using testosterone to treat thousands of men who have BPH and low testosterone. Debled, whose work is virtually unknown on this side of the English-French language gap, believes BPH is largely a result of an imbalance between testosterone and other hormones in the prostate. Specifically, he finds testosterone levels to be low relative to the normal levels of estrogens, sex hormone binding globulin (SHBG), and others.[19]

In a recent review of the literature on testosterone replacement, Dr. Lisa Tenover of the Emory University School of Medicine, who is a leading voice in prostate research in this country, seems to concur that testosterone may at least not be as bad as physicians have been taught (largely by pharmaceutical company-sponsored research) to believe. Of 11 studies in which an androgen (usually "testosterone") was given to older men, she found that only two reported any change in PSA (prostate specific antigen), an important early warning sign for abnormal prostate growth. In the five studies that evaluated prostate size or urine flow, androgen therapy caused no changes.[20]

# Is DHT a Therapeutic Option?

The French endocrinologist, Bruno de Lignieres, M.D., views prostate enlargement in much the same way as his countryman, George Debled, as an imbalance between androgens and estrogens. He has suggested that the best treatment for preventing prostate hyperplasia may be none other than DHT, currently cast as the villain of all villain hormones by advocates of 5α-reductase inhibition.[21] Dr. de Lignieres theorizes that the absolute level of testosterone or DHT may be less important for stimulating prostate growth than the balance between androgens and estrogens. (If this line of reasoning sounds familiar, you've probably read the earlier chapters in this book, where we point out that the *balance between androgens and estrogens* is also important for maintaining sexual function and cardiovascular health.)

Recall that some of the testosterone in the system is converted by the enzyme ***aromatase*** into estradiol, a high-potency form of estrogen (See Fig. 3-1). Dr. de Lignieres argues that those androgens that have been widely associated with prostate hypertrophy are the ones that are *aromatizable* – i.e., convertible to estradiol. The most important of these aromatizable androgens are testosterone and androstenedione. DHT is not aromatizable.

Supporting de Lignieres's view is an experiment in which either "testosterone" (testosterone propionate) or DHT was given to groups of Lobund-Wistar (L-W) rats. It is the misfortune of L-W rats to have been specially bred in laboratories to enhance their particular propensity for developing prostate cancer. Although there are important differences between human and rat prostates, these animals are often used as a model for the human male at high risk for prostate cancer. After 14 months of treatment, adenocarcinoma had developed in 24% of the testosterone-treated rats but not in one of the rats treated with DHT.[22] In another experiment, the same research team found that giving DHT to aging L-W rats actually *reduced* their risk of developing prostate tumors by 50%.[23]

These data suggest that the process of aromatization, which leads to an increase in estradiol relative to DHT, may be crucial for the initiation of prostate hyperplasia. The source of that excess estradiol, of course, is testosterone. According to de Lignieres, as men age, their prostate cells may tend to become slightly less sensitive to DHT and more sensitive to estradiol. "Following this theory," he writes, "a progressive imbalance between estradiol and DHT may appear in the prostate tissue of aged men." He considers this progressive increase in the estradiol:DHT ratio the "prime mover" for prostate changes in middle-aged men.[21]

In other words, when estradiol and DHT are in normal balance in prostate tissue, cell reproduction is controlled, and all is well. But as men age, their estradiol levels begin to rise relative to DHT, disrupting the normal hormonal milieu and shifting prostate growth into overdrive.

The most recent support for de Lignieres's position comes from an *in-vitro* experiment conducted by Dr. Atif N. Nakhla and his colleagues at New York's St. Luke's/Roosevelt Hospital Center and the Columbia University College of Physicians and Surgeons.[24] They took prostatic tissue – obtained during TURP surgery in men with BPH – and exposed it to various combinations of hormones and drugs, as well as to sex hormone binding globulin (SHBG). Their results clearly demonstrated that BPH was associated with elevated estradiol, decreased androgens, and increased SHBG. The accelerated growth of prostatic tissue, according to Nakhla's data, was due to estradiol acting "in concert with SHBG." Not only did DHT not provoke any new growth, it actually seemed to inhibit it by blocking the binding of estradiol to SHBG. In the authors' words, "[DHT] completely negates the effect of estradiol."

De Lignieres points out that conventional anti androgenic treatments including Proscar, leuprolide, and *high dose* estrogen (which shuts down testosterone production in the testes), tend to work only when they virtually eliminate androgenic stimulation.

$5\alpha$-reductase inhibitors may only be useful in the short term, he maintains. In the long run, they may be potentially harmful. By blocking the conversion of testosterone to DHT, they force testosterone down the aromatase-estradiol pathway – thus shifting the hormonal balance in favor of estrogen. Don't forget that, in addition to prostate problems, elevated estrogens relative to androgens in the human male have also been associated with sexual dysfunction, cardiovascular disease, and other serious chronic illnesses.

Dr. de Lignieres calls DHT treatment of BPH "an attractive possibility." In patients not taking a $5\alpha$-reductase inhibitor, testosterone therapy may sometimes be problematic, he explains, because it gets converted to both estradiol and DHT. If an imbalance is already in the making, extra testosterone may accentuate it. By contrast, DHT stimulates androgenic receptors, but it also *inhibits aromatase activity, potentially reducing the level of estradiol.* This would tend to shift the estrogen:DHT ratio back in a safer direction.

"In theory," writes de Lignieres, "[DHT] increases androgenic stimulation while preventing, or drastically reducing the age-related tendency to an increasing estradiol:DHT ratio." Regarding the safety of this treatment, he notes, "Reduction of estrogens, unlike reduction of androgens, has no visible side effects."[21]

A fascinating concept, but does it really work? De Lignieres reports on the results of a small study in which 37 hypogonadal men used DHT applied via a transdermal cream. Prostate size – as measured by ultrasound scan and PSA levels – decreased significantly in these men from 31 grams before treatment to 26 grams after a mean of 1.8 years of DHT treatment.

Unfortunately, hardly any other studies have been done to see what happens to the prostate when aging men take supplements of DHT. De Lignieres suggests that, if he is right, drugs that inhibit aromatase activity may be helpful. Little has been done to explore this option, but the few studies in the scientific literature are inconclusive regarding any therapeutic benefits of aromatase inhibitors.[25-30]

## Confused? Don't Worry, You're Not the Only One

*Which of the following statements is correct?*

A)  Testosterone helps cause prostate cancer

B)  Testosterone helps prevent prostate cancer

C)  Testosterone may help cause or help prevent prostate cancer depending on one or more other factors

D) There's no scientific certainty about the exact relationship (or relationships) of testosterone to prostate cancer

For the present, the answer is "D." So, what's a man to do?

It's apparent that this book supports the use of *natural* testosterone (NOT patented, previously patented, or otherwise altered, not-identical-to-natural testosterone) for men with symptoms of "male menopause" to help prevent cardiovascular disease, prostate disease, bone loss, impaired mental function, and other "infirmities of age." However, this support is presently a matter of "informed clinical judgement" and not "scientific certainty." The clinical judgement of other physicians may or may not concur. As you have read, on the Western side of the Atlantic Ocean, it most frequently does not.

So, if there's no scientific certainty, and (no matter how loudly opinions are stated) it's all a matter of clinical judgement, the question remains: what's a man (especially a middle-aged or older man) to do? First and foremost, no matter what course he chooses, a man should monitor himself (with and without a physician's help) for signs and symptoms of BPH and prostate cancer. Review the first part of this chapter. Is there:

- a weakening urinary stream?

- increased frequency of urination?

- hesitancy before urination?

- increasing dribbling?

If these signs and symptoms occur and then increase with whatever self-care course is chosen, it obviously isn't working and should be changed! Next, make sure to have the digital prostate exam (no, neither of this volume's co-authors enjoy this exam either!) with whatever regularity your physician recommends. Have your PSA test done regularly, and as soon as the cPSA or other more advanced test becomes more available, have that test done routinely. Once again, if the digital prostate examination or the PSA indicates a worsening condition, a different course of self-care needs to be chosen.

Dr. Georges Debled has treated more than 2000 men with testosterone over the past two decades. In a group of this size, statistically we would expect at least 50 to 60 would develop prostate cancer. According to Dr. Debled, prostate cancer has occurred in none of these men. Although my (JVW) clinical experience with natural testosterone is not as extensive as Dr. Debled's, it's been very similar; every man who's reported back to me has been pleased with his results. Combining this clinical experience with the studies noted (along with observations of nature, reason, and a little logic), I definitely recommend *natural* testosterone treatment at the appropriate time of a man's life.

While it remains scientifically uncertain how much, if any, therapeutic value testosterone supplementation has in treating BPH, it is evident that it is probably not risky unless a man already has prostate cancer. Thousands of men have been taking testosterone in its various forms for more than half a century without raising any particular alarms regarding the development of prostate cancer. Still, the kinds of large-scale, well-controlled studies that convince most medical authorities in this country are lacking. Given this uncertainty, conventional medicine on the western side of the Atlantic Ocean will likely to continue to view testosterone and DHT as enemies in the prostate wars for at least the next few years.

Nevertheless, there is good reason to be optimistic: A large amount of research supports the view that keeping testosterone and estrogens in balance is beneficial for prostate health and may prevent future problems.

And what about DHT? Is it a villain or hero hormone? While de Lignieres's hypothesis that transdermal DHT may be useful for preventing and treating BPH is intriguing, there is almost no solid clinical experience to back it up. Thus, it may be premature to start using DHT creams.

One thing that does seem fairly certain, however, is that the current enthusiasm among physicians and pharmaceutical companies for Proscar® and other 5α-reductase inhibitors is misplaced. At their best, these drugs appear to be only a partial, temporary solution for some men with BPH. They are probably useless for men with cancer and may even be dangerous for some of them. At least 5% of the men who use Proscar® can count on a disappointing sex life.

On the other hand, a handful of natural products appear to be at least as effective as Proscar® and certainly safer. We will discuss these in the following chapter.

# References

1.  Isaacs J. Role of androgens in prostatic cancer. In: Litwack G, ed. *Vitamins and Hormones, Vol. 49*. New York: Academic Press; 1994.

2.  McConnell JD, Wilson JD, George FW, Geller J, Pappas F, Stoner E. Finasteride, an inhibitor of 5 alpha-reductase, suppresses prostatic dihydrotestosterone in men with benign prostatic hyperplasia. *J Clin Endocrinol Metab*. 1992;74:505-508.

3.  Stoner E. The clinical effects of a 5 alpha-reductase inhibitor, finasteride, on benign prostatic hyperplasia. The Finasteride Study Group. *J Urol*. 1992;147:1298-1302.

4.  Gormley GJ, Stoner E, Bruskewitz RC, et al. The effect of finasteride in men with benign prostatic hyperplasia. The Finasteride Study Group [see comments]. *N Engl J Med*. 1992;327:1185-1191.

5.  Gormley G. Chemoprevention strategies for prostate cancer: the role of 5α-reductase inhibitors. *J Cell Biochem*. 1992;Supplement 16H:113-117.

6.  Cote RJ, Skinner EC, Salem CE, et al. The effect of finasteride on the prostate gland in men with elevated serum prostate-specific antigen levels. *Br J Cancer*. 1998;78:413-418.

7.  Levine AC, Kirschenbaum A, Kaplan P, Droller MA, Gabrilove JL. Serum prostate-antigen levels in patients with benign prostatic hypertrophy treated with leuprolide. *Urology*. 1989;34:10-13.

8.  Gabrilove JL, Levine AC, Kirschenbaum A, Droller M. Effect of long-acting gonadotropin-releasing hormone analog (leuprolide) therapy on prostatic size and symptoms in 15 men with benign prostatic hypertrophy. *J Clin Endocrinol Metab*. 1989;69:629-632.

9.  Bosch RJ, Griffiths DJ, Blom JH, Schroeder FH. Treatment of benign prostatic hyperplasia by androgen deprivation: effects on prostate size and urodynamic parameters. *J Urol*. 1989;141:68-72.

10. Walsh PC, Hutchins GM, Ewing LL. Tissue content of dihydrotestosterone in human prostatic hyperplasia is not supranormal. *J Clin Invest*. 1983;72:1772-1777.

11. Meikle A, Smith J, West D. Familial factors affecting prostatic cancer risk and plasma sex-steroid levels. *The Prostate*. 1985;6:121-128.

12. Gustafsson O, Norming U, Gustafsson S, Eneroth P, Åström G, Nyman C. Dihydrotestosterone and testosterone levels in men screened for prostate cancer: a study of a randomized population. *Br J Urol.* 1996;77:433-440.

13. Signorello LB, Tzonou A, Mantzoros CS, et al. Serum steroids in relation to prostate cancer risk in a case-control study (Greece). *Cancer Causes Control.* 1997;8:632-636.

14. Gann PH, Ma J, Hennekens CH, Hollis BW, Haddad JG, Stampfer MJ. Circulating vitamin D metabolites in relation to subsequent development of prostate cancer. *Cancer Epidemiol Biomarkers Prev.* 1996;5:121-126.

15. Kook N. *J Int Coll Surg.* 1944;7:129.

16. Queries and minor notes. *JAMA.* 1946;132:252.

17. Reiter T. Testosterone therapy. *Br J Geriatr Prac.* 1967;4:137-140.

18. Carruthers M. *Maximising Manhood.* London: HarperCollins Publishers; 1996.

19. Schachter M. *The Natural Way to a Healthy Prostate.* New Canaan, CT: Keats Publishing, Inc.; 1995.

20. Tenover JL. Testosterone and the aging male. *J Androl.* 1997;18:103-106.

21. de Lignieres B. Transdermal dihydrotestosterone treatment of "andropause." *Ann Med.* 1993;25:235-241.

22. Pollard M, Snyder DL, Luckert PH. Dihydrotestosterone does not induce prostate adenocarcinoma in L-W rats. *Prostate.* 1987;10:325-331.

23. Pollard M. Dihydrotestosterone prevents spontaneous adenocarcinomas in the prostate- seminal vesicle in aging L-W rats. *Prostate.* 1998;36:168-171.

24. Nakhla AM, Khan MS, Romas NP, Rosner W. Estradiol causes the rapid accumulation of cAMP in human prostate. *Proc Natl Acad Sci U S A.* 1994;91:5402-5405.

25. Zmuda JM, Fahrenbach MC, Younkin BT, et al. The effect of testosterone aromatization on high-density lipoprotein cholesterol level and postheparin lipolytic activity. *Metabolism.* 1993;42:446-450.

26. Schulze H, Berges R, Paschold K, Senge T. [New conservative therapeutic approaches in benign prostatic hyperplasia]. Neue konservative Therapieans atze bei der benignen Prostatahyperplasie. *Urologe [A].* 1992;31:8-13.

27. Levine AC, Kirschenbaum A, Gabrilove JL. The role of sex steroids in the pathogenesis and maintenance of benign prostatic hyperplasia. *Mt Sinai J Med.* 1997;64:20-25.

28. Kelloff GJ, Lubet RA, Lieberman R, et al. Aromatase inhibitors as potential cancer chemopreventives. *Cancer Epidemiol Biomarkers Prev.* 1998;7:65-78.

29. Friedl KE, Hannan CJ, Jr., Jones RE, Plymate SR. High-density lipoprotein cholesterol is not decreased if an aromatizable androgen is administered. *Metabolism.* 1990;39:69-74.

30. Ekman P. Endocrine therapy for benign prostatic hyperplasia in the 90's. *J Urol (Paris).* 1995;101:22-25.

# Chapter 9
# Protecting the Prostate: Natural Alternatives to Proscar®

If a man goes to a physician in the United States with symptoms of benign prostatic hyperplasia (BPH), odds are he'll come away with a prescription for the 5α-reductase inhibiting drug Proscar®. For the reasons discussed in Chapter 8 and in this chapter, Proscar® leaves a lot to be desired as a treatment for BPH, and it may even be dangerous for men at high risk for a certain type of prostate cancer.

Let the same man go to a European physician, and he is far more likely to be offered a natural extract of the dwarf palm *serenoa repens*, or *saw palmetto*, sold commercially as *Permixon®* and *Sereprostat®*, as well as other natural treatments. In Germany, about 90% of all men diagnosed with BPH are treated with one or more of these natural, botanical agents.[1] Numerous well-controlled scientific studies have shown these products to be quite effective for relieving the symptoms of BPH while causing hardly any unwanted effects.

## Saw Palmetto: The Multimodal BPH Therapy

Nothing focuses the differences between the pharmaceutical and natural approaches to health care more sharply than the treatment of BPH. Take finasteride (generic name for Proscar®), for

# First thing, get a prostate exam

Before beginning any kind of treatment for prostate disease, it is strongly recommended that every man should first have his prostate checked by digital rectal exam and/or a test such as the PSA to rule out the possibility that he might have prostate cancer. This is true even if there are no obvious symptoms of prostate enlargement. If cancer is present, most of the treatments described in this chapter will do little or nothing to slow its progress, but it is not known whether testosterone treatment would exacerbate it or not.

example. Designed by computer to fit a particular chemical receptor site, finasteride is a chemical laser-beam aimed at the metabolic juncture where testosterone turns into DHT – the enzyme $5\alpha$-reductase. By inhibiting the action of $5\alpha$-reductase, finasteride drastically reduces the amount of DHT formed in the prostate. This biochemical strategy has achieved a moderate degree of clinical success and a considerable degree of commercial success. More important, perhaps, it has helped pharmaceutical companies propagate the myth – among both the medical and general communities – that excess DHT is *the cause* of BPH. If you believe this myth, of course, then Proscar® is just what the doctor ordered. Isn't science great!

The problem, as we pointed out in Chapter 8, is that BPH is a lot more complicated than just too much DHT binding too many androgen receptors for too long. Effective treatment requires a strategy that approaches the problem from several different angles. As a complex, naturally occurring substance, you might expect saw palmetto to have a few more therapeutic tricks up its sleeve than a one-trick-pony like finasteride, and you'd be right.

Although saw palmetto extract is used widely in Europe, it is largely rejected by physicians on this side of the Atlantic Ocean. Ironically, it is derived from a plant native to the pine woods and sandy dunes of South Carolina, Louisiana, Georgia, and Florida. Saw palmetto seeds have a long history in Native American medicine as a treatment for irritations of the urinary bladder, urethra, and prostate.[2]

Exactly how saw palmetto works is not certain. What is certain is that, unlike finasteride, it appears to have a variety of different actions, any or all of which may be beneficial for prostatic health. These actions include an ability to:

- **Inhibit 5α-reductase.** Like finasteride, saw palmetto extract can inhibit the action of the enzyme 5α-reductase, reducing the conversion of testosterone to DHT, but it is thousands of times less potent than finasteride in this regard. The importance of 5α-reductase inhibition in relieving symptoms of BPH is unclear, however. Some research suggests that reduction of DHT levels seems to occur only at doses of saw palmetto far higher than those typically used to treat BPH.[?] Merck, of course, tries to paint finasteride's extremely high potency as a 5α-reductase inhibitor as an advantage. As we discussed in the previous chapter, though, lots of excellent research disputes this.

- **Block DHT binding to prostatic androgen receptors.** According to the conventional medical wisdom, the binding of DHT to prostatic androgen receptors is the central event in the proliferation of prostate tissue. Studies show that extract of saw palmetto competes with DHT for androgenic receptors, effectively blocking the binding of DHT.[3-6] Saw palmetto's anti-androgenic effects can be substantial. In one experiment, prepubertal rats and mice were castrated to remove the source of endogenous testosterone. The rats then received "testosterone" orally or by injection along with either saw palmetto extract or placebo for six to 12 days. Saw palmetto extract antagonized the prostate-stimulating effects of "testosterone," reducing prostate weight by 46%, compared with placebo.[2] Finasteride has never been shown to affect DHT binding. All it can do is keep DHT levels low.

- **Reduce prostatic edema (swelling) and inflammation.** A too often overlooked clinical element in prostate enlargement is edema and inflammation, a condition called *prostatitis*. In animal and *in vitro* (test-tube) studies, saw palmetto extract has been shown to reduce edema and suppress inflammatory mediators.[2, 7-9] Finasteride has no effect on prostate inflammation or edema.

- **Inhibit the effects of estrogens.** As noted in the previous chapter, it is becoming increasingly apparent that the potent estrogen *estradiol* can be a major stimulant for prostatic cell proliferation. The results of a double-blind, placebo-controlled Italian study have demonstrated that saw palmetto extract blocks estrogen receptors in the prostates of BPH patients, minimizing the growth-stimulating effects of estradiol.[10]

  Finasteride, of course, does not interfere with the actions of estradiol. In fact, according to Dr. Bruno de Lignieres, by blocking the conversion of testosterone to DHT, finasteride may make more testosterone available for aromatization, thus possibly *increasing* the amount of estradiol in the prostate. In the long run, this action might theoretically *promote* excess growth.[11]

- **Antagonize α-adrenergic receptors.** Stimulation of α-adrenergic receptors by noradrenaline causes smooth muscle cells all over the body, including the bladder and prostate, to contract.[12] Blocking α-adrenoceptors is a therapeutic option for BPH because it can relax these muscles, dilating the urethra slightly, thus permitting a reduction in symptoms. Saw palmetto has recently been shown to block α-adrenergic activity in animal smooth muscle tissue, suggesting yet another avenue by which it may help relieve BPH symptoms.[2]

Pharmaceutical drugs that block α-adrenergic receptors are sometimes used to treat high blood pressure, and one of those drugs, terazosin, has recently been approved by the FDA for treating BPH also. Others are likely to follow. According to U.S. government statistics, these drugs provide 51% symptomatic improvement for 59 to 86% of users, which is actually superior to finasteride (31% improvement for 54 to 78% of users).[13]

But α-blockers are awkward to use, in part, because of the difficulty in establishing an effective dose that does not cause unwanted adverse effects (which occur in as many as 43% of users). Also, there is no evidence they provide anything but short-term symptomatic relief. They have no effect on the progression of the disorder, as saw palmetto extract does. Needless to say, finasteride neither blocks α-adrenergic activity nor relaxes prostatic or bladder smooth muscle.

# Effects of Saw Palmetto Extract in Men With BPH

The vast majority of trials of saw palmetto extract in men with BPH have demonstrated it to be an effective and exceptionally safe therapeutic option. The most important of these studies are those that included large numbers of men and/or employed a double-blind, placebo-controlled, or comparative design.

In a large, multicenter, open-label trial* conducted in Belgium by 112 urologists, supervised by the University of Brussels urologist Dr. Johan Braeckman, 505 men with mild to moderate symptoms of BPH took saw palmetto extract (160 mg, twice daily) for three months. The results demonstrated impressive improvement in

---

* In an open-label study, both the investigators and the participants know what the experimental substance is. There is no placebo control.

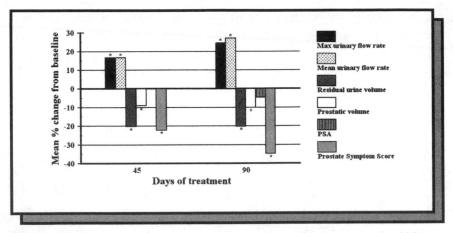

**Figure 9-1**. *Results of an open-label trial of saw palmetto extract in 505 men with BPH. Highly statistically significant improvement (\* p < 0.0001) in BPH symptoms, compared with pre-treatment baseline, was observed for all relevant measures. (Adapted from Braeckman, 1994)*

these men. As shown in Figure 9-1, the maximum urinary flow rate increased by 17% after 45 days of treatment, and by 25% after 90 days, compared with the pretreatment baseline. Similar increases were observed in mean urinary flow rates. Residual urinary volume (the amount of urine remaining in the bladder after a urination attempt) was 20% lower than baseline at both time points, and prostatic volume (the size of the prostate) was reduced by 9 and 10% after 45 and 90 days, respectively. The International Prostate Symptom Score (IPSS), based on a brief patient questionnaire, is a standardized measure of prostate symptoms. IPSS scores were decreased by 22 and 35%, respectively. All these differences were statistically significant. The only relevant measure that showed no significant change was PSA level.[14]

Braeckman's results may be discounted by some for the lack of a placebo control. This was not the case with a study by a French team headed by Dr. G. Champault, of l'Hôpital Jean Verdier in Paris. Using a double-blind, placebo-controlled design, these researchers asked 110 men with symptoms of BPH to take either saw palmetto extract (Permixon®) (160 mg, twice daily) or placebo for 30 days. Under these more rigorous experimental conditions, saw palmetto extract produced clearly superior results, compared with both pretreatment baseline and placebo. As shown in Figure 9-2, those taking saw palmetto extract experienced large, statistically significant improvements in the frequency of nighttime trips to the toilet, urinary flow rate, and residual urine volume.

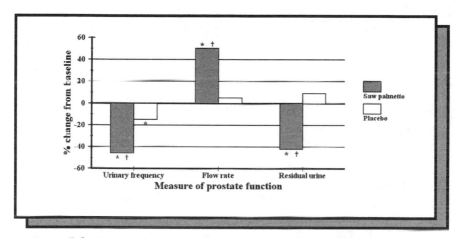

Figure 9-2. Comparison of the effects of saw palmetto extract (Permixon®) and placebo on three measures of prostate function in men with BPH. * p < 0.001 vs baseline; † p < 0.001 vs placebo. (Adapted from Champault et al, 1984)

# Saw Palmetto Extract vs Proscar®

How does saw palmetto extract compare with Proscar®? Only one published study has compared the two treatments in men with BPH. This was a very large, double-blind, French-based trial supervised by Dr. Jean-Christophe Carraro, of the Pierre Fabre Médicament, and conducted in 87 different urology centers in nine European countries.[9] The 1,098 men, all over age 50, were randomly asked to take either Permixon® (160 mg, twice daily) or Proscar® (5 mg, once daily) for six months. Neither the men nor the physicians who administered the treatments knew who was getting which treatment.

The results showed that both treatments were equally effective in reducing the symptoms of BPH. As shown in Figure 9-3, both treatments were associated with essentially equivalent improvements in prostate symptoms (about 22% at 6 weeks, 40% at 26 weeks), quality of life (about 54% at 6 weeks; 70% at 26 weeks), and urine flow rate (about 15% at 6 weeks, 25-30% at 26 weeks). The only significant difference between the two treatments on these measures was a slight advantage for Proscar® in peak urinary flow rate at 26 weeks.

In terms of sexuality, however, the Permixon-treated men fared significantly better. The Proscar-treated men complained substantially more about decreased libido, impotence, and ejaculatory disorders. As the authors wrote, "Patients receiving finasteride experienced statistically significant deterioration in sexual function score compared to those receiving Permixon®. The difference between the two groups, which was in favor of Permixon® for all four items of the questionnaire, was noted from the first follow-up visit at six weeks and remained significant at 26 weeks."[9]

Although both treatments were equally effective in decreasing symptoms of BPH, Proscar® was associated with a significantly greater (-16%) reduction in prostate size compared with Permixon® (-7%). How is this possible, if according to the conventional medical wisdom, BPH symptoms are a result of an enlarged prostate?

This finding underscores a fact, demonstrated by other research, that prostate symptoms and urinary flow rates are not necessarily directly related to prostate size. The authors suggest two possible explanations for this apparent discrepancy: 1) The decrease in prostate volume associated with 5α-reductase inhibition may not necessarily occur in the part of the prostate where BPH develops and obstructs urinary flow. 2) Intensified 5α-reductase activity may not necessarily be the sole or even the most important cause of BPH.

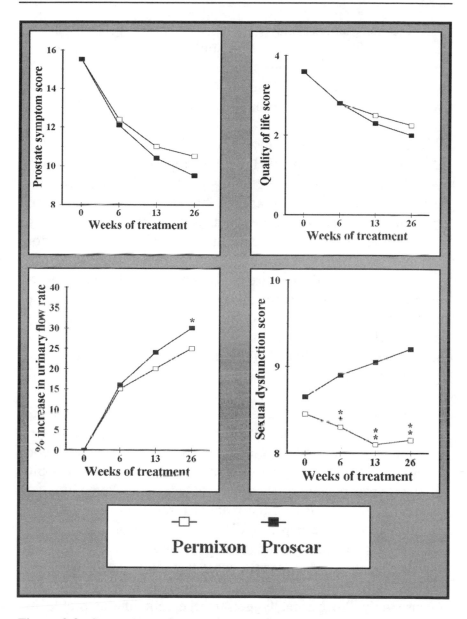

**Figure 9-3**. *Comparison of saw palmetto extract (Permixon®) and finasteride (Proscar®) in a multicenter, double- blind, study in over 1000 men with BPH. * p <0.05, Permixon vs Proscar; ** p <0.001, Permixon vs Proscar (Adapted from Cararro et al, 1996)*

Proscar® also caused a large drop in PSA levels, where Permixon® had no effect. The reason for this difference is also unclear (as is its clinical significance), but it may be related to the exclusion from the study of men with elevated PSA levels and/or a greater reduction in PSA-producing prostate epithelial cells by the 5α-reductase inhibitor.

Taken together, these results reinforce the contention that the laser-beam approach to BPH therapy represented by high-tech synthetic drugs, whose only effect is to inhibit 5α-reductase, may be misdirected. On the contrary, the broader therapeutic approach represented by saw palmetto extract, with its multiple avenues of attack, is not only equally effective in reducing symptoms, but more tolerable.

The results of the Carraro et al study essentially represent the European view of BPH treatment. What do scientists on this side of the Atlantic Ocean think about saw palmetto versus finasteride? Curiously, it is hard to find a positive word about saw palmetto in the U.S. literature. Unlike Carraro, the results of the only two other published comparative studies suggest that finasteride is the superior treatment.

You don't have to look too far to find the source of this apparent discrepancy. While the Carraro et al study was conducted by a large group of independent researchers (the paper was not supported by funds from any pharmaceutical company), the two pro-finasteride papers were published by scientists employed by – you guessed it – Merck & Co., the manufacturer of Proscar®. A close examination of these papers indicates that their primary purpose was to try to convince physicians – based on some very flimsy and contrived science – that, despite what they may have heard about saw palmetto, Proscar® was superior for treating men with BPH, because only Proscar really gets to the root of the problem – 5α-reductase inhibition. This is not to say that these researchers have lied, made up data, or otherwise misrepresented the facts. On the other hand, these papers are excellent illustrations of the way apparently good science can be manipulated to stack the experimental deck in favor of a particular point of view. Let's look at these two papers and see what was done.

*The Rhodes study.* The first study, by Rhodes et al,[4] was published in 1993 (three years before Carraro et al). It was an *in-vitro* (test tube) and *in-vivo* (lab rats and human subjects) comparison of the relative ability of finasteride and saw palmetto (and other plant extracts) to inhibit 5α-reductase.

In the introduction, the authors lay the groundwork for their ultimate conclusion by pointing out that, the "decrease in intra-prostatic DHT is thought to cause the decrease in prostate volume seen in men treated with finasteride." Their support for this statement comes from a 1992 paper by Stoner,[9] who coincidently, also worked for Merck. Given this "fact," it takes no great leap to conclude that anything that reduces DHT should also reduce prostate volume. The authors acknowledge that saw palmetto extract has been shown in European studies to have the ability to inhibit 5α-reductase.[3-6] They fail to note at this point,[*] however, that the same study (by Sultan et al) they cite to support saw palmetto extract's anti-5α-reductase activity also showed that it inhibits the enzyme 3-ketosteroid reductase and binding to androgen receptors.[5]

In the *in-vitro* studies, finasteride was found to be *5,600 times* more potent at inhibiting 5α-reductase than saw palmetto extract, but neither substance was found to have any ability at all to inhibit binding at androgen receptors. While the first result comes as no surprise (after all, that's what finasteride was designed to do), the second result is contradicted by several other studies.[3-6]

In Rhodes's animal study, pre-pubertal rats were castrated and then given doses of either "testosterone" (testosterone propionate) or "DHT" (DHT propionate). Half the animals in each androgen group also received either saw palmetto extract (Permixon®) or finasteride for seven days. Both the natural extract and the drug were given at doses that can only be described as "really high" and "unbelievably high," at least in human terms. The

---

[*]    They do mention it later in the Discussion section, but only to discount the reality of this effect.

dose of Permixon® given to these very young rats (weighing all of 50 grams) was either 180 mg or 1,800 mg per day. The low dose is just half the total dose normally given to a full-sized human being, while the high dose is *more than five times the **human** dose*. The doses of finasteride – 0.1 and 10.0 mg/day – were 2% and 200%, respectively, of the *human* dose. Whatever the results, given the magnitude of these doses, it's hard to imagine they could have any significance for human males aged 50 or older.

The results of the animal study showed that both "testosterone" and "DHT" stimulated rat prostate growth. As expected due to its mechanism of action, finasteride blocked prostate growth by 33% in the "testosterone"-treated rats, but not at all in the "DHT"-treated ones. Saw palmetto extract had no effect – "even at the highest dosage levels" – on prostate growth. Under these experimental conditions, finasteride, indeed, comes out smelling better. Seven days is a very short time when it comes to prostate growth, however. Recognizing this, most saw palmetto studies in the scientific literature have lasted for many months, even up to a year.

In the human phase of Rhodes's study, Proscar®, Permixon®, or placebo was given to 32 healthy young male "volunteers." This time standard human doses were used, but again, the duration of the study was just seven days. Predictably, the results demonstrated the superiority of finasteride for significantly *reducing the level of DHT in the blood stream*. In terms of clinical superiority, the relevance of these results for middle-aged or older men with BPH of a seven-day study in healthy young men is not really all that clear, especially if you question the importance of DHT for excess prostate growth.

Nevertheless, the underlying message of Rhodes et al couldn't be clearer:

1) If, DHT causes prostatic hyperplasia; and

2) if finasteride is thousands of times more potent an inhibitor of 5α-reductase than saw palmetto extract; and

3) if finasteride reduces DHT formation, while saw palmetto extract does not; and

4) if finasteride blocks "testosterone"-stimulated prostate growth, but saw palmetto extract does not; and

5) if neither treatment inhibits androgen receptor binding (despite what you may have read elsewhere about saw palmetto); then

6) finasteride must be the superior treatment for men with BPH.

Of course, Rhodes et al (and presumably Merck's legal department) are careful not go so far as to actually make any claims of clinical efficacy for finasteride based on these data,* but they pull no punches when it comes to saw palmetto extract. Let's analyze what they say in their **Conclusions** and see what it really means:

*What they say...*

"Based on our data, it is unlikely that Permixon...or other plant extracts assayed would cause prostate shrinkage via inhibition of $5\alpha$-reductase or binding to the androgen receptor."

*What it really means ...*

*It's true that Permixon probably does not cause prostate shrinkage by inhibiting $5\alpha$-reductase. That doesn't mean it might not work some other way, including via androgen receptor binding. It also assumes that prostate shrinkage is important for symptomatic relief. The authors' dubious conclusion that saw palmetto extract does not bind androgen receptors contradicts the European literature. They get away with this conclusion by using the "weasel" phrase, "Based on our data..." Good scientists do not draw conclusions based solely upon their own data. But what they have done here is to discount saw palmetto's other therapeutic effects by suggesting the possibility that the earlier European studies were somehow mistaken.*

---

* This article was published in 1993, before Merck had received official FDA approval to market – and therefore, make any therapeutic claims for – Proscar®.

### What they say...

"There are published results of multiple short-term clinical studies using various plant extracts, including Permixon . . . However, none have measured prostate volume effects or serum DHT in men."

### What it really means ...

*This statement is true. However, it fails to mention two important facts. First, saw palmetto extract is widely considered effective by physicians who use it. (It is officially "approved" for reducing BPH symptoms in Germany and several other countries.) Second, according to several studies, prostate volume and serum DHT levels may not be all that important in the etiology of BPH.*

### What they say...

"In contrast, finasteride is a potent, specific $5\alpha$-reductase inhibitor. It inhibits testosterone stimulated growth in the rat, inhibits human prostatic $5\alpha$-reductase in vitro at very low doses, and has been shown to shrink the human prostate and reduce serum DHT in long-term clinical trials."

### What it really means ...

*Having taken saw palmetto extract off the table as a therapeutic option, the authors now roll out their "superior," new alternative. In advertising-speak, this would be their "take-home" message. It reinforces the conventional wisdom that $5\alpha$-reductase inhibition is the key to the shrinking of hyperplastic prostate tissue, and the best way currently available to do that is finasteride.*

**The Strauch et al study.** The second Merck study, by a team of scientists headed by Dr. Georges Strauch, of the Hôpital Universitaire Cochin, in Paris, appears to be the same human clinical trial referred to in the Rhodes et al study. This paper simply gives more details about the study and a more intensive analysis of the results.[16] The trial was conducted in France, which may have aided its credibility among the article's more saw palmetto-sophisticated European audience (it was published in a European urology journal).*

The key details of Strauch et al have been discussed above. Suffice it to say, finasteride was found to be better at reducing blood levels of DHT as soon as 12 hours after treatment, while saw palmetto extract (Permixon®) had no effect on DHT even after seven days of treatment. While this appears to suggest that finasteride might be clinically superior to saw palmetto extract, don't forget that this conclusion rests on a very shaky foundation made up of false assumptions and selective attention to published scientific data:

- It assumes that $5\alpha$-reductase inhibition and DHT reduction are as important for BPH as they say they are.

- It ignores the fact that in many places in Europe, the clinical value of saw palmetto extract is unquestioned.

- It ignores the fact that clinical improvement with both saw palmetto extract and finasteride in their target population – middle-aged or older men with BPH – typically does not appear for weeks or even months. A trial of only seven days in healthy young men is irrelevant at best.

- *Relevant* clinical variables – prostate volume, urine flow rate, quality of life, etc. – were not measured and would have been meaningless anyway because the subjects consisted only of a few healthy young men, not older men with BPH.

---

* It is very unusual to publish the same experimental data in more than one scientific journal. Most well-respected journals will not publish data that have been previously published elsewhere. Other journals are not so choosy. The fact that Rhodes et al[4] was published in the U.S. and Strauch et al[16] was published in Europe may also have helped the study slip through the cracks.

The Strauch study may have had some validity as an early assessment of finasteride's and saw palmetto's mechanisms of action and short-term safety and tolerability. But to draw conclusions about the relative clinical efficacy of either treatment based on these data cannot be justified.

Yet, many physicians, especially those who may not be all that familiar with saw palmetto extract, will look at Rhodes et al and Strauch et al, and all they'll see are a pair of double-blind, placebo-controlled, comparative trials (a rare and desirable species) that *appear* to show that finasteride is superior to saw palmetto extract.* To many physicians, especially those in this country, and *especially* those who inhabit places like the FDA, the double-blind, placebo-controlled study is the *sine qua non* of medical research. Anything less raises the specter of possible experimenter bias or other undue influences on the results, thus lowering their credibility more than a few notches.

Many – but not all – of the European studies of saw palmetto extract have lacked the kinds of rigorous controls the American medical establishment typically demands. This should come as no surprise, since saw palmetto extract is an *unpatentable* substance. The enormous costs associated with conducting large, well-controlled clinical trials usually puts unpatentable (or generic) substances out of reach for most researchers.

For the most part, only large, multinational pharmaceutical companies like Merck have deep enough pockets to conduct these studies. They can afford it because they own the exclusive right to sell *patented* drugs like Proscar®. This means they can price their drugs as high as they want. If anyone could sell Proscar® (as will occur once the patent expires), prices would necessarily drop, and it would become far less profitable.

Since no such financial incentive to sell saw palmetto extract exists, large well-controlled human trials have been rare. Of the clinical trials of saw palmetto extract that have been conducted, a

---

* Rest assured that Merck sales reps probably hand out copies of these papers to every urologist and general practitioner they come across.

fair number have been published in languages other than English, essentially eliminating them from circulation among U.S. physicians. Against this background of largely "uncontrolled," "foreign" studies on saw palmetto, the "well-controlled" trial(s) of Proscar® are bound to stand out in sharp relief. Clinical relevance, however, is another matter.

The results of the Merck studies seem to suggest – without quite coming out and saying it – that saw palmetto extract has no useful pharmacologic purpose in BPH (after all, it doesn't block $5\alpha$-reductase as well as finasteride does), and therefore, it could not possibly have any therapeutic benefit in men with BPH. (What about all those European studies that say it works? Well, we won't look behind that curtain.)

At the same time, this new drug, called finasteride, researched and manufactured by a U.S.-based company you can trust, Merck, zeroes in on what is assumed, but not proven to be *the* causative mechanism of BPH (i.e., excessive $5\alpha$-reductase activity leading to too much DHT), essentially turning off the DHT spigot.

Comparing saw palmetto extract and finasteride under the conditions described above is akin to a sprinter racing a marathoner in the 100-meter dash. There's no doubt who will win. The race is rigged from the outset. Under these rules, the real question Who is the better runner? – must go unanswered. Just as a 100-meter dash can't possibly determine a winner between the two runners, neither can the Merck-sponsored research studies draw any meaningful clinical distinction between finasteride and saw palmetto extract. The Rhodes and Strauch studies have absolutely no relevance for the man with BPH and should be treated, not as important medical science, but as the pieces of pharmaceutical marketing they really are. The only well-controlled comparative study that was clinically relevant – because its subjects were men with BPH and it lasted six months – was the aforementioned study by Carraro et al.[9] It found that saw palmetto extract and finasteride were essentially equal for treating BPH symptoms, but that finasteride was significantly inferior in terms of adverse sexual effects.

Saw palmetto extract is widely available in health food stores and by mail order from nutritional supplement companies. *Caveat emptor* (buyer beware), however. Not all saw palmetto extracts are alike. It is important to make certain that the product label indicates that the saw palmetto extract is 85 to 95% fatty acids and sterol. Anything less may not have the potency to do any good. The dose most often found to be safe and effective is 160 mg twice daily. No serious side effects of saw palmetto extract have ever been reported at reasonable doses.

## Other Botanical Treatments for BPH

In addition to saw palmetto extract, a handful of other botanical products appears to have beneficial effects on the aging prostate. Among these are ***Urtica dioica (stinging nettle) root, Pygeum africanum bark***, and a flower pollen extract ***Graminaceae***, usually called by its brand name, ***Cernilton®***. Since each of these substances may have slightly different mechanisms of action, it is common to combine two or more of them to achieve an additive effect.

*Urtica dioica.* Extracts of the root of the *stinging nettle*, known as ***Urtica dioica***, are widely used as a treatment for BPH in Europe.* One laboratory animal study found that stinging nettle extract could inhibit experimentally induced BPH in mice.[17] In an open-label human study conducted in France, 67 men with various degrees of BPH took stinging nettle extract for up to six months. The treatment significantly reduced the number of nighttime trips to the toilet, especially in men with mild BPH. Symptom relief was achieved in as little as three weeks in those with the mildest BPH. Although stinging nettle extracts improved BPH symptoms, they had no effect on prostate volume, again emphasizing the disconnection between BPH symptoms and prostate size.[18]

Like saw palmetto extract, stinging nettle extract is a complex natural substance and probably has several relevant mechanisms of

---

* Stinging nettle extract, like saw palmetto extract, is an "approved" drug in Germany.

action in men with BPH. For example, the results of a Japanese *in-vitro* study suggested that certain components of stinging nettle extract may directly suppress prostate cell metabolism and growth.[19] Another study, conducted in Germany, showed that stinging nettle extract may inhibit the enzyme *aromatase*, which converts testosterone to estradiol.[20] (See Fig. 3-1.) Since elevated estradiol levels have been associated with BPH,[11,21,22] the resulting decline in estrogen levels may slow prostate growth. (See Chapter 8.)

Other studies have shown that stinging nettle extract binds to the protein *sex hormone binding globulin* (*SHBG*). SHBG permanently binds testosterone (and other "sex hormones"), and its levels increase with age, as testosterone levels decline.[23,24] (See Chapter 3.) To the degree that they bind to SHBG, the components of stinging nettle extract "crowd out" testosterone, which may raise the levels of free testosterone circulating in the body. Elevated free testosterone may have a variety of beneficial effects all over the body. Specifically in terms of the prostate, though, this added free testosterone may help restore the estradiol:testosterone ratio, thus removing an important stimulus to prostate growth.

Like saw palmetto, stinging nettle extract is available from health food stores and nutritional supplement suppliers. Combination saw palmetto/stinging nettle extracts are also available. The dose of stinging nettle extract used most often in clinical studies is about 300 mg per day. No serious adverse effects have been associated with reasonable doses.

*Pygeum.* Sometimes known as the African prune, *Pygeum africanum* is a tree that grows on the plateaus of tropical Africa. In the local folk medicine, Pygeum bark was powdered and drunk as a tea to treat genitourinary complaints. Standardized extracts are marketed mostly in Europe (but are also available in the U.S.) under various trade names (*eg*, Tadenan®).

Evidence suggests *Pygeum* by itself may provide symptomatic relief for men with BPH, although it seems to work best when combined with other modalities. In a large double-blind, placebo-controlled study conducted in Germany, France, and Austria, 263 men diagnosed with BPH took either *Pygeum* or

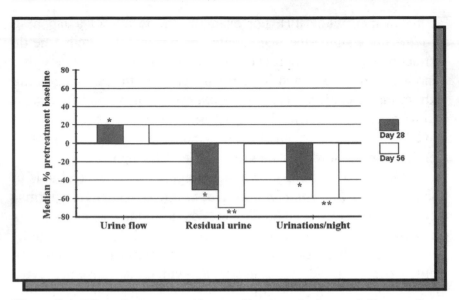

**Figure 9-4**. *Effect of treatment with a combination stinging nettle/Pygeum formulation in men with BPH compared with pretreatment baseline after 28 and 56 days. * p <0.0001vs baseline; ** p < 0.05 vs baseline. (Adapted from Krzeski et al, 1993)*

placebo for 60 days. The results showed statistically significant improvement in such measures as residual urine, urinary flow rates (which were described as near normal), and nighttime frequency.[25]

In a double-blind study conducted in Poland, 134 men (aged 53-84 years) with BPH symptoms agreed to take one of two doses of a stinging nettle/*Pygeum* preparation (either 300 mg or 150 mg of stinging nettle + 25 mg of *Pygeum*) twice daily for eight weeks. The researchers found that both doses were equivalent in significantly improving symptoms, including improved urine flow rate, decreased frequency, and reduced residual urine. Figure 9-4 shows the effects (relative to the pretreatment baseline) of the lower dose combination on three measures of prostate function after 28 and 56 days.[1]

***Cernilton®***. Cernilton is an extract of pollen from a species of rye-grass (*Secale cereale*) that grows in southern Sweden. Its therapeutic effects on the prostate were discovered by accident about 30 years ago, and it has since been approved for treating BPH symptoms in Switzerland, Austria, Germany, Spain, Greece, Japan, Korea, and Argentina.[26]

Several open-label and double-blind, placebo-controlled studies support the efficacy of Cernilton® in prostate conditions, particularly those characterized by inflammation and urinary obstruction.[26, 27] In one well-controlled trial, 60 men with BPH were asked to take either Cernilton® or placebo. After six months, 69% of the Cernilton-treated men reported subjective improvement, compared with only 29% of the placebo group. This difference was statistically significant. The researchers also found significant improvement in residual urine volume and prostate volume, and nonsignificant improvement in the urinary flow rate.[28]

A Polish study in 89 men with BPH treated over a period of four months found Cernilton® to be significantly more effective than *Pygeum* (Tadenan®). The authors reported statistically significant subjective improvement in 78% of the Cernilton group and only 55% of the *Pygeum* group. Cernilton treatment was also associated with significant improvement in objective measures of urinary flow rate, residual urine, and prostate volume.[29]

How Cernilton® works is still uncertain, although some evidence suggests that it might relax urethral muscle and the external urinary sphincter. Other evidence suggests that it might have anti-inflammatory and anti-androgenic effects, since it was able to block testosterone-induced prostate growth in castrated rats. At least part of this action may be due to inhibition of 5α-reductase.[26]

## Dietary and Nutritional Factors in Prostate Health

Chinese and Japanese men have among the lowest incidence of prostate cancer in the world. Yet, when men from these countries migrate to the West, their risk of developing prostate cancer soars. Japanese men living in Hawaii, for example, have 10 times the risk of their counterparts in Japan, and this rate is still about half the rate of Hawaiian white men. Although latent or clinically insignificant cancer of the prostate is found at autopsy at about the same rate in men from Asian countries and the U.S. (about 30% of men over age 50 years), the rate of prostate cancer cases that require treatment is 120 times higher in this country.[30]

These and many other lines of evidence strongly suggest that some important differences in life style and/or environment between Asian and Western societies may be influencing the risk of prostate cancer. Among the key factors is diet. Exactly what role diet plays is still being defined. Here is what scientific studies are suggesting so far.

*Dietary fats.* One of the prime dietary suspects in the etiology and/or progression of prostate cancer is fat. Japanese men living in Japan, who have among the lowest rates of prostate cancer in the world, typically consume far less fat than American men. When they move here, though, their fat intake increases – along with their risk of prostate cancer. Similarly, as Japan has begun to adopt a more Western style diet, with a higher percentage of animal fat, the incidence of prostate cancer in that country has increased.[31]

A large National Cancer Institute Study of more than 50,000 men aged 40 to 75 years came to the conclusion that animal fat, especially fat from red meat, was associated with an elevated risk of advanced prostate cancer. Fats from fish, vegetables, and dairy sources (except butter) were not related to elevated risk of prostate cancer and may actually be protective.[32] This conclusion is supported by other findings, such as a study showing that Alaskan Eskimo men who eat a lot of fish have a low risk of prostate cancer, while those who do not have a higher risk.[33] Laboratory experiments have shown that omega-6 fatty acids stimulate human prostate cancer cells *in vitro*, whereas omega-3 fatty acids inhibit these cells.[34]

Despite the enticing therapeutic possibilities these findings open up, virtually no systematic research has been done to investigate whether eating the "right" fats might actually offer a degree of protection for the prostate. Interestingly, though, one study, published in 1941, was conducted under the aegis of a foundation that supported nutritional research. In the report of their research, the authors, James Pirie Hart and William LeGrande Cooper, M.D., described the effects on BPH of taking supplements of what the authors called "vitamin F," but which is recognized today as *essential fatty acids.*[35]

Hart and Cooper asked 19 men with BPH to participate in their study. First, they established base lines for each man in terms of prostate size and consistency, residual urine, symptoms (e.g., dribbling, hesitancy, frequency, etc). Next, they asked the men to take capsules containing a mixture of essential fatty acids – *linoleic, linolenic,* and *arachidonic acid* – for several weeks.

Hart and Cooper report striking improvement in virtually every man, including: 1) Diminution of residual urine in all cases and elimination of residual urine in 12 of the 19 men; 2) elimination of nighttime trips to the toilet in 13 men; 3) decreased fatigue and leg pains in all men; 3) increased libidos in all men; 4) elimination of dribbling in 18 men; 5) generally increased force of stream; and 6) reduction in prostate size in all men. The few men who showed the least improvement, the authors noted, all had histories of gonorrheal infection in the genitourinary tract.

*Zinc.* Zinc is an essential trace element that is involved in the growth and development of many organ systems. Foods high in zinc content have been used therapeutically for thousands of years to promote general health, wound healing, various sexual and neurologic functions, as well as sperm physiology and maturation. Most recently, zinc has been in the news as a treatment for the common cold.

In the healthy human male, zinc concentrates in the prostate at levels about 10-fold higher than in other soft tissues.[36] Exactly what all that zinc is doing in the prostate is still not completely understood, although a few details are becoming clearer. For example, zinc concentrations in men with prostate cancer have been known for decades to be significantly lower than normal.[37] Less clear is what happens in BPH. Most studies show that prostate zinc levels in BPH are either normal or slightly elevated.[38, 39]

Evidence suggests that zinc may play an important role in modulating testosterone levels in the prostate, possibly by controlling the conversion of testosterone to DHT.[40] In one study in which rats were placed on a zinc-deficient diet, conversion of testosterone to DHT was significantly reduced.[41] In healthy men placed on a zinc-deficient diet, testosterone levels fell along with zinc levels.[42] Other research has found a decrease in the number of prostate androgen receptor sites in zinc deficient rats.[43]

Does increasing zinc intake help keep the prostate healthy? Surprisingly little research has been done to answer this question. In one study, injection of zinc directly into to rats' prostates led to a reduction in prostate weight.[44] A Chinese pilot study, in which men with BPH received a similar treatment, found that symptoms of obstruction and prostate volume decreased, while urinary flow increased.[44] Obviously, intra-prostatic injections are not a reasonable therapeutic alternative, but increasing dietary zinc is.

One small study of zinc supplementation was conducted by Irving M. Bush, M.D., Head of the Division of Urology and the Center for the Study of Prostatic Diseases, Cook County Hospital, Chicago, during the mid-1970s. Dr. Bush and his colleagues asked 19 men with BPH to take zinc supplements for two months. They found a reduction in symptoms in all 19 men. Shrinkage of the prostate, as measured by digital palpation, X-ray, and endoscopy was noted in 14 of the men.[39]

*Soy protein.* Another big difference between Asian and Western diets is soy protein. Asians eat a lot of soy in the form of tofu, soy milk, and many other products; Westerners don't eat much at all. The key protective components of soy seem to be to substances known as *isoflavones – genistein* and *daidzein*. The average daily isoflavone intake in Asian cultures is estimated to be 50 mg, compared with Americans, who typically ingest only a few milligrams each day.[45]

A variety of different mechanisms by which soy might protect against cancer have been proposed.[46, 47] In laboratory studies, both genistein and daidzein have been shown to inhibit the growth of prostatic cancer cells.[48] Genistein also inhibits the growth of blood vessels that supply malignant tumors, a process known as *angiogenesis*, that is critical for tumor growth and metastasis.[49, 50]

*Selenium.* Selenium is an essential trace element. Several very convincing lines of evidence support the notion that excessively low levels of selenium in the body predispose to a variety of cancers, including cancers of the breast, skin, and prostate.

- In "test tube" studies, adding selenium to prostate cancer cells growing in culture rapidly inhibits their proliferation.[51, 52]

- People who live in regions where the soil is deficient in selenium content have a higher incidence of prostate and other cancers. Their cancer risk drops significantly when they start taking selenium supplements.[53]

- When people with skin cancer took selenium supplements, their rate of recurrence of basal cell and squamous cell skin cancers did not change; however, deaths from all other cancers, including melanoma, prostate, lung, and colorectal cancer declined significantly.[53-56]

- Selenium blocked the occurrence of prostate cancer in men exposed to high levels of cadmium, a heavy metal.[57]

- Some evidence suggests that combining selenium with vitamin E results in a protective effect against prostate cancer greater than that provided by either agent alone.[58]

There seems little doubt that selenium supplements – 200 µg daily – should be part of every man's (and woman's) nutritional regimen. Selenium's protective effects against prostate and other cancers is unquestionable. So strong is the link that some researchers have suggested that cancer of the prostate ought to be considered a "nutritional disease."[59]

*Dietary fiber.* Dietary fiber, which, we are constantly reminded, has a broad range of health benefits for a number of systems, such as the heart and blood vessels, and the gastrointestinal tract, also appears to protect the prostate from cancer. Among the most definitive research in this area is that conducted among Seventh-Day Adventists, who generally follow a vegetarian diet. Seventh-Day Adventists who have the highest intakes of high fiber foods like beans, lentils, and peas also have the lowest risk of prostate cancer.[60]

*Lycopene*. A Harvard-based study published a few years ago found that eating at least ten servings a week of tomato-based foods – especially cooked tomato – could reduce a man's risk of developing prostate cancer by as much as 45%.[61] The ingredient in tomatoes that makes them so valuable for prostate health is *lycopene*, a carotenoid (a cousin of beta carotene), which provides the red color in tomatoes, watermelon, and pink grapefruit. Of the 600 to 700 natural carotenoids that have been identified so far, lycopene is the one that is present in human plasma in the highest concentrations. In males, lycopene tends to concentrate in the testes, adrenal glands, and prostate.[62, 63] According to one author in a recent review of lycopene research, *"Remarkable inverse relationships between lycopene intake or serum values and risk have been observed in particular for cancers of the prostate, pancreas, and to a certain extent, of the stomach. In some studies, lycopene was the only carotenoid associated with risk reduction."*[63] (Italics added.) While ten servings of cooked tomato dishes per week may be a bit much for most people, lycopene supplements are readily available.

*Vitamin E*. Vitamin E has achieved a well-deserved reputation as an antioxidant vitamin with a wide range of important health-promoting effects, including protection against atherosclerosis, heart attacks, cancer, Alzheimer's disease, Parkinson's disease, and enhancement of immune function. As mentioned above, vitamin E synergistically enhances the protection against prostate cancer provided by selenium. A recent *in-vitro* study found that vitamin E inhibits the proliferation of prostate cancer cells.[64]

*Vitamin D*. Although vitamin D was widely assumed to be a "vitamin," analyses of its chemical structure have now confirmed that it is, in fact, a *steroid hormone*, known more accurately as *calcitriol* (or in chemist-speak, as 1,25-dihydroxyvitamin $D_3$).[65] Recent evidence that a deficiency in vitamin D may play a role in promoting prostate cancer has generated much attention. Studies of vitamin D indicate that it is important for modulating the growth and differentiation of various tissues.[66] In the absence of testosterone, vitamin D appears to promote the abnormal growth of prostate tissue. In the presence of testosterone, vitamin D appears to promote normal prostate growth and differentiation. Moreover, increasing vitamin D intake is now thought to help prevent the growth of prostate tumors.[67-69]

In one study from the University of Southern California School of Medicine, the results indicated that the genetic predisposition for prostate cancer may be due in part to a defect in the vitamin D receptor in prostate cells.[70] A Czech study linked vitamin D deficiency with prostate cancer and high levels of PSA, which is currently considered an early and important marker of prostate malignancy.[71] Other research has demonstrated that vitamin D, along with its metabolites, and some synthetic analogues, can suppress the growth of prostate cancer cells.[72-74]

# Before you reach for the saw palmetto...

After reading through this chapter, most men (we hope) will be inclined to reach for saw palmetto (possibly along with Urtica dioica, *Pygeum africanum*, and Cernilton®) to relieve symptoms of BPH. Before doing that, though, it's always wisest to make sure that the essential nutrients are included in the diet (and are also supplemented) first. In 26 years of practice, it's been my (JVW) observation that men who try "diet and supplemental essential nutrients first" almost always experience a major improvement or even complete elimination of BPH symptoms without using saw palmetto or other botanicals.

Saw palmetto, Urtica dioica, *Pygeum africanum*, and Cernilton® are all valuable tools with practically no adverse effects, but none of us ever died or became seriously ill from a deficiency of any of them. By definition, though, illness or death is exactly what happens when we become deficient in essential nutrients. If we need more essential fatty acids (EFA) or zinc for our prostates, it's very likely we also need more of these essential nutrients for our eyes, brains, and many other body organs and tissues.

As noted above, there is at least some research showing that both of these nutrients can "shrink" enlarged prostates. In my clinical experience, EFA and zinc are the most important parts of a sup-

# And please don't forget ...

Although eating the suggested foods on one's own is fine, supplementation should only be done in consultation with a medical, osteopathic, naturopathic, or chiropractic physician (M.D., D.O., N.D., D.C.) or certified clinical nutritionist (C.C.N.) skilled and knowledgeable in natural and nutritional medicine.

And again, it is vitally important to get a prostate exam to eliminate the possibility of prostate cancer before beginning any regimen.

plement program designed to reverse BPH and its symptoms. Just these two essential nutrients (taken together as supplements) are all that most men with BPH need. [It's my opinion (no controlled research yet, however) that BPH may actually be a symptom of zinc and/or EFA insufficiency for some men.]

Two of the best and most easily accessible dietary sources of EFA and zinc are unroasted sunflower seeds and pumpkin seeds. Nearly all other unroasted seeds and nuts are also good sources of these two nutrients. Roasting of the seeds or nuts oxidizes and thus, destroys the utility of much of the essential fatty acid content; the zinc is basically unaffected.

While food sources of EFA and zinc (especially if included from childhood onward) may be enough to prevent BPH in the first place, they're usually not sufficient to reverse it. Once BPH and it's symptoms have occurred, I usually recommend zinc (from zinc picolinate or citrate) 30 mg three times daily to start, tapering down slowly as symptoms recede, along with one tablespoon (15 cc) of organically grown, carefully processed "high-lignan" flax oil, twice daily. [Each 30 mg of zinc should be "offset" with 2 mg of copper, and each tablespoon of flax oil accompanied by 400 IU vitamin E.]

.

What about selenium, and vitamins E and D? Although these are essential nutrients and should always be included in a diet and supplement program for the best of health (especially selenium for cancer prevention), there is as yet no evidence whether they're especially involved (as are EFA and zinc) in prostate "shrinkage" or enlargement.

Good dietary (food) sources of selenium include garlic, onions, tuna, wheat germ, broccoli, and cabbage, as well as most nuts and seeds. Although wheat germ oil, soy oil, peanut oil, and nearly all other nutritional oils are far and away the best dietary sources of vitamin E, unroasted nuts and seeds, sweet potato, green peas, brown rice, navy beans (steamed), eggs, and oatmeal are also "high" in vitamin E, at least when compared with other foods. There's practically no food source of vitamin D except cod liver oil and liver. ("Fortified" cow's milk products also contain vitamin D, but for many reasons, these are not recommended for good health.)

I usually also recommend daily amounts of at least 200 $\mu$g of selenium (up to 400 $\mu$g if there's a family history of cancer), at least 400 IU of vitamin E (as "mixed tocopherols"), and at least 400 IU of vitamin D.

Like the above-noted essential nutrients, soy protein with its genistein and daidzein, as well as lycopene (especially high in tomato sauce and other processed tomato products) are all important for the best of health, and can easily be included in the diet along with the many food sources of dietary fiber.

# Testosterone and Hair Loss?

There is a theoretical possibility that testosterone replacement may cause some men to begin losing hair. To minimize this possibility, it may be helpful to take saw palmetto (160 mg twice daily) along with natural testosterone.

# References

1. Krzeski T, Kazón M, Borkowski A, Witeska A, Kuczera J. Combined extracts of *Urtica dioica* and *Pygeum africanum* in the treatment of benign prostatic hyperplasia: double- blind comparison of two doses. *Clin Therap.* 1993;15:1011-1020.

2. Bombardelli E, Morazzoni P. *Serenoa repens* (Batram) J.K. Small. *Fitoterapia.* 1997;58:99-113.

3. Sultan C, Terraza A, Devillier C, et al. Inhibition of androgen metabolism and binding by a liposterolic extract of "Serenoa repens B* in human foreskin fibroblasts. *J Steroid Biochem.* 1984;20:515-519.

4. Rhodes L, Primka RL, Berman C, et al. Comparison of finasteride (Proscar), a 5 alpha reductase inhibitor, and various commercial plant extracts in in vitro and in vivo 5 alpha reductase inhibition. *Prostate.* 1993;22:43-51.

5. Carilla E, Briley M, Fauran F, Sultan C, Duvilliers C. Binding of Permixon, a new treatment for prostatic benign hyperplasia, to the cytosolic androgen receptor in the rat prostate. *J Steroid Biochem.* 1984;20:521-523.

6. Bolton NJ, Lukkarinen O, Vihko R. Concentrations of androgens in human benign prostatic hypertrophic tissues incubated for up to three days. *Prostate.* 1986;9:159-167.

7. Paubert-Braquet M, Mencia Huerta JM, Cousse H, Braquet P. Effect of the lipidic lipidosterolic extract of Serenoa repens (Permixon) on the ionophore A23187-stimulated production of leukotriene B4 (LTB4) from human polymorphonuclear neutrophils. *Prostaglandins Leukot Essent Fatty Acids.* 1997;57:299-304.

8. Tarayre J, Delhon A, Lauressergues H, Stenger A. Action anti-oedemateuse d'un extrait hexanique de drupes de *Serenoa repens*Bartr. *Ann Pharmaceutiques françaises.* 1983;41:559-570.

9. Carraro JC, Raynaud JP, Koch G, et al. Comparison of phytotherapy (Permixon) with finasteride in the treatment of benign prostate hyperplasia: a randomized international study of 1,098 patients. *Prostate.* 1996;29:231-40; discussion 241-242.

10. Di Silverio F, D'Eramo G, Lubrano C, et al. Evidence that *Serenoa repens*extract displays an antiestrogenic activity in prostate tissue of benign prostatic hypertrophy patients. *Eur Urol.* 1992;21:309-314.

11. de Lignieres B. Transdermal dihydrotestosterone treatment of "andropause." *Ann Med.* 1993;25:235-241.

12. Marshall I, Burt RP, Chapple CR. Noradrenaline contractions of human prostate mediated by alpha 1A-(alpha 1c-) adrenoceptor subtype. *Br J Pharmacol.* 1995;115:781-786.

13. Agency for Health Care Policy and Research. *Benign Prostatic Hyperplasia: Diagnosis and Treatment (Clinical Practice Guideline)*. Rockville, MD: U.S. Department of Health and Human Services; 1994.

14. Braeckman J. The extract of *Serenoa repens* in the treatment of benign prostatic hyperplasia: A multicenter open study. *Curr Ther Res*. 1994;55:776-784.

15. Stoner E. The clinical effects of a 5 alpha-reductase inhibitor, finasteride, on benign prostatic hyperplasia. The Finasteride Study Group. *J Urol*. 1992;147:1298-302.

16. Strauch G, Perles P, Vergult G, et al. Comparison of finasteride (Proscar) and Serenoa repens (Permixon) in the inhibition of 5-alpha reductase in healthy male volunteers. *Eur Urol*. 1994;26:247-252.

17. Lichius J, Muth C. The inhibiting effects of *Urtica dioica* root extracts on experimentally induced prostatic hyperplasia in the mouse. *Planta Medica*. 1997;63:307-310.

18. Belaiche P, Lievoux O. Clinical studies on the palliative treatment of prostatic adenoma with extract of *Urtica* root. *Phytother Res*. 1991;5:267-269.

19. Hirano T, Homma M, Oka K. Effects of stinging nettle root extracts and their steroidal components on the Na+,K(+)-ATPase of the benign prostatic hyperplasia. *Planta Med*. 1994;60:30-33.

20. Ganser D, Spiteller G. Aromatase inhibitors from *Urtica dioica* roots. *Planta Medica*. 1995;61:138-140.

21. Nakhla AM, Khan MS, Romas NP, Rosner W. Estradiol causes the rapid accumulation of cAMP in human prostate. *Proc Natl Acad Sci U S A*. 1994;91:5402-5405.

22. Henderson D, Habenicht UF, Nishino Y, el Etrohy MF. Estrogens and benign prostatic hyperplasia: the basis for aromatase inhibitor therapy *Steroids*. 1987;50:219-233.

23. Hryb D, Khan M, Romas N, Rosner W. The effect of extracts of the roots of the stinging nettle (*Urtica dioica*) on the interaction of SHBG with its receptor on human prostate membranes. *Planta Medica*. 1994;61:31-32.

24. Schöttner M, Ganser D, Spiteller G. Lignans from roots of *Urtica dioica* and their metabolites bind to human sex hormon binding globulin (SHBG). *Planta Medica*. 1997;63:529-532.

25. Barlet A, Albrecht J, Aubert A, et al. Efficacy of *Pygeum africanum* in the treatment of micturitional disorders due to benign prostatic hyperplasia. Evaluation of objective and subjective parameters. *Weiner Klinische Wochenschrift*. 1990;22.

26. Buck A. Phytotherapy for the prostate. *Br J Urol*. 1996;78:325-336.

27. Rugendorff E, Weidner W, Ebeling L, Buck A. Results of treatment with pollen extract (Cernilton® N) in chronic prostatitis and prostatodynia. *Br J Urol*. 1993;71:433-438.

28. Buck AC, Cox R, Rees RW, Ebeling L, John A. Treatment of outflow tract obstruction due to benign prostatic hyperplasia with the pollen extract, cernilton. A double-blind, placebo-controlled study. *Br J Urol*. 1990;66:398-404.

29. Dutkiewicz S. Usefulness of Cernilton in the treatment of benign prostatic hypertrophy. *Int J Urol Nephrol*. 1996;28:49-53.

30. Severson R, Nomura A, Grove J, Stemmerman G. A prospective study of demographics, diet, and prostate cancer among men of Japanese ancestry in Hawaii. *Cancer Res*. 1989;49:1857-1860.

31. Pienta K, Goodson J, Esper P. Epidemiology of prostate cancer: molecular and environmental clues. *Urology*. 1996;48:676-683.

32. Giovannucci E, Rimm E, Colditz G, et al. A prospective study of dietary fat and risk of prostate cancer. *J Natl Cancer Inst*. 1993;85:1571-1579.

33. Lanier AP, Bulkow LR, Ireland B. Cancer in Alaskan Indians, Eskimos, and Aleuts, 1969-83: implications for etiology and control. *Public Health Rep*. 1989;104:658-664.

34. Rose D, Connolly J. Dietary fat, fatty acids and prostate cancer. *Lipids*. 1992;27:798-803.

35. Hart J, Cooper W. *Vitamin F in the treatment of prostatic hypertrophy*. Milwaukee, WI: Lee Foundation for Nutritional Research; 1941.

36. Schrodt G, Hall T, Whitmore W, Jr. The concentration of zinc in diseased human prostate glands. *Cancer*. 1964;17:1555-1566.

37. Györkey F, Min K-W, Huff J, Györkey P. Zinc and magnesium in human prostate gland: normal, hyperplastic, and neoplastic. *Cancer Res*. 1967;27:1348-1353.

38. Habib F. Zinc and the steroid endocrinology of the human prostate. *J Steroid Biochem*. 1978;9:403-407.

39. Bush I, Berman E, Nourkayhan S, et al. Zinc and the prostate. Paper presented at the Annual Meeting of the American Medical Association; 1974.

40. Leake A, Chisholm G, Habib F. The effect of zinc on the 5-reduction of testosterone by the hyperplastic human prostate gland. *J Steroid Biochem*. 1984;20:651-655.

41. Om A-S, Chung K-W. Dietary deficiency alters 5-reduction and aromatization of testosterone and androgen and estrogen receptors in rat liver. *J Nutr*. 1996;126:842-848.

42. Prasad A, Mantzoros C, Beck F, Hess J, Brewer G. Zinc status and serum testosterone levels of healthy adults. *Nutrition*. 1996;12:344-348.

43. Chung K-W, Kim S, Chan W-Y, Rennert O. Androgen receptors in ventral prostate glands of zinc deficient rats. *Life Sci*. 1986;38:351-356.

44. Fahim M, Wang M, Setcu M, Fahim Z. Zinc arginine, a 5α-reductase inhibitor, reduces rat ventral prostate weight and DNA without affecting testicular function. *Andrologia.* 1993;25:369-375.

45. Messina MJ, Persky V, Setchell KD, Barnes S. Soy intake and cancer risk: a review of the in vitro and in vivo data. *Nutr Cancer.* 1994;21:113-131.

46. Kennedy A. The evidence for soybean products as cancer preventive agents. *J Nutr.* 1995;125:733S-743S.

47. Adlercreutz H, Mazur W. Phyto-oestrogens and Western diseases. *Ann Med.* 1997;29:95- 120.

48. Peterson G, Barnes S. Genistein and biochanin A inhibit the growth of human prostate cancer cells but not epidermal growth factor receptor tyrosine autophosphorylation. *Prostate.* 1993;22:335-345

49. Fotsis T, Pepper M, Adlercreutz H, et al. Genistein, a dietary-derived inhibitor of in vitro angiogenesis. *Proc Natl Acad Sci U S A.* 1993;90:2690-2694.

50. Schweigerer L, Christeleit K, Fleischmann G, et al. Identification in human urine of a natural growth inhibitor for cells derived from solid paediatric tumours. *Eur J Clin Invest.* 1992;22:260-264.

51. Redman C, Scott JA, Baines AT, et al. Inhibitory effect of selenomethionine on the growth of three selected human tumor cell lines. *Cancer Lett.* 1998;125:103-110.

52. Webber MM, Perez-Ripoll EA, James GT. Inhibitory effects of selenium on the growth of DU-145 human prostate carcinoma cells in vitro. *Biochem Biophys Res Commun.* 1985;130:603-609.

53. Fleet JC. Dietary selenium repletion may reduce cancer incidence in people at high risk who live in areas with low soil selenium. *Nutr Rev.* 1997;55:277-279.

54. Clark LC, Combs GF, Jr., Turnbull BW, et al. Effects of selenium supplementation for cancer prevention in patients with carcinoma of the skin. A randomized controlled trial. Nutritional Prevention of Cancer Study Group. *JAMA.* 1996;276:1957-1963

55. Combs GF, Jr., Clark LC, Turnbull BW. Reduction of cancer risk with an oral supplement of selenium. *Biomed Environ Sci.* 1997;10:227-234.

56. Combs GF, Jr., Clark LC, Turnbull BW. Reduction of cancer mortality and incidence by selenium supplementation. *Med Klin.* 1997;92 Suppl 3:42-45.

57. Webber MM. Selenium prevents the growth stimulatory effects of cadmium on human prostatic epithelium. *Biochem Biophys Res Commun.* 1985;127:871-877.

58. Horvath PM, Ip C. Synergistic effect of vitamin E and selenium in the chemoprevention of mammary carcinogenesis in rats. *Cancer Res.* 1983;43:5335-341.

59. Fair WR, Fleshner NE, Heston W. Cancer of the prostate: a nutritional disease? *Urology.* 1997;50:840-848.

60. Mills PK, Beeson WL, Phillips RL, Fraser GE. Cohort study of diet, lifestyle, and prostate cancer in Adventist men. *Cancer.* 1989;64:598-604.

61. Giovannucci E, Ascherio A, Rimm EB, Stampfer MJ, Colditz GA, Willett WC. Intake of carotenoids and retinol in relation to risk of prostate cancer. *J Natl Cancer Inst.* 1995;87:1767-1776.

62. Clinton SK, Emenhiser C, Schwartz SJ, et al. cis-trans lycopene isomers, carotenoids, and retinol in the human prostate. *Cancer Epidemiol Biomarkers Prev.* 1996;5:823-833.

63. Gerster H. The potential role of lycopene for human health. *J Am Coll Nutr.* 1997;16:109- 126.

64. Sigounas G, Anagnostou A, Steiner M. dl-alpha-tocopherol induces apoptosis in erythroleukemia, prostate, and breast cancer cells. *Nutr Cancer.* 1997;28:30-35.

65. Bouillon R, Okamura WH, Norman AW. Structure-function relationships in the vitamin D endocrine system. *Endocr Rev.* 1995;16:200-257.

66. Reichel H, Koeffler HP, Norman AW. The role of the vitamin D endocrine system in health and disease. *N Engl J Med.* 1989;320:980-991.

67. Getzenberg RH, Light BW, Lapco PE, et al. Vitamin D inhibition of prostate adenocarcinoma growth and metastasis in the Dunning rat prostate model system. *Urology.* 1997;50:999-1006.

68. Konety BR, Getzenberg RH. Novel therapies for advanced prostate cancer. *Semin Urol Oncol.* 1997;15:33-42.

69. Konety BR, Schwartz GG, Acierno JS, Jr., Becich MJ, Getzenberg RH. The role of vitamin D in normal prostate growth and differentiation. *Cell Growth Differ.* 1996;7:1563-1570.

70. Ingles SA, Ross RK, Yu MC, et al. Association of prostate cancer risk with genetic polymorphisms in vitamin D receptor and androgen receptor [see comments]. *J Natl Cancer Inst.* 1997;89:166-170.

71. Wilczek H. Importance of vitamin D in prostatic carcinoma. *Cas Lek Cesk.* 1996;135:716-718.

72. Skowronski R, Peehl D, Feldman D. Actions of vitamin $D_3$ analogs on human prostate cancer cell lines: comparison with 1,25-dihydroxyvitamin $D_3$. *Endocrinology.* 1995;136:20-26.

73. Esquenet M, Swinnen JV, Heyns W, Verhoeven G. Control of LNCaP proliferation and differentiation: actions and interactions of androgens, 1alpha,25-dihydroxycholecalciferol, all-trans retinoic acid, 9-cis retinoic acid, and phenylacetate. *Prostate.* 1996;28:182-194.

74. de Vos S, Holden S, Heber D, et al. Effects of potent vitamin D3 analogs on clonal proliferation of human prostate cancer cell lines. *Prostate.* 1997;31:77-83.

# Chapter 10

# Keeping Bones and Muscles Strong

*"Protein is the core substance of our bodies. And since testosterone is responsible for the building of protein from the point of conception to our very last breath, its anabolic function is an absolute precondition for the maintenance of life."*

— *Jens Møller, M.D., 1987*

For many men, the prospect of becoming "old and feeble," unable to work and stay active, is just as depressing as the loss of sexual capability. Although not conclusive, research suggests that testosterone replacement, when needed, may keep muscles and bones strong, helping to prevent loss of physical function.

In addition to its masculinizing properties (e.g., facial hair, deep voice, enlarged penis, etc.), testosterone has long been recognized for its essential *anabolic* role in building strong bones and muscles. A flood of testosterone (along with good diet, exercise and conditioning) is the primary reason why a boy can enter puberty as a frail, skinny, 98-pound weakling and leave a few years later as a linebacker. The fact that men have lots of testosterone while women have much less is why men are also generally much bigger and stronger than women.

But what testosterone giveth, the decline in testosterone can taketh away. As men age, the gradual downslide in testosterone levels slows the rate at which their bodies can rebuild and restore muscles and bones. The loss of bone density and strength with age, known as *osteoporosis*, is a "stealth" disease. It may take decades of gradual mineral loss before bones become thin and brittle enough that someone finally takes notice.

Osteoporotic changes do not become visible on ordinary X-rays until 30% of bone mineral is lost. More sensitive techniques, such as *DEXA* (dual energy x-ray absorptiometry) will pick up changes in density far earlier.

When a man reaches his 50s, his bone and muscle loss begin to accelerate, and so does his testosterone loss.[1] Weakened and increasingly unsteady, many elderly men first wake up to the fact that their bones are not what they used to be when they fall and break a hip after decades of slow, hidden, but steady bone loss.

Low testosterone is, without doubt, one of the major causes of osteoporosis in elderly men. In fact, the results of one study suggested that a low testosterone level may be a one-way ticket to a nursing home. The researchers were led by the late Daniel Rudman, M.D., of the Medical College of Wisconsin, who, just a few years earlier, had been the first to demonstrate the muscle and bone building properties of human growth hormone injections in elderly men.[2] In their later study, Rudman's team compared three measures – *bone mineral density* (*BMD*) (an important indicator of bone health), *muscle mass*, and *testosterone levels* – in 49 elderly men living on their own in the community with a similar group living in Veterans' Administration nursing homes. They found the BMD levels to be 4 to 20% higher in the free living men than in the institutionalized men. The best way to predict a free living man's BMD – short of DEXA – was to measure his testosterone level; 59% of the men with hip fractures had low testosterone, compared with only 18% of the controls. Among the institutionalized men, testosterone was less important; age, body weight, and immobility were better predictors of BMD.[3]

# What is Osteoporosis?

In osteoporosis, the bones lose calcium (as well as other minerals) and become thinner, weaker, and increasingly prone to fracture, even after mild impact, or even with no apparent impact. Both "fall-and-fracture" and "first fracture, then fall" are thought to be common ways for men and women with osteoporosis to break their hips.

The most vulnerable bones include those in the hip (femoral neck), wrist, shoulder, ribs, and spine, all of which contain relatively large amounts of sponge-like (cancellous or trabecular) bone. The longer bones of the arms and legs are much denser and stronger and consequently, are less likely to suffer the effects of osteoporosis.

Many years of osteoporosis are responsible for the "dowager's hump" in some elderly women (and men), a result of the fracture and subsequent compression of vertebrae. A broken hip due to a severely weakened femoral neck all too often marks the beginning of the end for many people with osteoporosis.

Osteoporosis occurs because bone, hard as it is, is a dynamic tissue that is constantly being "remodeled" throughout life. The remodeling process has two main phases. First, cells called *osteoclasts* travel throughout bone tissue. When they come upon older bone, they may dissolve or resorb it, leaving tiny, unfilled spaces, or pores, in its place.

Following in the wake of the osteoclasts are cells called *osteoblasts*, which enter these pores and begin construction of new bone tissue. Throughout youth and into middle age, bone remodeling reflects a healthy balance between these two processes. Osteoporosis means basically that the osteoclasts are outrunning the osteoblasts, resulting in a relative loss of bone tissue.

In another study, 68% of the men with hip fractures had sub-normal testosterone. Looking back over five years of patient records, Jeffrey A. Jackson, M.D., and Michael Kleerekoper, M.D., discovered that 30% of those men (most in their 60s) diagnosed with osteoporosis of the spine had long-standing testosterone deficiencies. In most of these men, symptoms of "hypogonadism" could be traced back 20 or 30 years.[4] Other studies have shown that osteoporotic fractures often occur in men who have no other signs of testosterone deficiency.[5]

Can replacing the missing testosterone resurrect lost bone and muscle in men like these? According to my own (JVW) clinical experience and that of many colleagues, which is supported by the results of hundreds of scientific studies, the answer is, "Yes, it can."

## Osteoporosis in Men?

Osteoporosis is a well-known postmenopausal disease in women. Who hasn't had a grandmother chronically hunched over due to the weakening and compression of her vertebrae, or an elderly aunt who fell and broke her hip and died soon thereafter? But in men?

People are often surprised to learn that osteoporosis is not just one of those "female" diseases but is very common in men, too. In fact, about one hip fracture in three occurs in a man, and when men do break a hip, they have a much greater risk of ending up permanently disabled or dead, compared with women. The death rate in men over age 75 with hip fractures was 21%, compared with just 8% in women.[6-8] Another study found that coexisting hip and spinal fractures increased a man's chances of dying by 17 to 20%.[5]

An important difference between men and women who get osteoporosis is that women begin experiencing fractures long before men do. As shown in Figure 10-1, however, by the time men reach their late 70s or early 80s, they catch up.[9-11] This delay is due in large part to the fact that  men generally start out with bones that are thicker and denser than women's. Therefore, they need to lose more bone before symptoms begin to appear.

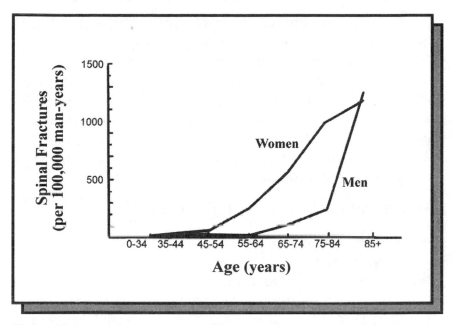

**Figure 10-1.** *Osteoporosis begins earlier in women than in men. This graph compares the frequency of vertebral (spinal) fractures according to age for men and women. (Adapted from Cooper et al, 1992)*

Of course, the male and female versions of osteoporosis also differ hormonally. In women, osteoporosis is a direct result of the loss of the estrogens and progesterone at menopause; in men, it is the gradual loss of testosterone.

Hormonal deficiencies are not the only cause of broken bones in elderly men and women. Also important are poor nutrition (especially too little vitamin D and calcium), immobilization, high blood levels of the amino acid homocysteine (easily treated with folic acid, vitamins B6 and B12, and betaine), cigarette smoking, and alcohol abuse, as well as the use of certain pharmaceutical drugs. These drugs include corticosteroids (e.g., prednisone), the blood thinner heparin (commonly given to people with certain cardiovascular diseases to reduce the risk of clot formation), and anticonvulsants.[4, 12] And we should not ignore the overuse of sedatives and hypnotics (sleeping pills). While they may not directly affect bone strength, these drugs seriously increase the risk of falling.

One often overlooked cause of osteoporosis is a common treatment for advanced prostate cancer, *castration*, either by certain drugs that drastically cut testosterone production or by the surgeon's blade. Removing the source of most endogenous testosterone may retard the growth of prostate cancer somewhat, but the cost, in terms of bone and muscle waste, not to mention increased cardiovascular risk, is very steep. In one study of 235 men who were castrated due to prostate cancer, severe osteoporosis developed in 14%, compared with 1% of healthy controls.[13]

## Testosterone, the *Anabolic* Steroid

"Protein is the substance on which all the biochemical and physiological activity of life is based. And testosterone is the hormone whose major role is to build up this core substance," wrote Dr. Jens Møller, the great Danish physician and testosterone researcher (see Chapter 7). Dr. Møller theorized that, from "birth until the prime of life," testosterone's *anabolic* – protein building – effects are balanced by the *catabolic* effects of another steroid hormone, *cortisol*. From the prime of life on, though, catabolism begins to dominate. "From this age onwards," wrote Dr. Møller, "we act as 'cannibals,' consuming our own bodies as the effect of cortisol gradually takes over. This process leads eventually to the extinction of life – if no accident or disease intervenes beforehand."[14]

Recent research, much of it conducted in the United States, supports the idea that supplemental testosterone may be capable of shifting the body's hormonal balance back in an anabolic direction, thus helping to build stronger bone and muscle tissue, among other benefits.[5, 15-20] In one important study, a group of researchers from the Harvard Medical School and the Massachusetts General Hospital, headed by Laurence Katznelson, M.D., examined the effects of "testosterone" (testosterone enanthate) injections on BMD (bone mineral density) and other measures in 29 hypogonadal men (mean age, 58 years).[19] A group of age-matched healthy (eugonadal) men receiving no "testosterone" served as controls.

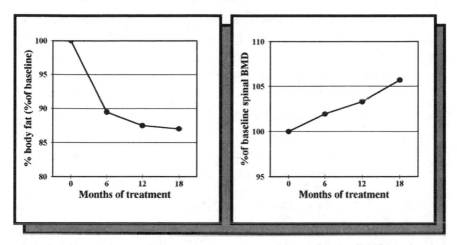

**Figure 10-2**. *Reduction in body fat and increased bone density (BMD) in hypogonadal men receiving treatment with "testosterone" (testosterone enanthate). Adapted from Katznelson et al, 1995*

The results (Fig. 10-2) indicated that "testosterone" treatment for up to 18 months was associated with a 14% decrease in body fat, a 7% increase in lean mass, and a 5% increase in BMD. Dr. Katznelson and his co-authors concluded, "The beneficial effects of androgen administration on body composition and bone density may provide added indications for testosterone therapy in hypogonadal men."

In a California-based multicenter study, 67 hypogonadal men (aged 19-60 years) were asked to take sublingual "testosterone" pills (testosterone cyclodextrin) for up to six months. The investigators, led by Christina Wang, M.D., of the Harbor-UCLA Medical Center, observed significant increases in lean body mass, leg muscle strength, and signs of increasing bone formation. Weight gain was accompanied by very small increments in arm, thigh, chest, and waist circumference. Skin thickness also increased slightly.[18]

High doses of "testosterone" (testosterone enanthate) injections, combined with strength training, have even been shown to increase fat-free mass and muscle size and strength in normal young men.[21] This study confirmed what thousands of athletes taking "anabolic steroid drugs" have known for decades. As we have

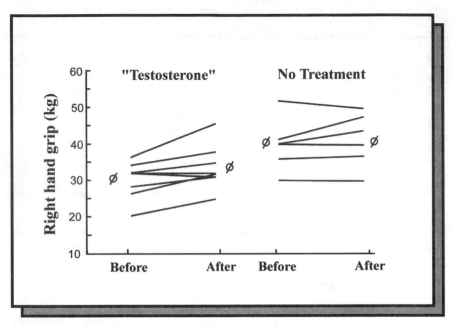

**Figure 10-3**. *Significant increase in right hand strength in elderly testosterone-deficient men receiving "testosterone" replacement for three months. Each line represents a different man. Ø = mean grip strength for each group. (Adapted from Morley et al. 1993)*

discussed in previous chapters, these drugs were developed as a means of mimicking the anabolic properties of natural testosterone while avoiding the masculinizing properties. Overall, though, they have been a disaster because of a high risk of serious toxic effects and should be avoided at all costs.

What about testosterone replacement in aging men? Surprisingly little has been done to answer this obvious question, although most evidence suggests it should work at least as well as natural estrogen and progesterone replacement in postmenopausal women. In one small study from the St. Louis University Medical School, eight men (mean age, 78 years) with testosterone deficiencies received "testosterone" (testosterone enanthate) injections every two weeks for three months.[15] Among the changes reported by John E. Morley, M.D., and his colleagues were increased right hand strength (Fig. 10-3), decreased cholesterol (no change in the

# Strength of a Stallion?

*W*ithania somnifera* is an important herb from the Ayurvedic medical system used in India for the treatment of debility, emaciation, impotence, and premature aging. Not surprisingly, it has been dubbed the "Indian Ginseng." Its Indian name, Ashwagandha, refers to the smell and strength of a stallion and alludes to its reputed aphrodisiac properties.

The effect of Withania on parameters of aging was studied in 101 healthy men, aged 50 to 59 years, under double-blind conditions. The men each took 3 grams of Withania root or 3 grams of starch (placebo) per day for a year. Withania caused a significant increase in hemoglobin and red blood cell count, and also significantly increased seated stature and hair melanin content (less greying) It significantly countered the decrease in nail calcium, and decreased serum cholesterol. Erythrocyte sedimentation rate, a reflection of non-specific inflammation, was also decreased. About 71% of the men receiving Withania reported improvement in sexual performance.[23]

"good" HDL-cholesterol), and elevated osteocalcin, an indicator of increased bone growth.

In another small, but well-controlled study, Dr. Joyce S. Tenover, of the University of Washington, asked 13 healthy men (aged 57-76 years) with low to borderline-low testosterone levels to take "testosterone" (testosterone enanthate) or placebo injections weekly.[22] After three months, she found, the "testosterone"-treated men had significantly more lean body mass (about 3-4 pounds), primarily from muscle, as well as indications of new bone formation, compared with their own pretreatment baseline and with placebo.

# Please Don't Move Too Fast...

One of the best-documented effects of testosterone replacement is a rapid improvement in mood, energy, and feelings of general well-being (See Chapter 11.) This is wonderful when it occurs, but men who have weakened bones and muscles due to years of testosterone deficiency need to take care that they do not push themselves too far too fast. This is because the anabolic improvements in bone and muscle take much longer to become manifest, perhaps several months or years, depending on how much has been lost. Thus, while men on testosterone replacement may soon *feel* like running up and down the stairs, they should try to contain their enthusiasm and avoid stressful activities until their bones and muscles have caught up.

Although this point has been made before, it's worth repeating here, too: Testosterone replacement alone is not likely to keep a man as strong and active as an overall "healthy aging" plan, including excellent diet, vitamin, mineral, and herbal supplementation, appropriate exercise, and testosterone replacement as needed.

# References

1.  Wishart JM, Need AG, Horowitz M, Morris HA, Nordin BE. Effect of age on bone density and bone turnover in men. *Clin Endocrinol (Oxf)*. 1995;42:141-146.

2.  Rudman D, Feller AG, Nagraj HS, et al. Effects of human growth hormone in men over 60 years old. *N Engl J Med*. 1990;323:1-6.

3.  Rudman D, Drinka PJ, Wilson CR, et al. Relations of endogenous anabolic hormones and physical activity to bone mineral density and lean body mass in elderly men. *Clin Endocrinol (Oxf)*. 1994;40:653-661.

4.  Jackson JA, Kleerekoper M. Osteoporosis in men: diagnosis, pathophysiology, and prevention. *Medicine (Baltimore)*. 1990;69:137-152.

5.  Anderson FH, Francis RM, Peaston RT, Wastell HJ. Androgen supplementation in eugonadal men with osteoporosis: effects of six months' treatment on markers of bone formation and resorption. *J Bone Miner Res*. 1997;12:472-478.

6.  Poor G, Atkinson EJ, O'Fallon WM, Melton LJ, 3rd. Predictors of hip fractures in elderly men. *J Bone Miner Res*. 1995;10:1900-1907.

7.  Poor G, Atkinson EJ, O'Fallon WM, Melton LJ, 3rd. Determinants of reduced survival following hip fractures in men. *Clin Orthop*. 1995:260-265.

8. Poor G, Atkinson EJ, Lewallen DG, O'Fallon WM, Melton LJ, 3rd. Age-related hip fractures in men: clinical spectrum and short-term outcomes. *Osteoporos Int.* 1995;5:419- 426.

9. Cooper C, Atkinson EJ, O'Fallon WM, Melton LJ. Incidence of clinically diagnosed vertebral fractures: a population- based study in Rochester, Minnesota, 1985-1989. *J Bone Miner Res.* 1992;7:221-227.

10. Seeman E. The dilemma of osteoporosis in men. *Am J Med.* 1995;98:76S-88S.

11. Seeman E. Osteoporosis in men. *Baillieres Clin Rheumatol.* 1997;11:613-629.

12. Ybarra J, Ade R, Romeo JH. Osteoporosis in men: a review. *Nurs Clin North Am.* 1996;31:805-813.

13. Daniell HW. Osteoporosis after orchiectomy for prostate cancer. *J Urol.* 1997;157:439- 444.

14. Møller J. *Cholesterol. Interactions with Testosterone and Cortisol in Cardiovascular Diseases.* Berlin: Springer-Verlag; 1987.

15. Morley JE, Perry HMD, Kaiser FE, et al. Effects of testosterone replacement therapy in old hypogonadal males: a preliminary study. *J Am Geriatr Soc.* 1993;41:149-152.

16. Griggs RC, Kingston W, Jozefowicz RF, Herr BE, Forbes G, Halliday D. Effect of testosterone on muscle mass and muscle protein synthesis. *J Appl Physiol.* 1989;66:498- 503.

17. Seidell JC, Bjorntorp P, Sjostrom L, Kvist H, Sannerstedt R. Visceral fat accumulation in men is positively associated with insulin, glucose, and C-peptide levels, but negatively with testosterone levels. *Metabolism.* 1990;39:897-901.

18. Wang C, Eyre DR, Clark R, et al. Sublingual testosterone replacement improves muscle mass and strength, decreases bone resorption, and increases bone formation markers in hypogonadal men—a clinical research center study. *J Clin Endocrinol Metab.* 1996;81:3654-3662.

19. Katznelson L, Finkelstein JS, Schoenfeld DA, Rosenthal DI, Anderson EJ, Klibanski A. Increase in bone density and lean body mass during testosterone administration in men with acquired hypogonadism. *J Clin Endocrinol Metab.* 1996;81:4358-4365.

20. Anderson FH, Francis RM, Faulkner K. Androgen supplementation in eugonadal men with osteoporosis-effects of 6 months of treatment on bone mineral density and cardiovascular risk factors. *Bone.* 1996;18:171-177.

21. Bhasin S, Storer TW, Berman N, et al. The effects of supraphysiologic doses of testosterone on muscle size and strength in normal men [see comments]. *N Engl J Med.* 1996;335:1-7.

22. Tenover JS. Effects of testosterone supplementation in the aging male. *J Clin Endocrinol Metab.* 1992;75:1092-1098.

23. Kuppurajan K, Rajagopalan SS, Sitaraman R, et al. Effect of Aswagandha (*Withania somnifera Dunal*) on the Process of Ageing in Human Volunteers. *J Res Ayurveda Siddha*. 1980;1:247-258.

# Chapter 11

# Improving Mood, Attitude, and Feeling of Well-Being

*Men who were stooped, slow-moving, slow-thinking, and consider-*
*ing retirement like old men came back for a check-up at two months*
*looking quite different. They walk well, hold themselves erect, and*
*talk and act like very young 50-year-olds instead of very old*
*60-year-olds. There is even a change in the voice, manner and*
*handshake.*

*Tiberius Reiter, M.D., 1963*

O ne of the most consistent findings in the scientific literature
on testosterone is the claim that it enhances feelings of
well-being. Such observations go back to antiquity a half a
world away. Chinese medicine more than 1,000 years ago
employed hormone-rich urine (collected from young men or
women) as a treatment for a variety of genitourinary ailments,
including prostatic hyperplasia and impotence in men, and menstrual irregularities and breast cancer in women. In addition to these
physical ailments, though, Chinese physicians also prescribed this
early form of "hormone replacement therapy" for treating disturbances of the psyche, including what has been described as the
"neuroses and psychoses of aging."[1]

Once scientists had isolated hormonal testosterone in the 1920s and '30s and began giving it to "hypogonadal" men, it quickly became evident that the ancient Chinese were onto something with their urine collection.* Testosterone-deficient men receiving androgen replacement really seemed to feel better, and it probably wasn't just because their sex lives had returned.

Wary of the Brown-Séquard effect (See Chapter 2), however, many physicians were loathe to exploit testosterone's apparent ability to help older men feel young again. One testosterone expert during the 1940s, Yale University Professor J.B. Hamilton, recognized that testosterone-related feelings of well-being were quite real, but he was suspicious that such feelings were necessarily such a good thing. He warned against "the deplorable and perhaps wishful thought that restoration of testis function produces rejuvenation." As Paul De Kruif tells the story:

> Professor Hamilton admitted that testosterone had that curious power to make old men, some old men, feel like singing "Oh, what a beautiful morning." It is the condition that is medically known as euphoria.... Professor Hamilton warned: "Euphoria is not uncommon (from testosterone) and should be guarded against by the strict insurance that the patient does not over-exert.... Stimulation of an older man with testosterone may cause him to feel younger and attempt to lead the life of a younger man."[2]

And we wouldn't want that, would we? It was the widespread belief among the physicians of the day – a belief that probably survives to a significant degree today – that old men should feel like old men and act like old men. Anything that makes them feel oth-

---

* Urine remains to this day a common means of collecting steroid hormones as well as of estimating an individual's hormone levels. The "estrogenic" drug Premarin®, for example, is extracted from the urine of pregnant mares. Hormone replacement using estrogens and progesterone extracted from the urine of ovulating *human* females, of course, would make just as much sense and a whole lot more sense physiologically for the woman who used it.

erwise, no matter how healthful it may be for them, may also be potentially dangerous.

Fortunately, not everyone thought this way. A number of studies demonstrating testosterone's ability to relieve depression and even psychosis in older, apparently "menopausal" men were published during the early days of testosterone experimentation in the 1940s. In 1944, Carl G. Heller, M.D., Ph.D., and Gordon B. Myers, M.D., whose landmark work in defining the hormonal basis of the "male menopause" syndrome was discussed in Chapter 5, reported on the effects of testosterone replacement in men with "psychic" symptoms such as depression, impaired memory, nervousness, and inability to concentrate. They found that 17 out of 20 such men responded to "testostcrone" (testosterone propionate) replacement with "complete abolition" of all symptoms.[3]

During the 1950s and '60s, the German physician, Tiberius Reiter, M.D., who practiced in London, reported on the results of intramuscular implantations of crystalline testosterone into 240 aging men. Dr. Reiter had his patients rate their mood on a scale from 0 (little or no depression) to 8 (suicidal thoughts) before starting them on testosterone and again after two and four months. Using this rather crude measure of depression, Reiter's patients appeared to experience a clear, dose-related decrease in feelings of depression (Fig. 11-1). Although it is impossible to dismiss the possibility that these results might be due, at least in part, to a "placebo" effect, the fact that the men generally felt better at four months than at two months and that higher doses appeared to work better than lower doses suggests that the benefit probably was real. "What the patient says is not objective evidence," acknowledged Dr. Reiter, "but many of them state that they have not felt so well and active for ten or twenty years. The improvement in potency and libido is important, but perhaps even more so is the disappearance of depression."

To doctors like Reiter, Malcolm Carruthers, and Jens Møller, who together have treated thousands of patients with testosterone, such improvements in mood, behavior, and even personality seem clear enough. Yet, when other, more traditional scientists have tried

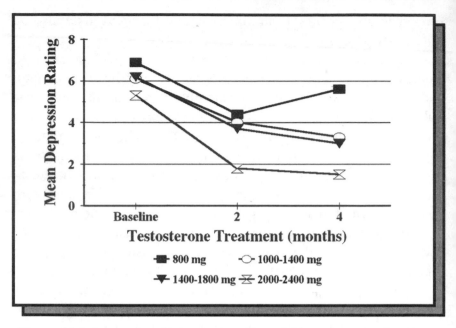

**Figure 11-1.** *Dose-related reduction in self-rated depression in men receiving testosterone implants for four months. (Adapted from Reiter, 1963)*

to quantify and analyze these effects, the results have often been contradictory. For every study showing a psychological or emotional benefit associated with testosterone replacement, there seems to be another that fails to find such an association.[4] The reasons for all this confusion are not to hard to understand.

First, it is almost impossible to conduct a placebo-controlled, double-blind experiment using testosterone. Such experiments are usually desirable to eliminate the risk that experimenter or subject bias could influence the results. Yet, on more than one occasion throughout the history of testosterone research, it has been noted that men "blindly" receiving testosterone supplements feel noticeably "better" in some way.[5, 6] This feeling immediately alerts everyone involved to the fact that these men could not be taking an inactive placebo, at which point the experimental "blinding" evaporates, rendering the placebo control futile.

Second, it is often very difficult to quantify something as vague as a feeling or mood. Sometimes standardized personality tests are used; other times men are just asked to rate feelings or mood on a crude numerical scale. Much depends on which method is used and how the relevant terms are defined and presented to the individual. One man's assertiveness can be another man's aggression.

Third, even if the problem of definition is solved, it is not always possible to separate one variable from another. Is a man feeling less depressed because testosterone replacement is exerting a direct physiological effect on his brain, or is it because his legs no longer ache when he walks, he's got new energy, and for the first time in 10 years he's able to have sex with his wife?

Fourth, aside from work like that done by Heller and Myers, Reiter, and Carruthers, almost no serious research has been conducted to specifically assess the behavioral and psychological effects of testosterone replacement in middle-aged or older men. In most studies, the researchers were more interested in the hormonal or physiological or sexual effects of testosterone and were not necessarily looking for any psychological or emotional changes in their subjects. Nevertheless, as noted above, several researchers have remarked, often in passing (because it was such a clear, yet unexpected finding), how the men who received testosterone replacement appeared to feel generally better, more energetic, more competitive, or more alive.

Fifth, most studies on the psychological correlates of testosterone have looked at the other end of the spectrum, teenaged boys, who sometimes seem to have testosterone oozing out of their pores. In most of these cases, the primary focus has been on the role, if any, of testosterone in aggression. Such studies have little or no relevance for grown men whose testosterone production has long since passed its peak and for whom excessive aggression is not the issue.

And finally, *many* studies have evaluated the effects of *anabolic steroid drugs* (e.g., methyltestosterone), *not natural testosterone*, on behavior. Some evidence suggests that these drugs *may* enhance aggressive tendencies in some males, most likely at the higher doses some body builders and athletes tend to use. There is no evidence that natural testosterone, or even testosterone esters (e.g., testosterone enanthate) have the same effect.[7]

In the end it probably matters little that there is so much disagreement. It is unlikely that a man would take testosterone supplements solely for their mood-enhancing value. If his low mood is related to low testosterone, it is more likely he'll also be taking it for its sexual, cardiovascular, or anabolic benefits. If he feels better in the process, all the better.

## How Testosterone Affects Mood and Behavior

No one denies that mood and behavior (not just sexual behavior) are profoundly influenced by testosterone. During the first half of this century, German researchers studying men who had been castrated or were simply testosterone-deficient found many important changes, in addition to the expected decline in sexuality. (See box.) In a major review of these data published in 1976, authors W.M. Herrmann and R.C. Beach, who worked for Schering Pharmaceuticals in what was then West Germany, hypothesized that testosterone may modify seven distinct facets of the human psyche:[8]

- **Sexuality**. Low testosterone levels consistently result in reduced libido, potency, and sexual activity. High testosterone, on the other hand, has no clear relationship to increased sexual interest or activity, except when testosterone replacement is given to men who are testosterone-deficient.

- **Aggression**. Low testosterone decreases aggressive behavior; whether increasing testosterone necessarily makes adult men more aggressive is doubtful.

- **Energy level.** High testosterone levels are generally associated with higher energy levels and more activity.

- **Psychomotor function.** In some studies, "testosterone" replacement has been associated with improved ability to

# Reported Effects of Low Testosterone

- Decreased libido and potency
- Early senility
- Memory failure
- Reduced "intellectual agility"
- Loss of ability to concentrate
- Moodiness/emotionality
- Depression
- Reduced activity
- Passive attitudes
- Reduced "pugnacity"
- "Great timidity"
- "General tiredness"
- "Nervousness"/anxiety
- "Touchiness"/irritability
- "Feeling weak"
- Reduced interest in surroundings
- "Hypochondria"
- "Inner unrest"

perform certain motor tasks and to reduce "psychomotor retardation."

- **Higher mental performance.** Elevated levels of "testosterone" in normal men have been associated with better performance on standardized cognitive tests and improved ability to concentrate.

- **Mood changes (depression).** Depression, as noted above, has been a consistent finding in testosterone-deficient older men. When treated with testosterone, these men have been reported to often (but not always) become less depressed. In younger "hypogonadal" men, testosterone replacement has been associated with reduced feelings of inadequacy, hopelessness, and withdrawal.

- **Personality characteristics.** In general, testosterone-deficient men have been described as more timid, passive, unsociable, withdrawn, shy, moody, nervous, anxious, and emotional. By contrast, those with high levels of testosterone tend to be more active, confident, aggressive, and assertive.

Can testosterone replacement actually bring about meaningful changes in the intellectual or emotional life of testosterone-deficient men? One of the few studies that has tried to systematically answer at least part of this question was a small 1992 National Institutes of Health (NIH) sponsored experiment, which set out to assess the relationship between androgen status and sexual function in *younger* "profoundly hypogonadal" men.[9]

The six men (aged 25-40 years) who participated were completely lacking in endogenous testosterone. Three of the men received "testosterone" (testosterone enanthate) injections every two weeks for a year. The other three men received hormones (not testosterone) designed to promote testicular growth, spermatogenesis, and virilization. All the men were asked to keep "sexual activity logs" before starting treatment and again at regular intervals. They were also asked to complete a "Profile of Mood States"

(POMS) questionnaire, a standardized test designed to assess such variables as anxiety, depression, anger, vigor, and confusion.

Dramatic differences were noted in the mental states of the hypogonadal men, compared with a group of hormonally normal men. As shown in Figure 11-2, the untreated hypogonadal men evidenced significantly higher levels of anger, depression, fatigue, and confusion. Within the first six months of the experiment, the three hypogonadal men treated with "testosterone" went through an accelerated adolescence, growing facial and body hair, developing body odor and acne, and learning that they could have erections and ejaculate. Two of the men described a "dramatic increase in sexual interest and potency" within the first month, while the third man described a more gradual sexual awakening.

Administration of "testosterone" to the hypogonadal men led to increased vigor (not shown) and reduced anger, compared with their pretreatment baseline, although they remained less vigorous and more angry than the normal control group. No other behavioral or mood-related differences were noted, however.

Although the NIH researchers reported no effect of "testosterone" replacement on depression (as measured by the POMS), various other researchers have shown a connection between testosterone and depression. In one study of 18 depressed men, who were

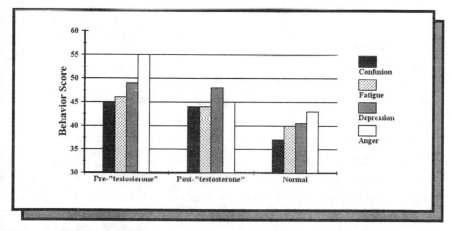

**Figure 11-2.** *Reduced anger in young hypogonadal men treated with "testosterone" for 12 months. (Adapted from Burris et al, 1992)*

described as having a wide range of ages and severity of illness, the researchers, led by Jerome Yesavage, M.D., of the Stanford University Medical Center, took blood samples from the men and evaluated their depression using the Hamilton Rating Scale for Depression (HRSD).* They found a highly significant negative correlation (-0.67) between the level of endogenous testosterone and HRSD score. In other words, the less testosterone the men had, the more depressed they were.[10]

Another experiment involved a group of six men with a congenital hormonal abnormality known as *Klinefelter's syndrome.* Males with Klinefelter's have a genetic aberration that

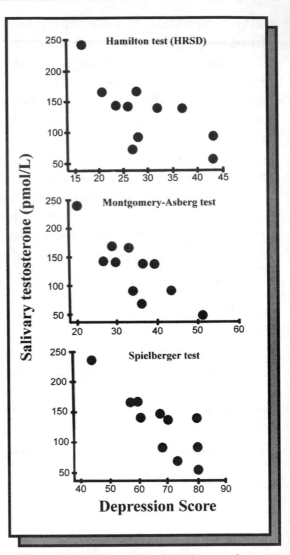

**Figure 11-3.** *In a study of 11 depressed men, lower levels of salivary free testosterone levels were associated with more severe depression. Each point represents a different individual; each graph represents the results on a different depression rating scale. (Adapted from Davies et al, 1992)*

---

* The HRSD is a commonly used measure for evaluating the degree of depression. It is probably more sensitive than the POMS or other crude rating scales.

leaves them with small testes and consequently, very little testosterone. They may lack many typical "masculine" features and may even have feminine features such as enlarged breasts. When adolescent boys with Klinefelter's are treated with testosterone beginning at what should be puberty, they tend to develop fairly normally, but must remain on testosterone replacement for the rest of their lives.

In this study,[11] which was conducted at the University of Washington, the men (in their 20s and 30s), were injected with "testosterone" (testosterone enanthate) at two- to four-week intervals and evaluated at these times on a number of different physical, hormonal, and psychological dimensions. Overall, the author noted, "testosterone" replacement resulted in "a significant psychological effect, including a change from feminine to masculine body image, increased assertiveness, increased goal-directed behavior and heightened sexual drive." No changes were observed in mood or energy; two of the men became more aggressive, but this effect disappeared when their dosing schedule was adjusted to allow more time between injections.

The relationship between testosterone and depressive illness was also investigated in a small study by a group of researchers from Wales.[12] They measured the levels of *free testosterone* (from saliva) in 11 men diagnosed with "major depression with melancholia." They also measured the men's degree of depression using three separate commonly used scales, including the HRSD. The results (Fig. 11-3) clearly supported the contention that lower testosterone levels were associated with more serious depression.

While considerable controversy still exists in scientific circles regarding the relationship, if any, between testosterone and the mood states of middle-aged and older men, those clinicians who have been prescribing testosterone for such men have little doubt that most do feel better. The most recent voice in the debate is a report of the clinical trials of the Androderm® testosterone patch, reported in the drug's (FDA-approved) official labeling. This study revealed that 12 months of Androderm® use resulted in statistically significant decreases in fatigue (from 79% before the patch to 10% after) and in depression score* from (6.9 before to 3.9 after).[13]

Only a couple of studies, conducted during the 1970s in Germany, have systematically examined the effects of testosterone treatment on men's cognitive function. In one experiment, normal, younger males receiving either "testosterone" or placebo via intravenous infusion were asked to perform a series of routine performance tests (e.g., serial subtraction). Over the course of a day, the performance of all the men deteriorated, but the performance of those receiving "testosterone" deteriorated significantly less.[14]

In a small double-blind, placebo-controlled study, normal male "volunteers" took a single dose of either the anabolic steroid drug Mesterolone or placebo. Before treatment and again at one, and three hours after treatment, the men performed a series of automated tests designed to evaluate higher mental function. The results suggested that Mesterolone treatment was associated with improved mental performance under conditions of psychological stress. The authors concluded that Mesterolone worked, at least in part, by stimulating psychomotor coordination.[8] Whether testosterone replacement would produce objective cognitive improvement in testosterone-deficient menopausal men has never been systematically investigated.

## Does Testosterone Cause Aggression?

One of the major obstacles (in addition to the fear of increased prostate cancer) that has probably slowed the acceptance of testosterone replacement therapy has been the fear of aggressive behavior, especially *sexually* aggressive behavior. Everybody *knows* that testosterone is the hormonal basis of aggression. Without testosterone, it is assumed there would be no overly aggressive behavior, certainly no rape or child molestation, and probably no Monday Night Football.

---

* As measured by the Beck Depression Inventory.

We like some aggression in our men, especially if they play for the home team or fight for our military, but too much aggression makes us uneasy. If testosterone causes aggression, won't giving men testosterone replacements push some over the edge? Might they turn kindly old Mr. Cooper from across the street into a "dirty old man" or even a sexual predator? Little girls walking home from school, *beware*!

While these fears are certainly exaggerated, there is no doubt that testosterone does help modulate the expression of feelings and behaviors that fall under the category of "aggression." As noted above, testosterone replacement has been associated with changes in men, such as increased assertiveness, energy, and self-confidence, which in some men may interpreted as increased aggression.

Unfortunately, there have also been numerous reports over the years in the scientific literature and especially in the news media of men taking "steroids" who apparently became violent and/or aggressive as a result. Since "anabolic steroid drugs" are widely, but mistakenly, equated with natural testosterone, it is *assumed* (because there is no direct confirmation) that raising a man's testosterone level would make him more aggressive. There are at least four things wrong with this assumption: 1) anabolic steroid drugs are *not* testosterone, 2) testosterone does not modulate aggressive behaviors as consistently in humans as it does in lower animals, 3) the scientific evidence linking anabolic steroid drugs and aggressive behavior is weak, and 4) the evidence linking natural testosterone replacement and aggression is practically nonexistent.

***Anabolic steroid drugs are not testosterone.*** As we have repeated *ad nauseam* in this book, *drugs are not hormones*. Anabolic steroid drugs (e.g., methyltestosterone, stanozolol, danazol, and many others) were developed with two primary goals in mind: 1) to mimic the tissue enhancing ability of natural testosterone without inducing further masculinization (especially in women), and 2) and second, to be patentable and thus, highly profitable. Drug company chemists took the testosterone molecule and twisted it a little, added an extra piece here, and trimmed a piece over there. The result is a molecule that looks like it might be a cousin of natural testosterone but clearly comes from a different side of the family. (See Figs. 3-8 and 3-9)

Having grown accustomed during eons of exposure to the natural androgenic/anabolic balance afforded by testosterone, the hormone, the human body finds the state of affairs created by anabolic steroid drugs highly *unnatural.* If the drugs cause unwanted effects like liver toxicity, why not excessive aggression, too? But just as liver toxicity has never been associated with the use of natural testosterone, neither has excessive aggression.

*Testosterone does not modulate aggressive behavior as consistently in humans as it does in lower animals.* The animals scientists like to study most when they're interested in the relationship of testosterone and aggression include mice, rats, birds, cattle, monkeys and apes, and of course, the favorite "lab rats" of human aggression studies, sex criminals and teenaged boys. From mice to cattle, raising testosterone clearly increases aggressive behaviors. Once we reach the primate level, though, the relationship starts to break down, and when you reach the human male, all bets are off. No consistent relationships have ever been found in humans.

In a thorough review of the scientific literature on testosterone and aggression, a group of Canadian researchers from the University of British Columbia and Simon Frasier University, concluded that human aggressive behavior, like human sexual behavior, is far too complex to be manipulated by the level of a single hormone. "When a wide array of relevant evidence is considered," the researchers, headed by Dr. D.J. Albert, wrote, "the biological basis of human aggression is not found in the gonadal hormones that modulate hormone-dependent aggression in nonprimate mammals."[7]

*The scientific evidence linking anabolic steroid drugs and aggressive behavior is weak.* Okay, you say, maybe testosterone esters or natural testosterone don't make men aggressive, but what about those anabolic steroid drugs? A fair enough question. If these drugs can build abnormally large muscles, it's not much of a leap to think they also turn men into belligerent monsters as well. The problem is that, again, myth, propagated largely by false or misleading news media reports, seems to have overtaken reality.

One of the few well-controlled evaluations of the psychological effects of anabolic steroids drugs was an NIH-sponsored trial, the results of which were published in the *Journal of the American Medical Association* in 1993.[15] The investigators, including Tung-Ping Su, M.D., and colleagues asked 20 healthy young (aged 18-42 years) men to spend two weeks on an inpatient research ward where they received (in a double-blind fashion) either methyltestosterone (40 mg or 240 mg per day) or placebo. Since this was a cross-over design, the men were blindly switched every three days to one of the other conditions.

The results indicated subtle, but significant changes in mood and behavior when the men were taking the high dose of methyltestosterone. These included significant improvement in both "positive" (euphoria, energy, and sexual arousal) and "negative" (irritability, mood swings, violent feelings, and hostility) moods. Cognitive function also appeared to deteriorate, with significant increases in distractibility, forgetfulness, and confusion.

Despite these and other similar results, though, a major review of the world's scientific literature on anabolic steroids, published in the journal *Sports Medicine* just three years later, came to a far different conclusion. The authors, Drs. Michael Bahrke, Charles Yesalis III, and James Wright, concluded that increased aggression in human males could not be firmly linked to the use of these drugs. "Information concerning the legitimate adverse behavioral effects of anabolic steroids has often been inaccurate and wildly speculative," they argue. "As a result, the frequent, often hysterical references by the media to unsubstantiated adverse behavioral effects of anabolic steroids has resulted in the loss of both media and medical/scientific credibility, deterring research on beneficial and legitimate uses, and as a stimulus and encouragement for litigation against physicians."[4]

Although there is much that is wrong with anabolic steroid drugs, and we never endorse their use, it seems likely that when it comes to turning men into aggressive animals, they have probably gotten a "bum rap."

*The evidence linking natural testosterone replacement and aggression is nonexistent.* Even if some uncertainty remains about the aggression-inducing ability of anabolic steroid drugs, no such doubt exists when it comes to natural testosterone or even testosterone esters. In their analysis of the biological basis for human aggression, Albert and colleagues reviewed 11 studies that set out to examine changes in sexual and aggressive behavior in a total of 187 hypogonadal men treated with either testosterone enanthate, testosterone undecanoate, or testosterone propionate. Although these studies uniformly reported increases in libido, sexual interest, sexual thoughts, and sexual activity, increased aggression was briefly observed in only two men.[7]

As Dr. Albert and his colleagues convincingly argue, testosterone esters produce levels of testosterone "above those of the most violent criminal offenders" without producing any consistent increase in aggression. Given this fact, it's hard to imagine how natural testosterone replacement at doses that reproduce youthful levels and mimic the natural circadian rhythm could have any adverse behavioral effect. Not surprisingly, increases in aggressive behavior have never been reported in men using natural testosterone in the form of a gel, cream, patch or sublingual tablet.

# References

1.  Needham J. *Science and Civilization in China (Vol. 5)*. Cambridge: Cambridge University Press; 1983.

2.  de Kruif P. *The Male Hormone*. New York: Harcourt, Brace and Company; 1945.

3.  Heller C, Myers G. The male climacteric and its symptomatology, diagnosis and treatment. *JAMA*. 1944;126:472-477.

4.  Bahrke MS, Yesalis CEd, Wright JE. Psychological and behavioral effects of endogenous testosterone levels and anabolic-androgenic steroids among males. A review. *Sports Med*. 1990;10:303-337.

5.  Tenover JS. Effects of testosterone supplementation in the aging male. *J Clin Endocrinol Metab*. 1992;75:1092-1098.

6.  Zorgniotti AW, Lizza EF. Effect of large doses of the nitric oxide precursor, L-arginine, on erectile dysfunction. *Int J Impot Res.* 1994;6:33-35

7.  Albert DJ, Walsh ML, Jonik RH. Aggression in humans: What is its biological foundation? *Neurosci Biobehav Rev.* 1993;17:405-425.

8.  Herrmann W, Beach R. Psychotropic effects of androgens: a review of clinical observations and new human experimental findings. *Pharmakopsych (Stuttgart).* 1976;9:205-219.

9.  Burris A, Banks S, Carter C, Davidson J, Sherins R. A long-term, prospective study of the physiologic and behavioral effects of hormone replacement in untreated hypogonadal men. *J Andrology.* 1992;13:297-304.

10. Yesavage J, Davidson J, Widrow L, Berger P. Plasma testosterone levels, depression, sexuality, and age. *Biol Psychiatry.* 1985;20:222-224.

11. Ruvalcaba R. Testoserone therapy in Klinefelter's syndrome. *Andrologia.* 1989;21:535- 541.

12. Davies RH, Harris B, Thomas DR, Cook N, Read G, Rlad-Fahmy D. Salivary testosterone levels and major depressive illness in men. *Br J Psychiatry.* 1992;161:629- 632.

13. Androderm® Testosterone Transdermal System. *U.S. Prescribing Information.* 1997;SmithKline Beecham.

14. Vogel W, Broverman DM, Klaiber EL, Abraham G, Cone FL. Effects of testosterone infusions upon EEGs of normal male adults. *Electroencephalogr Clin Neurophysiol.* 1971;31:400-403.

15. Su TP, Pagliaro M, Schmidt PJ, Pickar D, Wolkowitz O, Rubinow DR. Neuropsychiatric effects of anabolic steroids in male normal volunteers. *JAMA.* 1993;269:2760-2764.

# Chapter 12
# How to Obtain Natural Testosterone
## (and Other Natural Hormones)

A lthough you can get one of the new patented testosterone patch products at any pharmacy, natural testosterone creams, gels, and sublingual tablets may be a little more difficult to come by. Because they are not manufactured by multi-national pharmaceutical companies and endorsed with the FDA's incredibly costly stamp of "approval," natural testosterone and other natural hormones do not normally appear on the shelves of most ordinary pharmacies. You just have to know who to ask and what to ask for.

No matter what form it takes, natural testosterone is considered a "controlled substance" (Schedule III) and is available only with a prescription from a medical doctor (M.D.), osteopathic doctor (D.O.), or in some states, a naturopathic doctor (N.D.). All the other products mentioned in this book are available in most health food stores and from many companies that sell nutritional supplements.

## Compounding Pharmacists: Back to the Future

Unpatented natural testosterone creams, gels, and sublingual tablets are made from exactly the same hormone as that used in the patented high-tech patches and can be obtained on prescription from one of the growing number of compounding pharmacies in the United States. Compounding pharmacists prepare the hormones for each patient according to his doctor's prescription in the form best suited to the patient's individual needs.

In the centuries before the pharmaceutical industry took over the manufacturing of nearly all drugs, every pharmacist was a compounding pharmacist. As recently as the early 1940s, most drugs and natural compounds were prepared this way. By the 1990s, however, most pharmacists had been relegated to the role of pill counters.

As everyone knows, the current system basically works like this: the doctor writes a prescription for a standardized commercial drug like Androderm® and either calls the pharmacist or gives the prescription to the patient, who then hands it to the pharmacist at the local drug store. The pharmacist, who keeps a supply of Androderm® patches on hand, reads the prescription, grabs a box off the shelf, sticks a label with the patient's name and dosing instructions on it, and hands the box to the patient. In many cases, a vending machine could do the job just as well.

Fortunately, compounding pharmacies have been undergoing a rebirth, caused by rapidly growing public demand for more natural and more individualized health care, and by economic necessity for the traditional, small personal-service pharmacy. Consumers are increasingly dissatisfied with "nothing but drugs" and are seeking out natural remedies in ever-increasing numbers.

Compounding pharmacies are literally the only sources for prescription natural hormones and other prescription natural items. And many drug-prescribing doctors are increasingly frustrated with the limited selection of "approved" drug preparations and are working with compounding pharmacists in growing numbers to develop unique preparations and "delivery systems."

Many small, traditional, personal-service pharmacies were literally being driven out of business by cost-cutting insurance companies, managed care organizations, and HMOs that sign contracts with giant drugstore chains to provide massive quantities of deeply discounted drugs, and some have even opened their own mail-in drug outlets. With rapidly increasing consumer demand, the path to economic survival for smaller personal-service pharmacies became obvious: a return to traditional pharmaceutical compounding.

Today's compounding pharmacists can produce literally "whatever the doctor orders," usually in a variety of forms that best suit the individual patient's needs. Need some testosterone in a transdermal cream or in a sublingual tablet? You simply have your doctor write a prescription which you then present to a compounding pharmacist.

Compounding pharmacists have access to bulk quantities of high-quality natural hormones (and other substances) as well as the equipment to process them. They measure out appropriate doses and put them into whichever medium the doctor prescribes.

The pills, capsules, creams, etc., produced by a compounding pharmacist are virtually indistinguishable in chemical composition from the mass-produced variety, except that they usually don't come with the chemical colorings and shapes the pharmaceutical industry uses to distinguish its products from the competition and discourage "counterfeiting." As an added "bonus," a compounding pharmacist can leave out all unnecessary chemical flavors, preservatives, and adhesives (in patch products), as well as coloring chemicals, and can individualize "bases" according to a patient's allergies and sensitivities.

The quality of individually prepared natural hormones or drugs produced by a compounding pharmacist is generally excellent for several reasons:

- Compounding pharmacists are often more extensively educated than pharmacists who are just "pill-counters." They've taken special training in modern compounding methods.

- They have that extra motivation borne of having to satisfy each customer for his individualized prescription. A primary motivation for many non-compounding pharmacists is keeping a "third-party payer" happy. "Happiness" for third-party payers *always* means the lowest price possible, with "patient satisfaction" a distant secondary consideration.

- Every compounding pharmacy is licensed and inspected by its State Pharmacy Board, just like all other pharmacies.

- Materials used by compounding pharmacies are the same quality used by the major pharmaceutical companies. All materials used are subject to FDA inspection and the agency's Good Manufacturing Procedures code.

It's no surprise that the FDA and the pharmaceutical industry would like to see competition from compounding pharmacists eliminated, and they have made significant efforts to squash this valuable health resource. So far, this repression has been stalled in Congress, thanks to the vigorous lobbying efforts of representatives of the compounding pharmacists, knowledgeable medical professionals and consumers, and others concerned with preserving one of the last outposts of health care freedom in the U.S.A.

## How to Locate a Compounding Pharmacist

Compounding pharmacies are located all over the country, and finding one is not usually difficult. If there is no compounding pharmacy nearby, nearly all transactions can be carried out via mail, phone and/or fax.

The easiest way to locate a compounding pharmacist is to contact either the *Professional Compounding Centers of America, Inc.* (*PCCA*) or the *International Academy of Compounding Pharmacists* (*IACP*).

PCCA provides compounding pharmacists with support in the form of training, equipment, chemicals, and technical consultation on difficult compounding problems. At present, more than 1,900 compounding pharmacists in the U.S., Canada, Australia, and New Zealand are members of PCCA. For information about PCCA, including a listing of compounding pharmacists, you can contact them at:

## PCCA

| | |
|---|---|
| Telephone: | 800-331-2498 |
| Fax: | 800-874-5760 |
| Internet: | www.thecompounders.com |

IACP is more of a professional and political organization for compounding pharmacists. Its primary mission is to increase awareness of compounding pharmacies and to promote legislation that would protect this valuable resource. The IACP can be contacted at:

## IACP

| | |
|---|---|
| Telephone: | 800-927-4227 |
| Fax: | 281-495-0602 |
| Address: | PO Box 1365 |
| | Sugar Land, TX 77487 |
| Internet: | www.iacp.org |

# How to Get a Medical Doctor to Prescribe Natural Testosterone

Because most of their hormone- and drug-related information comes from pharmaceutical "sales reps," medical journals supported by pharmaceutical company advertising, or pharmaceutical company sponsored conventions, the average "conventional" medical doctor in the United States knows virtually nothing about using natural testosterone or other natural hormones. To many of these doctors, natural hormones sound like the latest natural food fad: "Natural testosterone cream for preventing heart or prostate disease? Give me a break! Let's see those placebo-controlled, double-blind studies. Let's see that FDA approval. Let's see those free samples!" Moreover, "conventional" medical doctors are all too often intimidated by their state medical boards, medical societies, or other peer groups, all of whom still disapprove of nonpharmaceutical "natural remedies."

Fortunately, like the rest of us, increasing numbers of medical doctors are seeing through the smoke and mirrors offered up by the government/pharmaceutical company complex. Many of these doctors have taken it upon themselves to learn about natural testosterone (and other natural hormones) and to recommend these to their patients in preference to expensive, patented pharmaceutical products.

Many other medical doctors, though perhaps less knowledgeable about the use of natural testosterone, are dissatisfied with the "approved" methods of treating the various age-related ailments in men (and women), because these so often prove to be unpleasant and possibly dangerous. These doctors are open-minded enough to recognize that the pharmaceutical industry does not have all the answers. If asked to prescribe natural testosterone and other natural treatments as described in this book, and provided with supporting documentation and dosing options, they're often happy to oblige, because they're always looking for better ways to help their patients.

If your doctor is interested but hesitant to prescribe natural products, it may help to put him or her in touch with a compounding pharmacist who can both reassure and provide education. Having such a consultation with a knowledgeable professional, who can explain the advantages of these products and provide some dosing guidelines, is usually enough to convince most skeptical doctors to at least give them a try.

The quickest and most efficient way to find a knowledgeable, open-minded doctor is to locate one who is a member of the American College for Advancement in Medicine (ACAM). All members of this professional organization are skilled and knowledgeable in the prescription and use of natural hormones, as well as various nutritional, herbal, and botanical products. ACAM members have studied and listened to discussions by dozens of experts (even including myself, JVW, on occasion) concerning the bio-chemistry, effects, and uses of these substances. For a referral to an ACAM doctor near you, contact ACAM at:

## ACAM

Telephone:     1-800-532-3688
Address:       23121 Verdugo Drive, Suite 204
               Laguna Hills, CA 92653
Internet:      www.acam.org

## Other Medical Alternatives

Although the American Medical Association would probably like you to believe otherwise, there are qualified medical professionals who have letters other than M.D. after their name. Many of these doctors, known as naturopaths and osteopaths, have a far better understanding of natural hormones, and usually considerably more experience in using them than the average "regular" M.D.

*Naturopathic Physicians.* Naturopathic medicine is based on the belief and observation that the human body possesses enormous power to heal itself when given the correct natural materials and energies.

After earning an undergraduate degree (B.A. or B.S.) includ-ing pre-medical requirements such as chemistry, biochemistry, biology, and physics, naturopathic physicians go on to a four-year graduate level, accredited naturopathic school of medicine, where, upon graduation, they earn an N.D. degree. N.D.s are educated in all the same sciences as M.D.s, although with less emphasis on drugs, radiation, and surgery, but much more emphasis on nutrition, botanical remedies, manipulation, homeopathy, acupuncture, psy-chology, and other holistic and nontoxic therapies. Naturopathic physicians place strong emphasis on disease prevention, lifestyle change, and optimizing wellness.

Before licensure, naturopathic physicians must complete at least 4,000 hours of study in specified subject areas and then pass a series of rigorous professional board exams. Although naturopathic physicians can be found in every U.S. state and Canadian province, they're currently licensed by state boards only in Alaska, Arizona, Connecticut, Hawaii, Maine, Montana, New Hampshire, Oregon, Utah, Vermont, Washington, and the District of Columbia. In Canada, naturopaths are licensed in British Columbia, Manitoba, Ontario, and Saskatchewan. To locate a naturopathic physician, contact the **American Association of Naturopathic Physicians (AANP)** at:

## AANP

Telephone:          206-298-0125
Address:            601 Valley St., #106
                    Seattle, WA 98109
Internet:           www.naturopathic.org

***Osteopathic Physicians.*** After earning an undergraduate degree (B.A. or B.S.), doctors of osteopathic medicine graduate from a 4-year osteopathic medical school with a D.O. degree. Their training and accreditation is similar to that which medical doctors receive.

Most osteopaths are primary care physicians, but many specialize in such areas as internal medicine, surgery, pediatrics, radiology, or pathology. Residencies in these areas typically require an additional two to six years of training beyond medical school.

Although many D.O.s are members of the AMA, generally they differ from M.D.s in their emphasis on the "whole person" and a preventive approach to the practice of medicine. Rather than treating specific symptoms, as many conventional "allopathic" M.D.s usually do, a D.O. is trained to focus on the body's various systems – particularly the musculoskeletal system – and how they interact with each other. Although D.O.s can and do prescribe conventional drugs, they are more likely to be open to and knowledgeable about natural remedies, including natural hormone replacement.

Osteopaths are licensed in all U.S. states and Canadian provinces to practice medicine and prescribe drugs. To find an osteopath, a good starting point is the American Osteopathic Association (AOA) or the Canadian Osteopathic Association (COA). The American Osteopathic Association can be contacted at:

# AOA

Telephone:      800-621-1773
Fax:             312-202-8200
Address:         142 E. Ontario Street
                 Chicago, IL 60611-2864
Internet:        www.am-osteo-assn.org

The Canadian Osteopathic Association can be contacted at:

# COA

Telephone:      519-439-5521
Address:         575 Waterloo Street
                 London, Ontario N6B2R2

## Laboratory Testing

Many laboratories test hormones in blood, and a few check levels in saliva. I (JVW) prefer to use the 24-hour urine test because nearly all hormones are secreted in "bursts" and "pulses," and a single "blood draw" or saliva collection (or even two or three of them) may not provide a representative sample.

There is some evidence that measuring free testosterone may be preferable to the measurement of total testosterone in helping to determine whether a man might benefit from testosterone replacement. Urine and saliva tests measure free testosterone; blood tests can measure either free or total testosterone, so it is important for the doctor to specify.

Dr. George Debled, the pioneering French andrologist, prefers a combination of laboratory tests including both free and total testosterone, serum sex hormone binding globulin (SHBG), luteinizing hormone (LH), follicle stimulating hormone (FSH), dihydrotestosterone (DHT), estradiol, and estrone. Some physicians may prefer to do two, three, or all of these tests as part of an overall evaluation.

The lab I work with uses the most up-to-date equipment (including mass spectroscopy, for the technically inclined) and offers multiple steroid hormone panels at exceptionally good prices. This laboratory is Meridian Valley Clinical Laboratories:

## Meridian Valley Laboratories

Telephone:     253-859-8700
Fax:           253-859-1135
Address:       515 West Harrison
               Kent, WA 98032

# Afterword

## We Need More Natural Testosterone Research

Some of the research and clinical experience we have reported in this book dates back more than 60 years. Some of it is quite recent. Over the course of these years, a remarkably consistent pattern has emerged. While testosterone is certainly not the "Fountain of Youth" once envisioned by some 19th century enthusiasts, it undoubtedly has some remarkable health-giving properties, most of which are not being made available to men today.

In typical pharmaceutical industry fashion, most drug company-sponsored research on testosterone replacement and other aspects of male menopause has focused on the largest and most lucrative portion of the market – sexual dysfunction or dissatisfaction. That's why the various testosterone patch products are being promoted largely for restoring libido and erectile ability, even though they are officially "indicated" for any physical manifestation of low testosterone levels.

But no one ever died of not having sex. Testosterone's benefit's for the heart and circulatory system and for bones and muscles, just like estrogen and progesterone in women, are hard to deny. But few doctors in this country are offering men the testosterone patch or other natural testosterone products to prevent or treat their angina, intermittent claudication, or osteoporosis.

Why not? The evidence is at least as strong for the cardiovascular and bone/muscle-building benefits of testosterone as it is for the sexual benefits, maybe stronger. It's largely because, so far, none of the drug companies that make patented testosterone replacement products has been willing to do the large-scale, long-term, double-blind, placebo controlled, prospective clinical trials to demonstrate to the satisfaction of the FDA, AMA, the AHA (American Heart Association), and others that testosterone replacement does in fact prevent heart attacks, etc, without causing any serious side effects. Instead they have opted to focus their consid-erable resources on a much easier target – sexual dysfunction.

And who can blame them? As the Viagra® experience has clearly demonstrated, there are millions, maybe billions, of men out there looking for an easy way to stay sexually active as they age.

Testosterone therapy for heart disease will likely be an exceedingly "hard sell" in this country, because the "heart disease industry" is firmly wedded to its drugs and expensive, dangerous surgical procedures, while giving lip service to diet and exercise. To accept testosterone therapy, the medical profession will need to substantially alter its views of the causes of and treatments for car-diovascular disease. Sex, as always, is a much easier product to sell.

All is not lost though. As more and more men use natural testosterone to enhance their sexuality, someone is bound to notice that these men are generally healthier, happier and "younger" for their age. Objectively, it will be easy to notice that their cardiovas-cular systems are in better shape, that their muscles are bigger and their bones stronger, compared with men their age who are not using testosterone.

Among conventional physicians, much of the hesitation to use testosterone comes from fear that it will *cause* heart disease and prostate cancer. Virtually no sound scientific evidence collected over the last 60 years supports these fears. *Anabolic steroid drugs* can cause heart disease, but natural testosterone does not. Nor have those researchers who have treated large numbers of men with testosterone over many years seen an increase in prostate cancer. It appears certain that, if no cancer is present, testosterone *will not cause it*; and if cancer is present, testosterone *may or may not pro-mote it*. There is good evidence that a normal androgen:estrogen balance may actually protect against heart disease, muscle and bone loss, and both benign and cancerous prostate overgrowth.

Pharmaceutical companies today are in a unique position with regard to testosterone replacement. Over 60 years ago, they abandoned natural testosterone in favor of a long series of patented synthetic testosterone-like drugs. While many men have benefitted from some of these products over the years, no synthetic "testosterone" was ever found suitable for everyday use. Researchers have never been able to synthesize a drug that can reproduce the normal, steady (with diurnal variations) hormonal environment over a long time period, and some of these drugs (e.g., methyltestosterone) have been found to be extremely dangerous.

With their new natural testosterone patches, the pharmaceutical industry has come full circle. Having devised a way to sell an unpatentable natural hormone in a patented, high-tech, transdermal "delivery system," their hormones, at least, are in the right place this time. If these products promote the widespread use of natural testosterone, and if the companies track users over the long term, as we hope they will, it will only hasten the day when testosterone replacement becomes as routine as good nutrition and exercise to help men over age 40 stay healthy, active – sexually and otherwise – and alive for a long, long time.

## Don't Forget Diet, Exercise and Nutritional Supplements

But even natural testosterone can't do everything. Although this book has concentrated on natural testosterone replacement, for best results, testosterone use should also be accompanied by an excellent diet, exercise, and the use of vitamin, mineral, and botanical supplements. Drug use (both legal and illegal) should be minimized or stopped as well. Although many of us have been hearing about diet and exercise from our wives for years, it's now time for us to act. Here are some important healthful steps we should all be taking:

- **Stop or reduce drug use**. If possible, prescription drugs of all types should be reduced or stopped. Of course, this should never be done without consulting with your physician. Chapter 4 lists certain types of drugs that are known to interfere with sexual function. If at all possible, stop them or switch to alternatives with less of this effect. Don't forget about tobacco, alcohol, and caffeine. These are all powerful drugs, too. It's best to stop tobacco entirely, use alcohol sparingly (no more than one drink a day), and minimize caffeine use. (Pesticides and herbicides are sprayed more heavily on coffee and tea than any other crops. Even if you continue to use small quantities of coffee and tea, "certified organic" sources are preferable.)

- **Eliminate junk food.** It's time to put aside all the junk food of youth! Besides, with the dozens of delicious natural products now available, it's no sacrifice to switch to natural alternatives. The goal should be a 100%-natural foods diet, processed as little as possible, with no chemical additives, flavorings, or preservatives. Remember to eat lots of vegetables and fruits, and don't forget *unroasted* nuts and seeds for snacks (the essential fatty acids in unroasted nuts and seeds are vital for promoting prostate health). Honey, molasses, pure maple syrup, and stevia* should be used instead of refined sugar or artificial sweeteners.

- **Take vitamin-mineral supplements.** *Minimum* vitamin-mineral supplementation should include **vitamin C**, which has been found to promote mens' longevity (1 gram twice daily); **vitamin E**, which is known to prevent a significant number of heart attacks (400 I.U. daily of mixed tocopherols); and a high-potency multiple vitamin/mineral combination (available from a natural food store or mail order supplement supplier, not from a grocery or drug store). Men "of an age" to think about testosterone replacement should also take **ginkgo biloba**, which has been shown in several studies to help preserve mental function in aging in both

---

* If you haven't tried this 100% natural, zero-calorie, entirely safe, and very intense sweetener, you're in for a delicious surprise! Due to unconscionable FDA harassment (including written threats of book-burning), suppliers are not "allowed" to inform consumers of the many ways stevia can be used as a sweetener. Despite this, stevia is legally available in nearly all natural food stores in liquid and powder forms.

sexes. As noted in Chapter 6, ginkgo may also help preserve men's sexual function.

- **"Special-purpose" supplementation.** If sexual function isn't all it should be, **L-arginine**, **yohimbine**, **ginseng**, **muira puama**, and **ginkgo biloba** have all been shown to be helpful. (Please see Chapter 6.) If the prostate is causing problems, extra **zinc, essential fatty acids (EFA)**, the botanicals **saw palmetto (serenoa repens)**, *Pygeum africanum*, *Urtica dioica*, and **Cernilton**® will all help greatly to reduce or eliminate symptoms of *benign* prostate enlargement. (See Chapter 9.)

- **Pure water.** Drinking water should be free of chlorine and fluoride (both increase the risk of cancer), and of course, free of other chemicals, herbicides, pesticides, or micro-organisms. Fortunately, several relatively inexpensive filtration systems are available for home use.

- **Exercise regularly!** A *minimum* of a half an hour four times a week.

- **Other** *natural* **types of health care.** Consider exploring other aspects of natural health care, such as chiropractic, acupuncture, homeopathy, and massage.

We are all "creatures of habit." Moving from old unhealthy patterns to new, more health-promoting ones isn't always easy and usually isn't accomplished overnight, but it definitely is worth the time and trouble. In addition to better health, vitality, and general enjoyment of life, these steps allow a man to improve his ability to care for and "be there" for his wife, children, and grandchildren...and have a greater chance of seeing his great-grandchildren!

# Index